D1091082

Other Books by Brock Yates

Cannonball!: World's Greatest Outlaw Road Race
The Hot Rod: Resurrection of a Legend
Outlaw Machine
Enzo Ferrari
The Critical Path
Indianapolis Five Hundred
Racers and Drivers
The Decline and Fall of the American Automobile Industry
Sunday Driver
Dead in the Water
The Great Drivers

Indianapolis Motor Speedway, 1954.

GATES

1 2 3 16TH GATE STREET GATE

4

SEC 57 · 48

PEDESTRIANS ONLY

SEC 76 · 87 D BOX 32 · 1 OFFICE

BOXES ONLY E BOXES ONLY

BOXES G

RESERVED BLEACHERS BOX 25 · 1 B BOXES ONLY

SEC 16 · 9 GEORGETOWN ROAD

BOXES A SEC 1 · 14 SEC 1 · 44

PITS PARQUET MAIN PADDOCK BOXES

SEC 42 · 1 GARAGES JUDGES STAND

GATE 6

SCORE BOARDS

INFIELD PARKING SPACE FREE

PARQUET STRETCH BOXES C SEC 24 · 37

SEC 51 · 92

SEC 38 · 47 F BOXES

PARQUET SEC 93 · 156 SEC

GATE 7

PARQUET SEC 66 · 75 H BOXES

RESERVED BLEACHERS SEC 8 · 1

GATES 8 9

10 GATES 11 30TH STREET

Denotes First Aid Stations

NORTH COUNTRY LIBRARY SYSTEM
Watertown, New York

796.72
YATE

"AGAINST DEATH and TIME"

ONE FATAL SEASON IN RACING'S GLORY YEARS

BROCK YATES

CENTRAL LIBRARY
WATERTOWN

THUNDER'S MOUTH PRESS
NEW YORK

AGAINST DEATH AND TIME

Copyright © 2004 by Brock Yates

Published by
Thunder's Mouth Press
An Imprint of Avalon Publishing Group Incorporated
245 West 17th Street, 11th Floor
New York, NY 10011

All rights reserved. No part of this book may be reproduced or transmitted in any form without written permission from the publisher, except by reviewers who may quote brief excerpts in connection with a review.

Library of Congress Cataloging-in-Publication Data

Yates, Brock W.
    Against death and time : one fatal season in racing's glory years / Brock Yates.
        p. cm.
    Includes bibliographical references.
    ISBN 1-56025-526-9
    1. Automobile racing—History. 2. Automobile racing drivers—Biography.
I. Title.
GV1029.15.Y35 2004   796.72—dc22

9   8   7   6   5   4   3   2   1

Designed by Kathleen Lake, Neuwirth and Associates
Printed in the United States of America
Distributed by Publishers Group West

To my beloved wife Pamela,
for her inspiration and
her passion for life.

PROLOGUE

HISTORIANS TEND TO DISMISS THE FIFTIES AS A decade of insipid, pastel-colored lassitude. Arthur Schlesinger Jr. described it as a period of "repose" following the cataclysmic decades of the Depression-ridden thirties and the war-ravaged forties. Yet the nation was evidencing a latent restlessness, led in part by veterans returning from World War II and Korea who found the pallid innocence of daily life boring in the extreme. Coffeehouses in the major cities were filling with angry young men soon to be known as "beatniks" while outside, the streets thundered with newly formed motorcycle gangs like the Hells Angels and the dreaded "hot-rodders" and their wild sport of "drag racing." A new generation of musicians were combining country music, western swing, and black rhythm and blues into a new sound called rock and roll. A struggling Kentucky-raised musician named Bill Haley and his new group, the Comets, had recorded "Rock round the Clock" in 1952. It was a modest success until a year later, when it became the theme song for *Blackboard Jungle*, Hollywood's first attempt to deal with disaffected youth and the newly discovered threat of "juvenile delinquency."

In 1955 James Dean and *Rebel without a Cause* shook the establishment along with a mass of young, flat-to-the-floor rock and roll musicians including Buddy Holly, Little Richard, Jerry Lee Lewis, Carl Perkins, Gene Vincent, Chuck Berry, and the immortal Elvis Presley.

Meanwhile, Detroit had discovered new sources of power through revolutionary, large-displacement V-8 engines, which triggered a "horsepower race" and prompted critics like writer John Keats to brand the chrome-encrusted monsters "insolent chariots." At the same time, Europeans were invading the shores with new "sports cars" and a strange, beetle-shaped economy car called the Volkswagen. On the race tracks, high technology was producing cars capable of doing 180 miles an hour with little or no commensurate concern for spectator safety. Death and injury on an unprecedented scale would be the result.

Four incidents shook the world of automobiles in the pivotal year of 1955. First came the shocking deaths of two of the world's greatest drivers at the peak of their powers—Italian former world champion Alberto Ascari and Indianapolis 500 superstar Bill Vukovich. Then came a gruesome disaster at Le Mans, France, when a Mercedes-Benz race car plunged into the crowded grandstands and killed at least eighty-eight people. Later that year, James Dean drove into immortality in what for a time was the world's most famous automobile crash.

In attempting to chronicle these incidents and the worlds they emerged from, I have employed what is referred to as "faction," in which a first-person, unidentified narrator is a witness to much of the action in an attempt to more intimately link the reader to the real and events. In so doing, the narrator meets and has an affair with a woman who in actuality is an amalgam of the wealthy, privileged women who followed the sport of automobile racing during that period. Aside from this pair, the rest of the characters in the story are real people. The events are as factual as I could make them, notwithstanding the passage of time and the blurring of memories. In working on this project, I have been particularly grateful to the following individuals who, over the years, have offered first-person accounts of the events portrayed. They include Tom Medley, John Fitch, Rodger Ward, Jim Travers, David E. Davis, Jr., Jesse Alexander, Lee Raskin, Jim Sitz, Dan Rubin, Phil Hill, Denise McCluggage, Donald Davidson, Chris Economaki, L. Spencer Riggs, Phil McCray, and the late Hans Tanner. A special thanks to John Fitch and his autobiography, *Adventure on Wheels—A Race Through Life.*

One note regarding poetic license. The character Peter Coltrin in chapters 9 and 10 did not actually arrive in Modena until 1957. However, Coltrin was a classic example of the many American journalists who went to Europe in the 1950s to immerse themselves in the world of high-speed automobiles and who became enamored of life around the Scuderia Ferrari. I have based my portrayal of Coltin's behavior and attitudes on numerous interviews with those who knew him.

I hope that in a small way, he and the other vivid characters on the following pages will help to bring alive one of the most tumultuous and riveting periods in automotive history.

Brock Yates
Wyoming, New York

CHAPTER ONE

VUKE

I MET HIM IN A TUSSLE FOR THE BATHROOM. HE was built like a middleweight. Forearms like bowling pins. His face was spread with a toothy smile, but his eyes, ink-black beneath a heavy brow, showed little amusement. It was obvious that his good nature would remain only so long as I gave him first shot at the shower.

We were on the third floor of a rooming house three blocks from the Indianapolis Motor Speedway on the second day of May in 1953. I was sharing a room with my old high school pal Tom Medley, a photographer and sometime cartoonist for *Hot Rod Magazine,* a Los Angeles–based monthly that had been started seven years earlier by a struggling Hollywood press agent named Bob Petersen. I had come east with Medley, having just been mustered out of the army and still bearing shrapnel scars picked up on the Yalu River. He had an assignment for the month at the place they called the "Brickyard." Unemployed as I was, I tagged along as his gopher, taking notes, running errands, and sharing what we considered to be the hefty room rate of twelve bucks a week.

"Who's that tough guy who just beat me out of the bathroom?" I asked Medley, who was sorting out Speed Graphic camera equipment on his single bed.

"Must be Vuke," he said.

"Vuke? Bill Vukovich?"

"That's him. Stays here every year with his wife."

"The guy they call the 'Mad Russian'? The guy who almost won the 500 last year? What the hell is he doing in a rooming house?" I asked. "I figured guys like him would stay downtown at a fancy hotel like the Claypool or the Riley."

"Let me tell you something," said Medley, laying down his camera. "Everybody thinks that guys who race at Indy are rolling in dough. Forget it."

"Come on," I protested. "This is big-time stuff."

"Maybe for the car owners. They're mostly rich guys in it for the sport. They get 60 percent of the purse. The driver gets 40. And if the car breaks, he gets zilch."

"I figured a guy like Vukovich would have money of his own."

"He's a car mechanic by trade. Got a little shop in Fresno. Wife. She's here somewhere. Stays out of sight. Two kids. No insurance. If he's hurt, he lays there until he gets better."

"It doesn't seem worth the risk."

"It isn't to a normal human being. These guys aren't normal."

"So the 'Mad Russian' is really mad."

"Hell, he isn't even Russian. Some press guy stuck him with that. Real name is Vucerovich. Czechoslovakian. Either way, don't mess with him."

I didn't mess with Bill Vukovich, although during that month our little races to the only bathroom became a small joke. He always won, partly because he was quicker afoot than I, but mostly because it seemed important to him. Second was not a place where Bill Vukovich wanted to be.

I first heard about Vukovich at an Indianapolis going-away party the racing fraternity traditionally held in late April at the Club La Rouge on Ventura Boulevard in West Los Angeles. It was a large, dark room lined with blue-upholstered vinyl booths and draped with red velvet curtains. The place was owned by a New Yorker named Shapiro whose idea of French decor no doubt came from second-rate Parisian brothels.

A swing band tooted away in a corner while the local Indianapolis crowd—mechanics, accessory manufacturers, rail birds, hangers-on, girlfriends, wives, and a few drivers—drank and bragged about their chances at Indy. Johnny Parsons, a chiseled movie-star type who had won the Indy 500 in 1950, was there, as was last year's winner, the young, strapping Troy Ruttman. He had to be six feet three and was still wearing a sling after breaking his arm in a freak accident in a Midwestern sprint car race.

Ruttman had won at Indianapolis driving for J. C. Agajanian, a big-time LA garbageman who strutted around the room in his omnipresent cowboy hat topping an immense Armenian hook nose. "Too bad Bill Vukovich isn't here," he said to Medley, placing a be-ringed paw on Tom's sloping shoulder. "I'd bet him a thousand bucks that we'll beat him again." Agajanian was choosing to forget that Vukovich had Ruttman doomed to a distant second until Vukovich's steering failed eight laps from the finish.

"Jesus. Everybody in the place thinks they're going to win back there," I said to Medley as a waiter planted two more Seven Crown and 7-Ups—"Seven and Sevens" were all the rage—in front of us.

"They think that way because they have to. If they didn't, they'd be in another line of work."

3

Chet Miller strolled in with his wife, Gertrude. A few scattered claps and whoops. He was a small man, slightly hunched and nearly bald. But he could drive. He had been in sixteen 500-mile races at Indianapolis since 1928 and had logged over 5,000 miles at the big track—but had never won. Third place was his best. This year was his biggest shot. He was driving a Novi, the fiercest, fastest, meanest race car in the world: 500 steaming horsepower that could make or break a man. The best had tried and failed. Ralph Hepburn had paid with his life. The Novi brooked no mistakes, yet had carried Miller to a track record just short of 140 miles an hour.

"If anybody's going to break 140, it'll be Miller," said Medley.

"A little guy. Looks like my tailor. That is, if I could afford a tailor."

"He's been doing this since the Depression. Fifty years old. Still hasn't made enough to retire. He runs a little upholstery shop for fancy cars over in Burbank. Business with the Hollywood types," said Medley. "But he can drive the shit out of those big Novis. Some say they're jinxed. Too much horsepower. Too radical. Faster than hell, but as evil."

"These guys are nutty about jinxes. Green cars. Peanuts. Black cats, woman in the pits. The number thirteen. All taboo. You'd be surprised what guys carry in their cars for good luck: St. Christopher medals, baby shoes, rabbit's feet, coins. Weird stuff. But I guess you've gotta be a little weird to even get in one of those things."

"What about that guy Vukovich?" I asked. "Sounds like he had it wrapped up until his steering broke."

"He'll be tough. Good car. Vuke calls it a roadster because he sits down low, deep inside the cockpit. Frank Kurtis built the thing up in Glendale. Another one of those Eastern European types. Croatia or somewhere like that. The car owner is Howard Keck. Superior Oil. Big money. Got two of the best wrenches in the business. Jim Travers. They call him Crabby. Got an attitude. His buddy is Frank Coon. Smart asses. Call 'em the Rich Kids.

"When Vuke first showed up at the Speedway two years ago, he had a shitbox car—an old stove entered by an Italian contractor from back in Ohio. A lot of other guys wouldn't get near it. A hoodoo car they called it. One that'd bite back and kill you. But when Vuke saw the thing for the first time he walked up to it and said, 'I can drive that pig.'

"He doesn't know the word fear. When he was a champion in the midgets, he'd run over the Russian army to win. Had some of his wildest battles with his own brother, Eli. No quarter. Eats nails and spits rust."

But during the first few days at the boarding house, run by a family named Manifold—which was such a weird coincidence that Tom and I wondered if they'd changed their name just for the racing crowd— Vuke and I somehow got along. He was generally distant and indifferent to anybody in the press, but us being hot-rodders from California and army veterans, he treated Tom and I with easy good humor.

Most mornings, the three of us walked the few blocks to busy Sixteenth Street and crossed into the immense Speedway. For most of its history, it had been paved with bricks— hence it's nickname (the Brickyard). But in the 1930s its owner, Eddie Rickenbacker, paved part of it with macadam.

The place was scary. The long front straight, still brick, was bordered by yawning grandstands on the outside along Georgetown Road and on the inside by the pits and a ramshackle five-story pagodalike timing tower built before World War I. The straight was 4,000 feet long, to be exact, with the back straight the same length, connected by four corners, each a quarter mile of a mile long, with two so-called short chutes at either end. Some of the faster cars, like Miller's Novi, would knock on 180 miles an hour before they swooped into the curves. One mistake, and three-foot-thick cement walls lining the track awaited, whitewashed to cover the deadly scars that pocked their surfaces.

It was on this ominous rectangle, which had consumed the lives of thirty-one men since opening in 1909, that guys like Miller and Vukovich were planning to average 140 miles an hour.

The weather stayed steamy for the first week of practice. Not much was going on, other than a few cars sporadically taking practice laps and some rookies being given so-called driver's tests, which mainly meant keeping their cars off the walls. The whole issue of safety was a bit of a joke. The rules were what you might call rudimentary. "Crash helmets" were required, but they were flimsy leather lids developed for motorcycle racing in the 1930s. It was recommended that "fireproof" clothing be worn. This involved soaking a shirt or a pair of coveralls in a boric-acid-and-borax solution to inhibit fire—the one component of the business that scared guys. Yet most of them, including the hot ones like Miller and Vukovich, drove in normal street clothes—usually a T-shirt during the hot months.

T-shirts were a major fashion item among drivers. Most displayed a Mobil flying red horse and a "Mobil Oil" logo on the front, courtesy of Mike Petrovich's Mobil station out on Sixteenth. Another favorite was the T-shirt handed out at Mate's White Front Saloon, a racer's hangout across from the Speedway.

As a final precaution, the Speedway rules stipulated that all dentures and false teeth be removed, lest they be swallowed in a crash.

There was no mention of seat belts, which were optional. Most drivers wore them—surplus webbed types from World War II aircraft—although it was known that most European drivers still refused to belt themselves in, figuring it was better to be thrown clear in case of a crash.

Nobody had even considered using a seat belt until 1941, when a Cherokee Indian driver named Joie Chitwood found that his car bounced so violently on the brick surface of the Speedway that he couldn't keep his foot on the throttle. As a remedy, he tied himself into the cockpit with a rope. This caused major concern among the officials, who openly worried that the young driver would "wear the car" in the event of a rollover. Some star drivers, like the great Rex Mays, were ardently against such a device.

Then came a 100-mile dirt track race at the Del Mar, California, horse track in late 1949. Mays was tossed from his spinning car and run over by a competitor. His death throes were featured in a shocking two-page spread in *Life* magazine. A year earlier, the national champion, Ted Horn, had died a similar death after spilling out of his car at the DuQuoin, Illinois, dirt track.

Slowly, the reality that staying inside a crashing car was safer than being pitched out of it like a rag doll began to make sense. Yet nearly a decade would pass before seat belts became mandatory in racing cars.

Practice went well for the first nine days, with only minor spins and some dented aluminum. Everybody was getting serious in preparation for the first big weekend of qualifying when Cliff Griffith, a twenty-seven-year-old Hoosier, took out one of the new Kurtis-Kraft roadsters for some hot laps. He'd been running over 137 mph in his black number 24, sponsored by Bardahl, an engine performance additive.

Tom and I were hanging around the little Associated Press hut in the garage area. The AP guys sat there, smoking cheap El Productos and playing gin rummy when a light bulb went on. The light bulb was connected to the network of caution lights around the track, and when it flashed, it usually meant a crash.

Because the AP was really only there to record wrecks, when the lightbulb flashed, the reporters and photographers would drop their cards, grab their notebooks and Speed Graphics, and run like a bunch of firemen to the scene of the accident.

"Griffith's into the wall in the first turn," somebody yelled. The mad rush. Tom had a little CZ single-cylinder motorcycle, and we piled on and skittered across the vast, manicured lawn of the infield to the scene.

7

The sweet smell of fresh-mown grass and dandelions mingled with the smoky odor of fire issuing from Griffith's car.

The ambulance and safety crews were there. Somebody was spraying carbon dioxide on the Bardahl Kurtis-Kraft, which was sitting, its front wheels splayed in odd directions, in the middle of the track. Fuel dripped out of its innards like the spoor from a wounded animal. Covered with white CO2 powder, it looked more like a beached whale than a race car.

Griffith was already in the ambulance—called "the crash wagon" by the racing guys—and about to be hauled off to Methodist Hospital. "He hit a ton," said a tall man with navy tattoos on his forearms holding a pair of stopwatches. He was one of the many crewmen stationed inside the first turn to clock speeds through the corner, which were clear indications of how quickly various drivers were negotiating the entire track. "He lost it. Got it sideways and couldn't get it back. Then it caught on fire. Cliff got out, but he looked like hell."

He should have. Somehow Griffith, an ex-soldier like virtually every driver in the place, had managed to climb clear of the flaming car, despite having broken his pelvis. His Mobil Oil T-shirt was burned away in the fire.

Unlike gasoline, the methanol alcohol used in race cars burned with a light blue flame that could barely be seen in daylight. The Bardahl's fuel tank had been split open by the impact and Griffith had been engulfed in fire. He suffered horrible second- and third-degree burns over much of his upper body and would spend four months in the hospital. Yet, like most drivers, he couldn't—or wouldn't—stop. He returned to drive again the next year.

They dragged the Bardahl back to the garage area, better known as "Gasoline Alley"—like the cartoon strip. Nobody could remember if the cartoon had been named after the place, or the place named after the cartoon. The car's owner, a wealthy guy from St. Louis named Ed

Walsh, wasn't giving up. Although his driver had been burned, his crew dove into the wrecked car and started to make repairs. The rumpled aluminum body was ripped off—revealing the charred, skeletal remains of the frame—and the rebuilding began.

Gasoline Alley was like that. Death and injury all around, and yet life went on, rife with gallows humor and a mordant sense of reality. Live or die, the race goes on.

The area consisted of rows of wooden garages with green-and-white-trimmed doors that housed the race cars and the necessary tools. The work benches generally had coffee pots brewing and snacks scattered around, creating a relaxed, homey feel to the spaces where crewmen and drivers joked and horseplayed their way through the long days. At noon, various teams would light up charcoal grills and roast corn. Late into the night, the little alcoves would be jammed with mechanics hammering and wrenching on the cars. Many would then simply fall into cots and sleeping bags to be ready for an early next day.

Gin rummy was the game of choice in Gasoline Alley, and somewhere, twenty-four hours a day, a serious game for serious stakes would be under way. Usually in the game was Rodger Ward, a chunky little former P-38 pilot who was known to have tons of talent, provided he could knock off the booze and the cards and quit chasing the babes. He was a smart guy, maybe too smart for his own good, and he radiated a cockiness that had yet to pay off on the race track.

It was a man's world. Women were forbidden to enter Gasoline Alley, a last bastion of male misogyny. Old-timers recalled that when French driver Louis Chiron entered the race in 1929, he brought along his mistress, Alice Hoffmann, who customarily did his timing and scoring in the pits. In Europe woman were allowed in restricted areas, but not at Indianapolis. In deference to the visitors, the Speedway officials constructed a small platform for her on the edge of the pits, where she would not sully the hallowed precincts.

This archaic tradition would not be broken until the realities of the women's movement finally overwhelmed the Speedway's establishment. In 1976, Janet Guthrie became the first woman driver allowed to compete at Indianapolis.

Griffith's crash was quickly forgotten. It was simply part of doing business in big-time automobile racing. "You pay your money. You take your chances," said one crewman as he walked away from the scene. "Cliff knew what he was doing. Today it didn't pay off."

Sometimes Tom and I would walk across Sixteenth Street at the end of practice for a few beers at the White Front, a stark, concrete block-house that consisted of little more than a few beat-up tables, a long bar, and a half-broken piano. The drink of choice was the Boilermaker, composed of a draft beer and a shot of cheap whiskey. Woman were not banned from the White Front, but were seldom seen inside its grim precincts. The talk consisted of the endless rumors and gossip at the Speedway and the outrageous spike in prices that awaited visitors to Indianapolis during the month of May. That year it involved the scandalous inflation of the price of gasoline, which had been bumped from 23.5 cents per gallon to a stratospheric 26.9 cents.

Rain and drizzle descended on the Speedway for nearly two weeks. Because the cars' tires were not capable of gripping a wet track surface, the days devolved into endless gin rummy games in Gasoline Alley and chatter the guys called "bench racing" in the cafeteria and across the street at the White Front.

Jimmy Bryan, a tough guy from Phoenix generally described as "brave as Dick Tracy," was more dangerous in the garage area than on the race track. A relentless practical joker, Bryan packed an arsenal of powerful M-80 firecrackers and was known to unload them on friends in phone booths, under dinner tables, and in automobiles. Two years earlier, Bryan had closed down the entire Pennsylvania Turnpike by pitching an M-80 into a toll booth.

While guys like Bryan horsed around and drove like wild men, others were deeply serious and seemed wary of the Speedway. Indianapolis was like that—some drivers accepted its challenges without the slightest hesitation, while others, perhaps more cerebral, viewed it with rightful anguish. It was not a matter of courage, but rather of motivation. Indianapolis was a place that demanded more than bravery. To be successful, a level of audacity bordering on insanity had to be called forth, a fevered urge for speed that transcends logic—which, at 180 miles an hour, becomes a useless component of the human mind.

To hurtle into the Speedway's sweeping corners knowing that the slightest error would send you into the outer walls required a reflexive suspension of reason, forcing a driver to rely on pure passion and mindless, desperate desire.

On the Friday before the first day of qualifications, the weather cleared. A warm sun blossomed over the Indianapolis skyline when Medley and I left the rooming house and began walking toward the track. Then we heard it: an unearthly bellow, punctuated by a faint, bancheelike screech. "A Novi. Come on," he said, breaking into a sprint toward the track entrance.

We got into the garage area to find a crowd gathered around a fierce, white, tubular-shaped car. The war whoop of its monstrous V-8 engine was a siren song for the racing crowd, laden with mystique and danger.

The Novis were the fastest cars ever to appear at the Indianapolis Motor Speedway—and perhaps the most lethal and star-crossed. The Speedway crowd called them "hoodoo machines," jinxed and permeated with death. The first of the two Novis, built by Glendale's Frank Kurtis in 1946, had already claimed the life of veteran Ralph Hepburn—after he had set the track's lap record. He made a tiny error entering the third turn. The Novi nosed onto the infield grass. Hepburn, fifty-two years old and a veteran of eighteen 500-mile races, did what was expected of a front-wheel-drive machine at speed; he applied power to pull the car back into line. But the explosive 550 horses of the Novi overwhelmed him. The car arrowed across the track and bunted the wall head on. Hepburn was killed instantly.

Two years later Duke Nalon, another veteran driving the second Novi, was leading the race when the right rear axle snapped. Nalon skated backward into the wall, where the eighty-five-gallon methanol fuel tank burst open and engulfed the car in flames. Nalon somehow wriggled loose and escaped, although the burns he suffered would keep him hospitalized for months. The Novi meant rampant, haunted horsepower to many at the Speedway, and its legend was only enhanced when the car's designer and creator, W. C. "Bud" Winfield, a technical genius, was killed in a highway crash near Clovis, California. There were two Novis, identical in form and shape. Lean and low, they looked like massive French baguettes on wheels. Both were painted refrigerator white, with "9" and "15" painted on their enormous hoods.

They were officially called Novi Governor Specials. Their owner, a Michigan industrialist named Lew Welch, built, among other things, speed governors for Ford tractors. Welch's relationship with the aging, eccentric mogul dated to the 1920s and was cloaked in mystery. Some believed that Ford money backed the two cars.

The pair were parked outside their garages, glinting in the sunshine as crewmen worked among a swirl of bystanders.

"See that young guy in the sport coat and open shirt?" said Medley.

I spotted him, a plain man with dark hair and a large, flat nose.

"Yeah, so what?"

"Henry Ford's bastard son, Ray Dahlinger."

"Cut the shit," I blurted.

"True fact," said Tom. "Everybody knows it but never talks about it. They say ol' Henry had an affair with a Detroit babe named

Evangeline Cote. He got one of his senior employees, named Roy Dahlinger, to marry her. Her father and brother both got Ford dealerships in Michigan as payoffs to shut them up. That's Ford's kid, Ray Cote Dahlinger. He hangs out with the Novi team here at Indy."

"Jeez, and I thought old Henry was this Bible-thumping puritan."

"And a Jew-baiter to boot. But the old son-of-a-bitch put America on wheels," said Medley.

"And the Dahlinger family in high cotton."

A small man wearing a beret and wire-rimmed glasses stood over the open engine bay of the number 15 Novi. He was Jean Marcenac, the brilliant Frenchman who crew-chiefed the two cars. A crewman named Radio Gardner struck a large starting motor into the blunt snout of the Novi. Race cars carried no starters, and the unit looked like a giant Electrolux vaccuum cleaner. It whined for a moment, before the engine blurted into action. The noise sent men reeling, covering their ears against the primordial shrieking. Acrid methanol fumes poured out of the twin exhaust pipes, causing eyes to water and noses to smart, adding to the Mephistophelian aura of the machine.

"That thing even sounds like death," muttered a reporter from the *Indianapolis Star* standing next to me. "It already killed Hepburn. Its sister tried to kill Nalon. Wonder how much time Miller's got."

Marcenac was unperturbed as he fiddled with the throttle linkage, blipping the engine to warm the oil.

Back at his Pasadena, California shop, he had agreed to start the Novi engines at odd hours, after neighborhood complaints about the noise and concerns from a nearby pottery store owner that the awesome harmonics might shatter his more delicate pieces.

As the engine was warming, Chet Miller sidled out of the darkened garage and into the sunlight. He donned a crash helmet, a dome-shaped object resembling a kitchen pot. He had trouble with the chin strap, thanks to a permanently bent left arm, the relic of a major crash at the Speedway in 1938. Miller had swerved off the backstretch during the 500 in order to avoid fellow driver Bob Swanson, who was sprawled in the middle of the track following a melee that had killed the defending champion, Floyd Roberts.

"Chet's going for the record," said a short man standing behind me. "They say he went over 140 on some stopwatches this morning. Now he's gonna make it official."

Miller climbed into the giant machine, sliding deep into the leather seat and grasping the flat steering wheel, which appeared to have been salvaged from a Greyhound bus. He crammed the beast in gear, idled out of the garage area through a canyon in the grandstands, and disappeared. The crowd stampeded off toward the pits, expecting to see history made as the first 140-mile-per-hour lap was recorded at Indianapolis.

Medley and I reached the pits—no more than a wide apron on the inside of the front straightaway—as Miller rumbled off the fourth turn and arrowed toward us. The shriek of the Novi V-8 bounced and rattled off the high roof of the grandstands, echoing across the Indian flatlands. The Novi rushed past and squirted out of sight into the first corner.

Another lap. Miller gaining speed. Stopwatches clicking along pit row. "One thirty-eight!" somebody shouted.

"He's still warming up," came another voice. "Next lap he'll stand on it."

The drum roll of power. A flash of white at the far end of the straightaway. The ungodly howl of the Novi's supercharger blended with the ominous rumble of its exhaust to create a deafening racket. Miller blazed past, hunched over the steering wheel as he had done thousands of times. If anybody knew how to get around the dreaded rectangle, it was Chet Miller. Or so everyone thought.

The screech of agonized rubber on pavement.

"Oh, oh, the voice of Firestone," said Medley. "I hate that sound."

"The Voice of Firestone" was Speedway slang for the howl that Firestone racing tires emitted during a spin, filched from the title of a popular NBC Radio classical music program sponsored by the Akron company.

Another screech, and then a hollow, thumping explosion unique to the impact of soft metal on concrete.

A track official ran onto the front straight, waving a black flag. Practice was stopped. An ambulance bolted out of Gasoline Alley, its light flashing, and rushed toward the first turn. A thousand faces along pit row gaped in silence.

A woman screamed. I turned to see Miller's wife, Gertrude. She was sitting in the low bleachers behind the pits, the closest a woman could get to the all-male action. She slumped in tears into the arms of a younger woman beside her. Others gathered around her, all wives of drivers who sat in tormented isolation. Sobbing uncontrollably, Gertrude Miller was led away by her friends. As drivers' wives, they were all potential victims of instant tragedy.

Medley and I turned and trudged back to the garage area. A pall hung over the place. The racing fraternity, as it was called, had a sixth sense about serious crashes.

Something serious had happened to Chet Miller. He was dead.

His accident was identical to that which had killed Ralph Hepburn in the same car six years earlier. The Novi had bobbled slightly entering the turn, then dove to the inside apron. Partially on the grass, Miller had repeated Hepburn's error by nailing the throttle. Again the beast seized its reins and arrowed into the wall at 120 miles an hour. Chet Miller died with the same basal fracture of the skull that had killed his teammate.

One second, Miller was chasing the fastest lap in Indianapolis Speedway history. Another second, and he was dead.

Engines were silent. A pall hung over the entire track. Mechanics, crews, members of the press, and the various manufacturer's reps who infested the place, stood zombie-like, each digesting the tragedy in his own way.

We headed instinctively toward the Vukovich garage. Travers and Coon were laboring, heads down and mute, on the Fuel Injection Special—the number 14, battleship-gray Kurtis-Kraft that Vuke was to drive. He lurked in the back, shielded from the press. We were among a select few allowed into his private space.

"Tough deal about ol' Chet," mumbled Medley.

"Yeah, he was a good guy," answered Vukovich.

"I wonder what happened?" I asked.

"Nothin' happened," snapped Vukovich. "He made a mistake. He got killed. That simple. You don't make a mistake in this place. Some days you eat the bear. Other days the bear eats you."

He turned away and began to sort through a mass of spark plugs on the bench. "What are you gonna say to the press? They're sure as hell gonna ask your opinion about the crash," I said.

"They can write whatever the hell they want. They don't need me," he grumbled.

A scrawny man with streaky gray hair walked up as we left Vukovich in his sullen isolation. It was Ken Purdy, the editor of *True Magazine* and an accomplished writer about motor racing.

"You've gotta wonder about all this dying. When's it gonna stop?" I said.

Purdy, who was given to literary references, fired back, "Probably never. Ernest Hemingway said there are only three real sports— bullfighting, mountain-climbing and automobile racing. The rest are children's games played by grown-ups."

"You've got to die to make it a sport?" I countered.

"Let me put it this way. Tazio Nuvolari was maybe the greatest race driver who ever lived. Someone once asked him why he risked his life in a racing car. 'How do you want to die?' he asked his inquisitor. 'In bed, in my sleep,' was the answer. 'Then how do you find the courage to turn out the lights at night?' said Nuvolari. Ironically, Nuvolari died in bed, but his point pertains," said Purdy.

Seemingly satisfied that he had answered my question, Purdy began framing pictures with his trendy new Nikon 35 mm single-lens reflex camera and wandered back into the crowd.

Somewhere, as if by a signal, an engine fired up. It was the guttural rumble of an Offenhauser. Another joined in. Then two more. Crew chiefs were back at it, warming up their engines in preparation for the track to reopen for more practice.

The debris of the Miller crash would be swept up, and business would begin again, as if nothing at all had happened.

The bark and roar of the big engines spoke of a new beginning. Chet Miller was dead. A race car was wrecked. It was time to begin the resurrection.

Rumination over a tragedy would not be tolerated. Any reflection might bring into harsh light the potential futility of the entire enterprise—that seeking unseemly speed for a few moments of glory and a pocketful of money bordered on insanity. Death was a partner in big-time automobile racing. To exclude it somehow unraveled the meaning of the contest. This was a war against fear and reason, and to pause, much less to wave a white flag, meant weakness, capitulation, and defeat.

Within an hour, the track was open again. Other men were charging past the ugly smear on the turn-one wall that marked Miller's last moment on earth.

The rains came again the following day, which was supposed to be the start of qualifying. Each entrant would be given four laps on the Speedway. The thirty-three drivers recording the quickest times would make the 500-mile Memorial Day race. The rest would load up their cars and go home.

The low-pressure system that had cursed the Midwest for most of the month of May ended by early afternoon. The grandstands filled with perhaps 100,000 fans, each of whom had paid fifty cents for the privilege of watching one car at a time circulate the track.

The gloom hung over the Speedway until mid-afternoon, when the American Automobile Association officials judged the track dry enough for qualifications. Freddy Agabashian, a mannerly northern California veteran, managed to gain quick time in a new Kurtis roadster entered by the Chicago-based Granatelli brothers.

An ugly bank of rain clouds loomed in the west as the Fuel Injection Special was rolled out of its garage and Vukovich climbed aboard. Running in the rain was sure disaster, yet he headed onto the Speedway for his four-lap run against the clock.

"This looks like *To Please a Lady*," cracked Medley as we sprinted to the pits. He was referring to the 1951 MGM feature starring Clark Gable and Barbara Stanwyck, wherein Gable had braved a rainstorm to qualify for the 500.

"Life imitating art," I mused.

Vuke reeled off three perfect laps. The Fuel-Injection Kurtis, smaller, lower, and narrower than the rest of the entrants, seemed planted to the track, its driver in a long-sleeved denim shirt, leaning aggressively over the steering wheel.

"Oh, shit, here it comes," shouted a photographer as he attempted to shield his Speed Graphic from the cloudburst that suddenly pounded the Speedway. The torrent sent the bleacher crowd scurrying for cover as the growl of Vukovich's engine rose in the distant back straight.

"He's gotta lift. That thing will think it's on an ice rink," said Medley.

"No way he'll finish the lap," I agreed.

Standing in the monsoon, we awaited the silence signaling that Vukovich had cut his engine and was coasting into the pits.

Wrong. This was the Mad Russian, not some featherfoot tyro. The Offy's thunder racketed off the grandstands as the car, sluicing and yawing on the rain-soaked bricks, roared out of the mist and skated past the checkered flag, rooster-tails of spray spewing off its wheels.

"Holy shit! Now I've seen it all!" exclaimed a reporter from the *Toledo Blade*. "Nobody ever ran this joint at full speed in the rain. That Vukovich has cast-iron balls, I'll give him that!"

He also had the pole position for the 1953 Indianapolis 500-mile race, based on one of the most audacious driving exhibitions ever witnessed in the thirty-seven-year history of the Indianapolis Motor Speedway.

CHAPTER TWO

THE FRESNO
TRACTOR DRIVER

IN A RARE MOMENT OF REFLECTION, THE SPEEDWAY management stood down for part of a day to honor Chet Miller. On the Monday following Vukovich's daredevil drive in the rain, practice was suspended for Miller's funeral services, which were held at the Speedway City Funeral Home nearby. Father Leo A. Lindemann, the Catholic track chaplain, gave the eulogy. It was announced at the ceremony that the Chevy Chase Country Club in Glendale, California, planned to erect a water fountain in the seventh hole in memory of Miller, who was a devoted golfer and a longtime member member of the club.

Six of Miller's rival drivers, including Wilbur Shaw, were pallbearers. Shaw was an icon in Indianapolis. Not only had he won the 500 three times, with a fourth in his pocket until a wheel broke, but he was the Speedway's President. He worked for owner Anton "Tony"

Hulman, the Terre Haute sportsman who had purchased the track from Eddie Rickenbacker in 1946. Yale man Hulman's family owned Terre Haute, for all intents and purposes, as well as the Clabber Girl Baking Powder Co. and Indiana's Coca-Cola distributorship.

Following the funeral service, the engines were back at full cry. As if to take a chunk out of the bear, Duke Nalon was among the first on the track to make some practice laps in the second Novi. To climb into a sister car that had killed two of his teammates and had tried to burn him alive was an act of pure defiance. Nalon was a crafty, low-key Chicagoan, not given to big talk. Like many Indy veterans, he had abandoned the sport full-time for a job with Ford Motor Company in its aircraft division, and only drove once a year at Indianapolis. Many believed that his deft touch with the evil Novis came as close as possible to maximizing the car's potential. Only one Novi remained. Owner Lew Welch announced that the Hepburn/Miller machine would never be repaired. Enough was enough.

With Vuke on the pole for the race, he was able to relax as seventy-six drivers hammered around the track seeking the remaining thirty-two positions. He remained reclusive, choosing to confine his limited conversations to Travers and Coon and a few other drivers. Some believed him to be an angry man, full of venom and hatred for strangers, but this was not the case. In private he was affable and easygoing. But he sought no public image and asked for none in return.

One morning we were hanging around his garage when a writer for *Life* magazine approached me and asked if I might intercede to arrange an interview. I told him the possibility was unlikely, but that I would ask.

"Hey Vuke, a guy from *Life* magazine would like to talk with you. What do you think?"

"This does my talking," he said, a wry smile crossing his face. He was pointing to his right foot.

In fact, Vukovich's entire mind and body were able to talk racing at a level of intensity seldom seen in the sport. He trained vigorously for the ordeal, both back home in Fresno and at the Speedway, where he ran the 2.5-mile track each morning and flailed away steadily on an exercise machine mounted in his garage. Like many drivers, he had fashioned a steering wheel mounted on a shaft connected to a friction shock absorber. Twisting on the wheel developed upper-arm and shoulder strength, a critical component in controlling a nose-heavy, one-ton race car at speed during an era when power steering was only available on a few luxury sedans. Born in Alameda, but raised in Fresno where his immigrant father had run a small vineyard, when he was sixteen he and his two older brothers were orphaned and had raised themselves on the tiny spread on the edge of town.

He drifted into the world of motor racing before the war, fascinated by the fierce competition and lured by the possibility of making a living away from the hardscrabble farm. He made little impact prior to his military service in World War II, but returned a stronger, brighter, more focused competitor; and by 1950 he had won the national midget racing championship in the face of fierce competition from masses of hungry, restless veterans like himself. Vukovich's dream was to race at the Indianapolis Motor Speedway, the Mount Olympus of the sport, and he took an instant liking to the foreboding rectangle. He felt no fear of the place.

For others it was not so easy. John Fitch was a P-51 fighter pilot, prisoner of war, and an expert sports car driver with the top-notch Cunningham team. He had just won the arduous Sebring 12-Hour endurance race and had returned to Indianapolis, his native city, where his father was an executive with the now-defunct Stutz motor company. He planned to race in the vaunted 500, but like many, this courageous and skilled driver simply could not get comfortable in the vast arena. After attempting to run competitively in two different cars, he left quietly to return to the amateur sports car world, whose drivers Rodger Ward and other pros lampooned as "strokers and bro-kers"—i.e., rich playboys lacking the cojones to run with "real" men.

This was surely unfair, although in Fitch's case, it was true that he was unable to exceed 129 mph in a new Kurtis roadster while forty-six-year-old Bill Holland, who had been suspended from the Speedway for two years after running a so-called outlaw (unsanc-tioned) race, easily qualified the car at 137 mph. Holland, a former winner of the 500, was clearly someone who had no trouble running the big track at record speeds. Yet Fitch's career in motor sports would be long and distinguished, despite his failure to crack the mental bar-rier at Indianapolis.

Somehow an eastern Brahmin was at a massive disadvantage in professional automobile racing. Of the thirty-three men who made up the starting field in 1953, more than half were native Californians. Eight had either won the 500 or were destined to win it during the fifties.

All were working-class Anglo-Saxons, with the exception of Vukovich. All had been trained in the crucible of competition like the booming midget racing leagues, where competition was carried on around the Los Angeles basin seven nights a week, or in the crazed California Roadster Association, where wheel-to-wheel hot-rod rac-ing took place at the elemental level of survival of the fittest.

They were hardly boys of summer. Of the thirty-three, only two, at twenty-four years of age, were young enough to play major league baseball in their prime. A few others were in their late twen-ties or early thirties. Three were in their forties, bringing the aver-age age to twenty-eight. All had been in racing since their teenage years, bouncing around the dirt and asphalt bullrings of the nation, honing their skills behind the wheels of lethal, unhinged semi-wrecks owned and campaigned by local gas station and garage owners, all dreaming of a shot at Indianapolis. All had suffered injuries ranging from broken noses and teeth and cheekbones, to horrific arm bruises from flying clots of dirt, to multiple fractures and burns. Many were unmarried, content to live out their lives drifting from racetrack to racetrack, with cheap hotels and tourist homes offering the only respite from the noise and violence. Weeks on end might be spent sleeping in the backseat of a car towing a race car known simply as "the Ford motel."

A man of Fitch's background, where gentlemanly amateur motor sports was the fashion, could not easily adjust to the fanatic level of driving to be found among the Californians. So it would come to pass that Golden Staters like Johnny Parsons, Oklahoma transplant Troy Ruttman (absent from the 1953 starters due to an arm injury), Vukovich, Bob Sweikert, Sam Hanks, Rodger Ward, and Jim Rathmann would win at Indianapolis while gentlemen sports car racers, the "teabaggers" and "strokers and brokers," were resigned to secondary status, at least in the deadly game being played out each May at Indianapolis.

As an example of how unforgiving professional racing at the Indianapolis level was: among the thirty-three men who started the 1953 Indianapolis Motor Speedway International Sweepstakes (the official name of the event), seventeen would die in racing accidents. Another would be permanently disabled. Four would meet death at Indianapolis, while the rest would die at various dirt track and asphalt speedways around the nation. By contrast, in Fitch's world of sports cars, death and injury were both rare. The racing speeds were slower, and the environment was more relaxed.

Medley and I ate dinner the night before the big race with a few journalists at a little downtown steak house called St. Elmo's, famous for its mouth-frying shrimp cocktail sauce and tender beef. We planned to rise early and be at the trackside long before the prerace festivities got underway at ten o'clock. But I was awake far earlier than expected, when a hot breeze rolled into my bedroom. I checked the clock: 3 a.m. and already it was stifling. Unless a cold front arrived,

Indianapolis would be blanketed in insufferable humidity by the time the green flag fell.

The cavernous grandstands were slow to fill, the throng (estimated at two-hundred thousand) perhaps sensing that a late arrival would minimize exposure to the heat. By ten o'clock the thermometer outside the Associated Press hut read 88 degrees. A steamy layer of soft nimbus clouds hung over the track, and people were already dabbing their foreheads with soaked handkerchiefs.

The Purdue University marching band was a traditional performer at the prerace ceremony. It would accompany Martin Downey in his rendition of local favorite "Back Home in Indiana." The program went according to plan until a pretty blonde drum majorette keeled over with heat prostration. She was followed by four band members, who went down like tenpins in heat-induced faints.

The cars were rolled out of their garages and pushed onto the front straightaway, there to be swallowed up by a sea of sweating pit crewmen, VIPs, journalists, and track officials. The drivers, sensing a long, hot ride, were wearing polo shirts, ignoring fire protection in favor of simple ventilation.

Whistles blew and a battalion of track guards wearing blue shirts and yellow ties—a uniform resembling the Indiana State Highway Patrol began to clear the grid.

Only the cars, their drivers, and the crews stood on the bricks. Then came the world-famous words from speedway boss Wilbur Shaw: "Gentlemen, start your engines."

Starters whined. Engines blurted into life. A cheer swept through the grandstand. William Clay Ford, the son of the founder of modern automotive transportation, eased onto the track at the wheel of his white Ford Sunliner convertible pace car. Ford slowly accelerated to lead the field on a pair of pace laps. Vukovich's gray Fuel Injection Special was flanked by fellow Californians Freddy Agabashian in the Granatelli brothers' Kurtis-Kraft roadster and

Jack McGrath in Jack Hinkle's narrow, bright maroon, upright dirt-track Kurtis.

Meldley rushed off to the first turn with his camera, hoping to get some early race action. Dripping sweat, I made off to the pits to await any emergency stops.

The race started. Deafening thunder as the field pounded past and slashed out of sight. A minute later they reappeared, with Vukovich already well out in front. Lap one of two hundred.

Four laps and a yellow flag. Caution. Andy Linden, a burly ex-navy boxer from Manhattan Beach, had started fifth among the fast guys, but had lost control in the second turn and slammed into the wall. I headed for the infield hospital, where the chief doctor, C. B. Bohner, had set up a small army of physicians, nurses, and ambulance drivers to handle the inevitable crunch of injuries among the massive crowd and the competitors.

As I trudged through the infield, I passed a row of bizarre scaffolds that had been erected along the main straightaway. They looked like medieval assault towers, built out of spindly pipe frames used as temporary construction and painters' platforms, and enterprising fans had erected them for better race viewing. Though they were guy-wired, they looked over-packed and dangerously wobbly. A year later, one such structure would topple, killing several people. The towers were subsequently banished from the Speedway.

Seven tents had been erected around the infield hospital. Already a cluster of cots was occupied by victims of the rising heat. Nurses were applying cold packs and offering water to patients as the ambulance hauling Linden arrived. He staggered out, apparently not seriously injured, although an ugly burn on his right arm needed treatment.

The thermometer on the door frame of the hospital read 91 degrees. It was not yet noon. Linden's wife arrived, crying hysterically. It was the wives who had it worst of all.

Beyond the rickety towers and the grandstands, the deathly roar of the engines was omnipresent. I could see flashes of color as the cars arrowed past through breaks in the crowd. It was clear that Vukovich was in the lead and unchallenged.

Word spread through the staff that Carl Scarborough was being brought in with heat prostration. He was a veteran of the so-called outlaw circuits that were unrecognized by the American Automobile Association, and had run the 500 only once before. He claimed to be thirty-eight years old.

He arrived on a stretcher, looking beet-red. An ambulance attendant came out of the hospital. "He's got a temperature of 103.6. His crew accidentally doused him with CO2 trying to put out a fuel fire. Damn near suffocated him. He ain't good."

Gene Hartley, a kid from Indiana, arrived soon afterward. He had hit the wall, but appeared unhurt. It was getting hotter. Two more drivers showed up on stretchers. Johnny Parsons, who had won the race in 1950, and Jerry Hoyt, a newcomer, were wrapped in wet sheets and given intravenous salt solutions.

The din went on.

A male nurse came out. "Scarborough's real bad. They've opened up his chest and are massaging his heart. Three doctors working in teams."

Another ambulance. Pat Flaherty had gotten woozy from the heat and lost control in the third turn. He was unconscious. After a short interlude inside the hospital, he was reloaded into the ambulance and sent on to Methodist Hospital.

A reporter from Chicago said, "It's a war zone on pit road. Guys are falling out of the cars like flies. It's over 130 degrees on the track. Nobody can handle it."

"What about Vukovich?" I asked.

"Except him. Hasn't slowed a bit. The guy isn't human."

Father Lindemann, the Catholic priest who had conducted the service for Chet Miller, blew through the crowd and went into the hospital.

"Bad sign. He's giving Scarborough last rites," somebody said.

Spider Webb, another veteran, showed up, also wrecked by the heat. Then came Tony Bettenhausen, the former national champion, and Rodger Ward, the cocky ex–fighter pilot. All were wrapped in cold sheets and seemed to be recovering. Would this nightmare never end? Word went around that only a few drivers, including Vukovich, who was far in the lead, could continue without relief. Drivers were piling in and out of the steaming cockpits to the point that no one was sure who was driving what car. Art Cross, an Indiana driver who started the race in a car owned by tiny blond Bessie Paoli, operator of a welding shop in Springfield, Illinois, quickly gave in to the oppressive heat. His car's cockpit was so poorly ventilated that four other drivers relieved him at the wheel during the race. The Springfield Welding Special finally finished second, marking the only time in the history of the race that five drivers shared in one car's prize money. Several other cars had three drivers, while young Bob Scott carried on for Scarborough. In the face of the choking heat, no one was quitting.

Linden was back. He had crashed a second time. He had shrugged off his earlier injuries and gone back to drive relief, only to bunt the wall again. Dr. Bohner yelled at Linden for such idiotic behavior. "Hey, Doc, you can't let your buddies down," pleaded Linden.

Carl Scarborough was dead. It was announced to the press as the final laps unwound.

Four laps from the end, another yellow flag. Hartley again. Like Linden, he had gone back for more, relieving his friend Chuck Stevenson, who was driving the Agajanian 98 that had won the race the year before. Exhausted and heat-ravaged, Hartley had smacked the wall a second time. Miraculously, he was not seriously injured. Duke Nalon, cautiously driving the remaining Novi, had intentionally spun to miss Hartley and ended up stalled on the track apron. This would mark the final appearance of front-drive Novis in the Indianapolis 500.

A distant cheer echoed from the grandstands as Vukovich took the checkered flag. He had led all but five laps of the two hundred. Then silence. The engines were dead. Only the rustle of the crowd heading for the gates rose above the stifling breeze.

A doctor and a nurse rushed toward an ambulance. "Russo and Daywalt," said the Chicago reporter. "Both in bad shape from the heat. Stuck in Gasoline Alley. Too much traffic and crowds. They can't get here. The docs are going to them with adrenaline and salt solutions. This place is nuts."

I had spent the entire race—all of its insane, boiling, metal-shredding three hours and fifty-three minutes—hanging around the hospital. I had seen little or nothing of the track action, although the endless detonations of the racing engines still rang in my ears. Feeling sorry for poor Scarborough and the chaos he was surely leaving behind for his family, I worked my way back to Gasoline Alley. It was slow going against the tide of spectators heading for the parking lots. My plan was to meet Medley at the Vukovich garage.

The place was mobbed with reporters and bystanders jammed ten deep in front of the Fuel Injection Special. The car, smeared with rubber dust and oil, was parked outside. A large victory wreath hung on its cowling.

I spotted Medley on the edge of the mob.

"Let's get outta here," he said. "The heat's killing me. Vuke's not around. Must be with the VIPs or the big-time press. You know that ice cream parlor near the rooming house? Man, I'd die for a malt right now."

With that, we fled the hellish scene.

It took nearly an hour to poke our way through the glut of people trying to wedge their way out of the gates and onto Sixteenth Street. Cars were everywhere, jammed in honking masses. "The main highways for a hundred miles in every direction are in gridlock," said a Speedway City cop, soaked in sweat as he directed traffic.

We trudged down a tree-lined street in silence. One driver was dead, and many were injured, albeit not seriously, while our rooming house–mate had won the biggest motor race in the world. Even in the shade, the heat was unrelenting. Our pace increased as we spotted the parlor ahead.

Wheeling through the door, we spotted a couple sitting at a corner table. The woman, dark blonde, was wearing a white sleeveless summer dress. The man, swarthy and well-muscled, was in a filthy, sweat-soaked polo shirt and grimy white pants that appeared to have been worn in a grease pit.

"Holy shit, that's Vuke!" exclaimed Medley.

"What the hell is he doing here?"

We approached the couple, who were drinking large milk shakes.

"Jeez, Vuke. I thought you'd be over at the Speedway with the big-wigs, celebrating like a real hero driver," I said.

"You can't believe how hot it was out there. Like driving a tractor in Fresno in July. For the last hundred miles all I could think of was a cold shake in this place. As soon as I could, I got Esther and we scrammed. I'll do that hero stuff when they give me my check."

So there he was, the winner of the Indianapolis 500, sitting in an ice cream parlor, far from the screaming masses, from the press and the autograph hunters.

Tomorrow his name would be plastered all over every newspaper in the world and a big payday awaited him at the victory banquet.

By that time we had packed up and headed out on the long drive back to Los Angeles. Vuke's take was big: $89,496 in prize money, which he would split with the owner, Howard Keck, and his crew. But he would also get the Ford Sunliner convertible pace car, a special winner's wristwatch, a year of free meals from a local catering service, a tool set, and a cocker spaniel puppy with a case of Ideal dog food.

And one very cold milk shake.

CHAPTER THREE

EVERYWHERE, THUNDER

FOLLOWING HIS DECISIVE VICTORY AT INDIANAPOLIS, Bill Vukovich was content to remain out of the public eye, refusing the corporate endorsements that came the way of an Indianapolis champion, and all offers for public appearances. One exception came when Firestone flew Vukovich and his crew of Jim Travers and Frank Coon, plus three-time Indy winner and track manager Wilbur Shaw, to the Big Apple. The occasion: a special appearance on the *Voice of Firestone* television show. Harvey Firestone, the scion of the great tire company family, hosted the trip. Prior to the show he ordered a cab to take Vukovich, Travers, and Coon on a tour of the city. Travers recalled, "We told the driver to take us to Broadway. When we rolled down the Great White Way, I turned to Vuke and said, 'When Frank and I hired you, we promised we'd get you on Broadway. Well, here you are.' Vukovich lifted up his right foot and said, 'Cut the shit, Smokey'—that's what he called me—'this is what got us to Broadway.'"

When he quietly returned to his small ranch to help his wife, Esther, raise their two children, Vukovich's absence from the rest of the AAA national championship schedule was a disaster for race promoters across the country. They depended on the presence of the Indy 500 champion to boost the gates at the ten other races leading to the national title. All were held on fairground dirt tracks, ancient one-mile ovals that had been designed for horse racing. Most of them, like the Michigan State Fairgrounds in Detroit, the New York State Fairgrounds at Syracuse, the Indiana Fairgrounds at Indianapolis, and the Arizona State Fairgrounds at Phoenix, had been built between 1880 and 1910.

The dirt miles were insanely dangerous. Lined with board fences or chain-link barriers, they offered no protection to the drivers. Shredded wood or jagged steel could easily kill a man on impact. The clay surfaces were either deeply rutted and layered in powdery, blinding dust or polished to an ice-rink sheen by the spinning tires. Flying clots of dirt and stones did terrible damage to the drivers, sitting upright and exposed in their cars. They wore nothing but light clothing, a thin leather helmet, and goggles. Broken noses and jaws, and shattered teeth were common during the running of the 100-mile endurance tests, during which the track surface could change radically based on the heat, sunshine, and humidity.

The drivers made feeble attempts to protect themselves from the debris. Some wore bandannas over their mouths and noses to keep out the dust. Others wrapped cardboard around their midriffs and their right arms, which were most vulnerable during the broad slides that pitched the cars sideways. Some bit down on rags to keep their teeth from rattling loose. Others simply faced the raging dirt, knowing that by the end of the season their entire upper bodies would be a mass of welted, black-and-blue flesh.

As brave as he was, Vukovich hated the mile tracks. "You get really tired out there over a hundred miles," he'd say. "Or else the car does. You make one slip and you're done. You couldn't pay me enough to get me on that circuit."

Those words were spoken after his 500 victory, when his nearly $40,000 share of the winnings had given his family a sufficient cushion to restrict his race driving. Prior to winning the 500 he had run the lethal miles, driving with his usual relentless style and winning his share of races.

Late in the year he did relent, at least theoretically. J. C. Agajanian, the Los Angeles promoter, staged a 100-mile championship race in late October at Sacramento's California State Fair and proudly announced that Vukovich had entered. This was a pure publicity stunt, since he had been paid a hefty sum merely to appear in a second-rate car and attempt to qualify. His time was over 3.5 seconds slower than the pole winner, Jimmy Bryan, and too slow to make the eighteen-car starting field. Having collected his "appearance" or "deal" money, Vukovich headed back home to Fresno no worse for the wear and indifferent to his slow time. Already he was in training for his next race, a defense of his Indianapolis 500 title. When a reporter asked him about his disappointing time at Sacramento, he shrugged and grumped, "Write whatever you want, you don't need me."

By the summer of 1953, Los Angeles had gone crazy over cars. Since the population boom of the twenties, when the great western migrations reached full stride, the entire basin had become an automobile paradise. Perfect weather, vast open acreage, the nearby mountains with their miles of twisty roads, and the great dry lakes beyond the mountains had produced an environment in which automobiles of every size, shape, and design could thrive.

The plutocrats of the movie colony had been ideal customers for the flashy Duesenbergs, Rolls-Royces, and Mercedes beyond the reach of ordinary citizens. The automobile industry had created a style revolution when the Fisher Body Division of General Motors hired young, brash Harley J. Earle, who was then customizing Cadillacs for members of the movie colony at the Don Lee Agency in Los Angeles. Earle was transforming drab, monochromatic roadsters and sedans into flashy, multicolored rolling stock that altered the entire consciousness of the industry. He would later become chief of the General Motors Art and Color Section, which grew into the giant, corporate styling department that created the incredible two- and three-tone, be-finned "insolent chariots" of the car-crazed 1950s. Earle would be but the first of many designers and stylists to rise out of Los Angeles, both from the hot-rod and custom-car movement and from the more formal precincts of the Art Center School in Pasadena.

By the twenties, a fledgling hot-rod culture had formed, in the main by young men who took their modified Model T roadsters to the mud-baked, high desert lake beds at Muroc, Russetta, and Rosamond for high-speed runs. Other race cars still ran at dangerous ovals like Ascot long after the multimillion-dollar, ultra-high-speed board tracks built in the 1920s had either burned down or rotted away.

Following the end of World War II, thousands of veterans returned with fevered enthusiasm for fast sports cars like the British MGs and Jaguars they had discovered during their European tours of duty. The sports car craze joined hot-rodder madness to infest the streets of the entire basin, from the San Fernando Valley in the north to the eastern Los Angeles suburbs to the surfer beach towns in the south.

In an effort to limit the outlaw world of street racing, the National Hot Rod Association was formed to organize the "drag races" so reviled and feared by the citizenry. The races slowly migrated onto airport runways and special drag stops and off the public streets.

In a parallel movement, the California Sports Car Club organized races staged on closed public roads and on airport runways as far south as Torrey Pines outside San Diego and as far north as Pebble Beach on the Monterey peninsula.

Thanks to the Southern California aircraft industry, which had boomed during the war, thousands of young men were now skilled in the arts of welding, lathe work, metal-crafting, tool-and-die-making, drafting, and other skills necessary to build, modify, and maintain high-powered automobiles.

As a nascent high-performance industry rose out of gas stations, auto dealerships, and backyard garages, self-taught craftsmen began manufacturing exhaust systems, camshafts, cylinder heads, carburetors, fuel-injection systems, magnesium wheels, custom bodies, chassis, and even entire cars. By the end of the twentieth century, such pioneering names as Cragar, Bell, Edelbrock, Iskenderian, Halibrand, and others served as the cornerstone of a speed-equipment industry that generated over 30 billion dollars in annual revenues.

Meanwhile, master metal men, working with little more than tin-snips, a bag of sand, and a hammer, were creating aluminum masterpieces. Artisans named Kurtis, Kuzma, Lesovsky, and Deidt were pounding out stunning race cars from sheet aluminum and chrome-molybdenum steel tubing. Meyer-Drake manufactured powerful four-cylinder racing engines in Glendale that were first designed by Harry Miller and perfected by his shop foreman Fred Offenhauser in the early 1930s.

In July of '53 the savagery of the Korean War finally ended, with an uneasy armistice. Stalin was dead and a new, smiling president named Ike promised a term of endless rounds of golf and evenings of television laughs with Uncle Miltie while the nation supped on Swanson's revolutionary frozen TV dinners. *Reader's Digest* scolded smokers with a breakthrough series titled "Cancer in a Carton." The tobacco industry and Liggett & Myers countered the blow with a new L&M brand marketed with the slogan "Just what the doctor ordered."

The Dow Jones sat in the mid 250s—within striking distance of the pre-crash high of 1929. The Yankees dominated baseball and Hillary and Tenzing conquered Mount Everest. Hollywood was about to revolutionize the picture business with Cinemascope and 3-D. For the first time since Pearl Harbor, the world seemed to be back on its axis.

Medley and I had returned to Los Angeles after the 1953 Vukovich victory at Indianapolis and drifted our separate ways. He continued his photography and his cartooning for *Hot Rod* magazine while my freelance writing career began to bear fruit. I sold a screenplay to Warner Brothers that was never produced, along with several stories to *Colliers* and *Look*, two of the largest and flashiest weeklies in the business. I soon had enough money to afford a small apartment in Studio City and a used MG TC roadster that I bought from Competition Motors, a hot dealership on Vine Street in North Hollywood owned by a wealthy Austrian émigré and race driver named Johnny Von Neumann.

The sports car crowd gathered at places like "Hollywood" Bill White's Ascot Cafe on Slawson and the Coach & Horses on Sunset Boulevard in Hollywood to discuss racing exploits and nighttime adventures on the twisty Mulholland Drive in the hills above the Cahuenga Pass.

The hot-rodders hung out at the area's drive-in restaurants—which had become a Southern California fad—between their endless street races and stoplight shootouts. Favorites included the In-n-Out on Valley Boulevard in El Monte, Farmer Boys on Colorado, Bob's Big Boy in Glendale, and Henry's in Arcadia, all of which would form the basis twenty years later for George Lucas's classic movie about the hot-rod culture, *American Graffiti.*

A flock of magazines were published to serve the various enthusiast groups. By far the largest was Medley's *Hot Rod* magazine and its sister, *Motor Trend*, published by the Petersen Group, which had taken up high-rise headquarters on Sunset Boulevard. Serving the sports car scene was *Road & Track*, where, from its Playa del Rey headquarters, it lavished praise on the European machinery pouring into the basin. Other, smaller publications concentrated their coverage on the oval-track racers who remained active in the region, although the famed Gilmore Stadium had been torn down in 1951, to be replaced by the CBS television studios. Built in 1934 on the corner of Fairfax and Beverly boulevards by oil baron Earl Gilmore, it was the first stadium dedicated to the booming sport of midget auto racing—the competition that spawned great stars like Vukovich.

While automobile enthusiasm percolated, there was little crossover among the various subspecies. The hot-rodders laughed at the sports car set, with their English-style driving gloves and woolen caps, calling them "tea-baggers," "strokers and brokers," and "sporty car drivers," while the MG and Jaguar aficionados denounced professional Indy types as "circle burners" and "roundy-rounders."

It was into this world of car nuts of all types that Detroit made its entrance in early 1953. Cadillac and Oldsmobile had been producing high-performance V-8 engines since the late 1940s but had been reluctant to abandon their giant, soft-spring sedans in order to compete with the sports cars pouring into the American market from Europe.

But in January 1953, the Chevrolet division of General Motors entered the fray when new GM models were shown at the corporation's "Motorama," held annually at New York's Waldorf-Astoria hotel. Among the flashy machinery was a svelte two-door roadster called the Corvette. Its body was fiberglass and its power plant a modified six-cylinder—the "Blue Flame Six" used in the division's mundane passenger sedans. There had been little choice, in that Chevrolet's arch rivals within the corporation, Cadillac and Oldsmobile, refused to share their powerful V-8s with the struggling, entry-level brand. Chevrolet, under siege at the time from Ford—which had a new V-8 of its own—was left with its own tepid six-cylinder tied to a two-speed "Powerglide" automatic transmission. This immediately handicapped the Corvette in the marketplace against rivals like Jaguar, which employed a high-performance, double-overhead, camshaft six that produced 180 horsepower versus the Corvette's 150. Moreover, the Jaguar used a four-speed manual transmission of the type preferred by enthusiasts. Worse yet, the new XK 140s from Jaguar boasted a top speed easily 25 mph higher than the Detroit upstart. Despite high hopes that the Corvette would penetrate the import sports car market, only 183 were sold in 1953 and rumors drifted through the automobile industry that the project would be cancelled.

The hard-core sports car crowd who gathered regularly at the Coach & Horses scoffed at the Corvette. Bar talk denounced the "fiberglass flyer" powered by a "shushbox automatic." It made no impact on the anointed, who understood the value of a "real" sports car. Ford then countered with plans for a two-seater called the Thunderbird to be introduced in 1955. It would be described not as a sports car, but as a "personal car," with emphasis on creature comforts and smoothness as opposed to the more elemental pleasures to be found in the Corvette.

The great Detroit horsepower race was about to accelerate. It had begun in 1948–49, when Cadillac and Oldsmobile developed powerful overhead-valve V-8s that almost doubled the output of the aged in-line six- and eight-cylinder engines that had been the industry standards for decades. These revolutionary new units were quickly imitated throughout the industry, leaving only Chevrolet with their antiquated six. Yet rumors arose that a revolutionary lightweight Chevrolet V-8 was in the works for 1955.

Already, Chrysler and Lincoln had engines producing well over 200 horsepower, and both were major contenders in the violent, high-speed Carrera PanAmericana, a 1,500-mile open road race that ran the length of Mexico. Other manufacturers were hastily creating big, thirsty, high-compression V-8s that would easily surpass the 200 hp and soon would nudge past 300.

Mounted as they were in giant, three-ton sedans and coupes

equipped with smallish drum brakes, vague steering, and soft suspensions, these behemoths were far from sports cars. Much of their surplus horsepower was employed in such avante-garde gadgetry as power seats, steering, windows, and automatic transmissions. Still, 100-mph road speeds were common, and accident rates soared as drivers across the nation unleashed their newfound power.

While the Indianapolis professionals were running a series of 100-mile races sanctioned by the American Automobile Association for the national championship, the sports car set was competing on open roads and airport runways converted for racing, with hay bales and rubber cones to mark the corners. The oval-track pros were woolly, intense young men racing for a living. The sports car drivers were simon-pure amateurs competing on the English model, which strictly forbade prize money. Theirs was a "gentleman's" sport. It was believed that money would corrupt the atmosphere, although it was an open secret that many wealthy sportsmen hired drivers with under-the-table payments of hard cash.

While the gentlemen who ran sports cars were in fact as fiercely competitive as the professionals in some respects, the generally lower speeds and lesser horsepower of their cars (excepting a few ultra-fast and exotic Maseratis and Ferraris that were reaching American shores) made the competition much safer. While the professionals labored on dusty, rutted dirt tracks and a few high-banked macadam speedways, the amateurs played on natural road courses lined with trees, telephone poles, ditches, and, in some cases, houses. Protection involved a few hay bales laid around significant hazards and flagmen to warn drivers of other cars. While off-road excursions were common, the low cornering speeds—generally in the 50–70 mph range—kept injuries to a minimum. This was in part God's grace, because the drivers were as vulnerable as the professionals—at least those driving open roadsters. Seat belts were required, but rollover protection was unknown. In fact, any suggestion of "roll bars" was rejected by all parties, based on the reasoning that the aesthetics of the car would be ruined by such appendages. "We don't race our cars upside down" was the standard response among the AAA professionals, and this mantra was repeated among the amateur ranks.

On the whole, safety, both for the drivers and the spectators, who often watched road races from behind snow fences and other flimsy barriers, was a minor consideration and would remain so until the end of the decade. Modest efforts to protect spectators had been made after an incident at Watkins Glen in 1952, when a Cadillac-Allard driven by millionaire Chicago sportsman Fred Wacker hit a child sitting on a curb between the legs of his father. It happened on the opening laps of the Watkins Glen Grand Prix, a race started in 1948 in the tiny upstate New York village around a 6.6-mile network of public roads. The Allard had skidded while slowing for a corner on the village's main street. It struck the seven-year-old, killing him instantly. The ensuing outrage prompted the state legislature to outlaw further competition on state highways and forced the Watkins Glen organizers to move the Grand Prix to local county and town roads until a permanent, closed circuit could be built.

A year later, AAA champion driver Chuck Stevenson lost control during the annual 100-mile race at the nearby Syracuse State Fairgrounds and tumbled upside-down into a group of spectators. Miraculously, no one was seriously injured, although when the Stevenson car was righted, a small boy was found crammed in the cockpit. The Stevenson car had made a perfect landing on top of the child, leaving him uninjured. These and other incidents were essentially ignored, and the issue of crowd safety would have to wait until a shocking disaster rocked the world out of its apathy.

The sports car craze was attracting an entirely new demographic mix. Because the automobiles were expensive, high-speed toys, with little utility for everyday life, higher-income customers made up the market. Upper-middle-class enthusiasts were buying the British and

German imports, which generally cost three times as much as a basic Chevrolet or Ford. Sports car ownership was instantly appealing to upwardly mobile men and women, and the presumed sophistication embodied in the ownership of a European sports car—as opposed to mundane "Detroit Iron"—packed tremendous social cachet.

This trendiness was affirmed by the presence of the celebrities who populated the pits of the sports car races and who often competed themselves. In the east, TV broadcasters Walter Cronkite and Dave Garroway drove in races, while bandleader Paul Whiteman and opera star James Melton were regular attendees. On the West Coast, superstar Clark Gable was often seen at the races, as was fellow actor Keenan Wynn. Competing in his own Maserati and Ferrari was international playboy Porfirio Rubirosa, the ex-husband of Barbara Hutton (whose son, Lance Reventlow, would become a major presence in the sport). Sexpot actress Zsa Zsa Gabor often accompanied Rubirosa, adding a glitter and panache virtually unknown in the grittier world of AAA championship competition, where the likes of Vukovich, Bryan, and McGrath went to war.

While the schism between the two forms of the sport would remain unbridgeable, the entry of such mainstream companies as Chevrolet, with its new Corvette, indicated that Detroit now recognized that the dynamics of the automobile market were quickly changing. The enthusiasm for imported sports cars was growing by the day. Tiny firms like MG, Jaguar, Porsche, and even Volkswagen imported only a handful of automobiles, but they were making steady inroads among many influential customers. While many Detroit executives laughed at these "silly" little machines and predicted that they would soon wither away, others, like GM's Ed Cole, who had ramrodded the Corvette, realized that America's new fascination with power, speed, and performance would not abate and that European sports cars had awakened an enthusiasm in a critically important segment of the market.

Cole, among others, understood that motor racing was about to explode in interest among the public and that, if exploited effectively, it could become a major sales tool for the industry. Lincoln and Chrysler were already using success in the Mexican road race as sales promotion, while the entire industry was looking south at the struggling but growing world of stock car racing. A former Daytona Beach service station operator named Bill France had formed the National Association for Stock Car Automobile Racing (NASCAR) and was steadily expanding his rough-and-tumble "Grand National" series from the Piedmont Plateau of the Carolinas up and down the East Coast. Already, Hudson, Ford, and Plymouth were entering cars in the series. Other Detroit brands were sure to follow. "Win on Sunday, sell on Monday" was about to become a mantra for Detroit in the booming world of stock car racing.

In the meantime, the Indianapolis 500 remained the pinnacle of the sport. Men like Vukovich offered the only recognizable racing names to the general public, whose sporting distractions were mostly restricted to major league baseball and college football. There was a small claque of enthusiasts who followed the various forms of motor racing, but their numbers were minuscule compared to the multitudes who followed the fortunes of such household names as the New York Yankees, the Brooklyn Dodgers, and the Fighting Irish of Notre Dame.

Years would pass before the rising thunder of motor sports would be heard by more than just a tiny percentage of the American public. That is to say, until the sport grabbed headlines through its single unique component—the omnipresent chance for violent and sudden death.

As the nation eased out of the traumas of World War II and Korea, a new Eisenhower-style brand of optimism swept the public. Breakaway pastel colors displaced the gray, woollen drabness in women's clothing, while gadgetry infused the households of the nation. Fancy refrigerators, electric carving knives, bigger, clearer televisions, FM radio, and Waring blenders joined nylon, Dacron vinyl, and other synthetics to make easier living through chemistry. With this new technological exuberance came a fascination with power and speed on the highway. That in turn energized technology, where competition within the automobile industry and on the racetracks of the world caused quantum leaps in performance. The advances would not come without penalty.

CHAPTER FOUR

THE POWER ELITE

BILL VUKOVICH RETURNED TO INDIANAPOLIS IN May 1954, loaded for bear. His crewmen, Jim Travers and Frank Coon, had modified the three-year-old Kurtis-Kraft roadster with an advanced fuel-injection system developed by them and their friend Stuart Hillborn. The car's owner, Howard Keck, remained the same elusive personality, still insisting that his name not be associated with the car and remaining in the shadows as he opened his Superior Oil Company in Los Angeles. Other than the old machine being painted a pale yellow to replace its original battleship gray, the Fuel Injection Special number 14 appeared outwardly unchanged from its two earlier appearances at the Speedway.

While the "Mad Russian" or the "Fresno Flash," as the press chose to call him, remained a favorite, other serious men were posing a challenge. Jack McGrath, at thirty-four, was a year younger than

Vukovich and also a veteran of the California midget and hot-rod wars. The son of a successful Los Angeles meat packer, he was not only a brilliant driver, but an accomplished mechanic and engine builder who maintained his own race cars. He had been recruited in 1949 by wealthy Wichita oilman Jack Hinkle to run his Indianapolis cars. Unlike Keck, Jack Barron Hinkle was a likable extrovert who got deeply involved with McGrath's racing efforts. Working with another mechanic, Jack Beckley, the trio was known as the "three Jacks" around the big-time racing AAA championship trail.

While McGrath drove the dirt miles with expertise, his métier was Indianapolis, where raw speed on the paved rectangle appealed to certain drivers. Many others were awestruck by the place, fearing the blinding speeds required on the long straights and the blind, sweeping corners bordered by starch-white cement walls. But not McGrath. From the moment he first saw the Speedway in 1948, he relished its special challenge. After hooking up with Hinkle a year later, he became a major force in the 500—always among the fastest, but never yet able to win.

"Gentleman Jack," as he was known among the press, was tall, lean, and courtly, a soft-spoken Californian who seemed to have nothing in common with the rough-hewn Vukovich. Despite this, they were friends off the track and often exchanged thoughts on race tactics and car setup. They were members of a rare and exclusive fraternity—men willing to face the ultimate challenge in seeking glory in the most dangerous race devised by man.

While McGrath and Vukovich were at the peak of their powers, other, younger, more restless men were ready to make a challenge. Jimmy Bryan was a rangy, brush-cut, cigar-smoking Arizona native known among his peers as the "the Cowboy." Brash and good-humored, Bryan was an ex World War II pilot. He had come up the hard way, cadging rides in junk race cars, living in the backs of station wagons between races, and even scavenging corn from farmer's fields and trading empty soda bottles for eating money. Bryan had migrated across the country, racing sprint cars in the East, midgets in the East and West. He was a vagabond in a helmet, ready to manhandle any car that would withstand his heavy foot.

Unlike Vukovich, who hated the dirt fairground miles, and like McGrath, who excelled on the smooth expanse of the Indianapolis Motor Speedway, Bryan loved the rough-and-tumble world of dirt tracks, where his audacious, never-lift driving style worked to his advantage. After several seasons spent struggling with second-rate machinery, he had broken out in late 1953 with a win in the Sacramento 100-miler at the wheel of Bessie Paoli's Springfield Welding Kurtis-Kraft. Even better days lay ahead.

Another young lion, Bob Sweikert, a twenty-eight-year-old charger from Hayward, California, had at the end of the 1953 season abandoned the seat of the Dean Van Lines dirt car—a stark white, upright Offy-powered machine built by Los Angeles craftsman Eddie "Zazoom" Kuzma. Owned by Southern California sportsman Al Dean, who operated the prosperous coast-to-coast Dean Van Lines moving company, the Kuzma was regarded as one of the finest race cars in the nation. Its owner quickly replaced Sweikert with Bryan, thereby setting the stage for his breakout into the top ranks of the sport.

McGrath and Hinkle arrived at Indianapolis in early May 1954 ready for war. They unloaded a spanking-new, bright yellow Kurtis-Kraft 500B roadster, an updated and improved version of the now-aging Keck car assigned to Vukovich. Bryan appeared with the Dean Kuzma, a car intended more for the dirt tracks than for the Motor Speedway, but nonetheless a contender thanks to the man behind the wheel.

McGrath was fast in practice. An expert engine man, he seemed to have perfected the use of the explosive engine additive nitromethane—"nitro" or "pop," as it was known in the garage area.

The stuff was so potent than only a few drops in a tank of methanol were needed to add an instant 50 horsepower. But if used imprudently, pistons would be fried, crankshafts cracked in half, and blocks shattered. Only a few men, including McGrath, seemed to understand the nuances of its use. With a dollop of "pop" in his car's tank, he quickly dominated practice, rushing past the vaunted 140-mph barrier and winning the pole position with ease. His time for the four laps against the clock was a record-shattering 141 mph.

Meanwhile, there was endless grief in the Vukovich garage. Broken piston rings became a curse for the crew, and several practice runs for the defending champion ended with the car being towed into the pits with a broken engine. Tensions were rising as Vukovich watched men like McGrath and Bryan rush around the Speedway at speeds far in excess of those recorded by him and the Fuel Injection Special the year before.

In frustration, he began to demand that Travers use nitro. Travers refused, claiming the stuff was an aphrodisiac offering quick bursts of speed but hurting the reliability needed in a 500-mile endurance contest. Loud arguments could be heard behind the closed doors of the Keck garage as pressure mounted.

Vukovich finally managed to qualify the car, in nineteenth place, deep in the thirty-three-car starting field. The so-called railbird experts among the press and opposing crews claimed that his run with the old Kurtis was over; newer machinery, the gossip went, and more audacious drivers were prepared to displace him and end his brief reign. No one had ever before won the big race starting so far back in the field. The Mad Russian, they said, was finished.

Not quite. Driving with an intensity and an audacity seldom seen in motor racing, Vukovich attacked as soon as the green flag fell. His driving was relentless. He passed cars low in the corners, his left wheels on the grass; then high, his right wheels nearly scraping the retaining walls. He was a hunter. The rest of the thirty-two drivers were helpless prey. By the half-way point, he was leading, with only McGrath and Bryan capable of hanging onto the frenzied charger.

Bryan had long ago learned from Vukovich's style and his fearless, defiant approach to driving.

It had happened in a midget race years earlier in Vukovich's hometown of Fresno. Bryan had come north from Los Angeles to run at the local track, where the Vukovich brothers, Bill and Eli, were famous for their brawling tactics. During the race, Bryan was slammed by Vuke as they fought for the lead—typical Vukovich intimidation move. But rather than back off and give way, Bryan slammed back, shoving a wheel nearly into Vukovich's cockpit. A small war began. Wrestling for the lead, the pair repeatedly ramrodded each other in a raging metal-to-metal duel.

When it was over, young Bryan climbed out of his car to see Vukovich coming at him, his helmet still on. There would be a fight—a tough middle-weight against a tall, raw-boned kid from Arizona. Ready for war, Bryan was stunned when Vukovich's face spread into a toothy smile and he exclaimed, "Son of a bitch. Now that's how I like to race!" The pair shook hands, and a bond of mutual respect was established.

As the 500 thundered into its final laps, McGrath had been forced out of contention by two long pit stops. Bryan was left to fight the champion with a crippled car. The front spring had broken, as had a rear shock absorber. The Kuzma had become a high-speed coal cart, unleashing merciless damage on Bryan's body. The pounding of the cobbled bricks on the front straightaway caused the seat bolsters to gnaw at his midriff, opening up bloody welts. His ribs near the breaking point and his hands worn bloody from fighting the steering wheel, Bryan refused to lift, even when the throttle pedal shattered. On the verge of collapse from the pain, the pounding, and the violent shuddering of the wounded car, he soldiered on in second place. Somehow he managed to keep pace with the flying Vukovich, who held the lead with his unique style, which embodied high-speed power and grace.

As the checkered flag fell, the pair crossed the finish line almost nose to nose—except that the struggling Bryan was a full lap behind the winner. McGrath came in a few seconds later, in third place.

As Vukovich was receiving his winner's trophy and a long kiss from Marie Wilson, the star of the popular TV show *My Friend Irma*, Bryan was sprawled on the floor of his garage, semi-conscious.

His crew called for medical help. The Speedway medical staff dispatched a young nurse to take a look at the wounded driver. When she entered the dark space, Bryan was lying next to the grimy, oil-soaked Kuzma that had almost beaten him to death.

She leaned over and asked, "How are you feeling?"

Bryan's eyes opened to spot a pretty face a few inches away. Suddenly a broad smile swept over the grime. "Hey, babe, I'm doing great! How about you?"

Such was the way of men who rode next to death, but refused not to seize the essence of life in every moment. Bryan was a towering physical presence with incredible hand-eye coordination. He was able to adjust his expert dart-throwing skills so that he could pop carnival balloons, despite the fact that the game's operators had purposefully made their darts out of balance. He loved outrageous practical jokes, including his notorious employment of powerful M-80 firecrackers at unexpected moments.

But Bryan's injuries were too severe for him to run the next weekend at the Milwaukee 100-miler. Because the track had been paved after seventy-seven years of running as a dirt horse track, and because the Fuel Injection Special was being retired from competition by its owner, Howard Keck, Vukovich was persuaded to take Bryan's place in the Dean Van Lines cockpit.

He qualified the car on the pole, then retired with steering problems and returned to Fresno, where he opened his Vuky's 500 Service station. He had plans to open more around the Fresno area, and often could be found pumping gas for his customers. He drove to and from work in one of the two Indianapolis 500 pace cars that he had won.

In the meantime, Bryan regained his health and the Dean race car seat, where he went on a late-season tear, winning four 100-milers in a row and claiming the national driving championship with a burst of audacity that elevated him to Vukovich's top contender for the 1955 Indianapolis 500 title.

In September I returned to upstate New York to celebrate homecoming at my alma mater, the tiny but respected Hobart Collage in Geneva, a lovely little city planted on the shore of Lake Seneca, the largest, deepest, and perhaps the most beautiful of the five Finger Lakes. It had been five years since I had partied my way to a "Gentleman's C" in English and History, and a reunion with my classmates seemed in order following my ordeal in Korea. During my sojourn, friends suggested that I attend a pair of automobile races that might offer background for a story I was researching for *Liberty* magazine on risk-taking in sports.

My first stop would be Syracuse, where the New York State Fair was staging its annual 100-mile AAA championship race. I drove north from Manhattan on the newly opened New York State Thruway, a 559-mile toll road that ran the length of the state and would serve as a prototype for the $101 billion, 40,000-mile Interstate system the Eisenhower administration would launch two years later.

The Syracuse State Fairgrounds sprawled on the edge of little Lake Onondaga. The fair had been held each year since the early 1800s and many of its pavilions, horse barns, and arcades dated to the turn of the century, as did the one-mile horse track that served as a centerpiece for the vast acreage. Men had raced cars there since 1907, but like all the dirt miles it had been designed specifically as a horse track in 1880.

The state fair was in full swing when I arrived. I had to park miles away from the giant, arched grandstand that lined the front staightaway. I was late and had to rush through the jumble of midways to reach the gate. The carny barkers, food vendors, ride operators, and side-show shills were all barking their wares to the throngs. The heavy aroma of burgers and fries, sugar cones, and stale beer attacked my nose. Calliope music belched mechanically from the innards of the merry-go-rounds, thrill rides, and Ferris wheels that dotted the luridly colored casbahs.

I reached my seat in the upper rows of the grandstand, protected from the hot afternoon sun, to find the race cars already lined up on the track. There were eighteen tall, audacious machines with glistening paintwork and swooping tails. They bore the brands of industrial, hard-knuckled Americans: "Lutes Truck Parts," "Schaefer Gear Works," "Auto Shippers," "Federal Engineering," "Springfield Welding," and "Central Excavating" were painted on their long hoods—gritty businesses with links to the tough-guy segments of the American economy, segments that made things, hauled things, repaired things. All the cars were hand-built, for the most part in the Los Angeles shops of master craftsmen. They were working-class, self-taught artisans who could fabricate, through sheer inspiration and innate technical brilliance, an entire automobile from sheet aluminum, chrome-molybdenum steel, and magnesium bar stock— within a matter of months. With a muscle-bound, 300-hp Meyer-Drake/Offenhauser engine packed in their innards, these beautiful but lethal machines were capable of speeds over 140 mph on the lumpy straights of tracks like Syracuse.

The drivers lounged against their cars, awaiting the call to action. They were all young, tanned, raw-boned men with flinty expressions of faint defiance earned by those who face death on a regular basis. The same look can be found on the faces of fighter pilots, bullfighters, high-steel workers—those who know they are tougher, braver, and bolder than normal men and are prepared to die to prove it.

They moved among the gaunt, bare-wheeled machines, occasionally joking with one another as they checked tires and steering link-ages in preparation for the ugly battle that lay ahead.

All were dressed in wrinkled khakis, short-sleeved pullovers, and T-shirts. They had names like Sweikert, McGrath, Bryan, Reece, Thompson, Boyd, and Parsons—Anglo-Saxons from the California suburbs and backwater middle America towns, where automobile racing served as a way out, like boxing for ghettoized big-city Irish, Italian, and black kids of the day.

Among them was a nail-hard ex-marine from Bellmore, Long Island, and a hero of Bougainville, named "Iron Mike" Nazaruk; and a pudgy Armenian kid from Oakland whom the other drivers gave extra room. Ed Elisian was known as "Illusion" and had a reputation for being unstable both on and off the racetrack.

At the back of the field, leaning against the battered blue number 81 Central Excavating Special, was another rebel. Rodger Ward was the ex-pilot known for his incendiary temper, his profligate gam-bling, and his bad manners on the racetrack. Only five days earlier, during the latter stages of a similar 100-mile championship race at DuQuoin, Illinois, Ward had barreled off the fourth corner and lost control of the Central Excavating Special. It plowed into the pits and instantly killed Clay Smith, the much-liked and widely respected chief mechanic for the Agajanian team. Before the car tumbled to a stop, it had injured eight more bystanders—including two children.

But that was five days ago. Ancient history. The car had its dents pounded out and the blood wiped away, and the old warrior was ready for another battle. Like most of the cars at Syracuse, number 81 had been around for years. Built in 1951 by Ohio craftsman Floyd Trevis for Cleveland contractor Pete Salemi, the car had been Bill Vukovich's first ride in Indianapolis and had carried a number of drivers, both fast and slow, over its four-year career. Unlike modern racing cars, which are replaced after a few races, cars like the Central Excavating Special labored on for years—sometimes decades—until their innards fell apart and they were scrapped. Many would carry more than one driver to his death or shatter his bones, yet would return to the tracks.

For some, it was too much. Following the DuQuoin death of Clay Smith, his driver and friend, thirty-five-year-old Chuck Stevenson, quit racing on the spot. His car and Ward's had touched wheels, which is what caused the fatal spin into the pits. Shattered by the experience, the 1952 national AAA champion and two-time winner of the stock car class in the Mexican road race would not climb into a race car for another six years.

Syracuse, too, had taken its toll. In 1911 Lee Oldfield (no relation to the legendary Barney) lost control of his car and plunged into the crowd, killing eleven spectators. Nine years later, the track claimed the life of Indianapolis champion and French Grand Prix winner Jimmy Murphy. Scores of others would be badly injured, in part because the track funneled from a wide front straightaway into a back chute barely more than two cars wide. Yet, skating on the hard cinder surface—which became like polished black granite after 100 miles of scuffing by the racing tires—average speeds were climbing to 100 mph.

At the head of the pack was the cream-and-white Bob Estes Special, the entry of Inglewood, California, Lincoln-Mercury dealer Bob Estes. Its driver was a hard-eyed Angeleno named Don Freeland who had savaged the car around the evil old track to win the pole position. Next to him on the front row was the burly ex-sailor Andy Linden, who packed a reputation as a first-class bar fighter and something of a loner. Behind Freeland in the second row, driving the Lute's Truck Parts car, was handsome, cocky Bob Sweikert. Considered a major talent, the brash twenty-seven-year-old had often trenchantly remarked, "I'll never live to retire." Back in eighth, in the cream-and-red Hinkle, was McGrath, while near the back was Bryan, chewing a cigar and waving a hand still raw from his Indianapolis trial at a young woman in the stands.

It would have been hard to believe that among these eighteen young men, eleven faced early, grisly deaths in race cars. One other, Linden, would suffer debilitating injuries. Imagine a sport like football or hockey, both considered to be violent tests of courage, in which *half* of its participants would die while playing. The risks faced by those men on that sunny day in Syracuse seem, in retrospect, intolerable in a civilized society. They even equaled—or exceeded—the toll taken in the man-on-man gladiatorial contests popularized during the Roman Empire.

The crowd crushed into the rickety grandstands were like the drivers—blue-collar mechanics, carpenters, farmers, welders, hoary-handed workers of all kinds who understood the skills demanded of their heroes. As the giddy beat of a Sousa march pounded through the loudspeakers and mingled with the faint screams of riders on a Ferris wheel in the distant midway, the drivers flicked away their cigarettes and eased into their leather-upholstered seats. They pulled on leather crash helmets of the type long favored by motorcyclists, a feeble nod to safety they had resisted for years—much as hockey pros like Gordie Howe and Bobby Hull would sneer at protective headgear two decades later. When a local dignitary sounded the traditional call—"Gentlemen, start your engines"—the drivers snapped aircraft-style seat belts around their waists, knowing full well they would be essentially useless in the event of a flip. Behind each of them was mounted a seventy-five-gallon tank of methanol capable of incinerating a man with its nearly invisible, iridescent flame.

Like Hemingway's bullfighters, they faced unspeakable danger, not from a raging one-ton animal, but from an equally savage machine twice that weight. The car could kill in the same abstract fashion that the face of a granite cliff might a misstepping mountain climber. Such were the penalties for men who chose the great writer's three sports over "children's" games. The engines, guttural, unmuffled, fierce, rattled through the grandstands as the cars rolled away, slowly at first, then gaining speed during the two pace laps to align the field, two by two, to take the green flag.

Then mayhem. Thunderous noise. A swirl of color as a wall of dust and the reek of methanol overwhelmed the crowd. Linden barged into the lead for a few laps, angling through the corners in wild slides before being overtaken by Freeland, then by Sweikert, who seized the lead in a fiercely executed pass at the exact spot where Jimmy Murphy had lost his life thirty years earlier.

Both Freeland and McGrath challenged Sweikert in the latter stages, swapping the lead before the gritty surface began to shred their tires. That left Sweikert unchallenged, thereby avoiding a repeat of his crash the year before, which had taken both him and McGrath into the fence. His payoff was $3,750, 60 percent of which would be shared with the car owner and crew.

Checkout completed at the Onondaga Hotel, where most of the teams stayed—often three and four to a room—and it was off to the next race the following weekend at the Indiana State Fairgrounds in Indianapolis. The Lutes Special, its nose scoured clean from the flying cinders, was loaded onto an open trailer and hooked to a road-worn Ford station wagon, then aimed west for the 500-mile trip to the Hoosier State. Five more races remained on the AAA championship schedule, which would ultimately take Sweikert and the Lutes across the country, to Las Vegas, Sacramento, and Phoenix before season ended that November.

On balance, 1954 would be a good year for the professionals. Just two men, both rookies in over their heads, had lost their lives. Bob Scott, an eager twenty-five-year-old from the West Coast hot-rod ranks, had died of head injuries when his car rolled onto him during the Darlington, South Carolina, 100-miler. Wally Campbell, a hot-headed kid from the eastern sprint car circuit, had burned to death when his car leapt the outside fence at Williams Grove, Pennsylvania. In a macabre scene, the car had continued to run in tight circles as its

unconscious driver was consumed in flames. Considering the potential for death and injury on the championship trail, most of the
young lions had dodged a bullet. So too for the professional
European road racers, among whom only young Argentinian Onofre
Marimon, a protégé of the world champion, Juan Manuel Fangio,
had died during practice on the notoriously twisty, up-and-down,
fourteen-mile Nürburgring in Germany.

I took a week to laze around Geneva, staying at my fraternity on
South Main Street, a tree-lined avenue bordering the western shore of
Lake Seneca that F. Scott Fitzgerald once called one of the most beautiful streets in America. I would rush to the front porch when I heard
local sportsman George Harris running his incredible, thundering
Cadillac-Allard J2X up South Main, no doubt headed to the local
hills for a mad drive across the golden woodlands of early autumn.

The following weekend a friend and I drove his new Austin-Healy
100S to Watkins Glen, a tiny village at the southern end of Lake
Seneca. The largest of the five Finger Lakes, which dented the central
New York landscape like a giant handprint, Seneca was forty miles
long, with cold, impenetrable depths reaching seven hundred feet.
Route 14 meandered along a ridge hundreds of feet above the cleft of
the lake, offering a spectacular vista of woodlands bright with the
crimson and lurid oranges of turning leaves and a sweep of the vine-
yards that were springing up throughout the region. At roadside fruit
stands, homegrown pumpkins, squash, gourds, late-season tomatoes,
and jugs of cider were piled high and offered at bargain prices.
Watkins Glen had subsisted for decades solely on its salt mine and on
a modest tourist business based on a spectacular shale ravine carved
out during the same ice age retreat that had formed the lakes.

In 1948 young Cameron Argetsinger, the son of a Youngstown,
Ohio, steel executive whose family had a vacation home on the
Seneca shore, convinced the village elders that if a European-style
road race could be run through the streets and a network of nearby

Schuyler County roadways, a giant tourism boom would ensue. His efforts, aided by the local Chamber of Commerce and other civic groups, resulted in the first "Grand Prix" being run on October 2 of that year. The eight-lap race around the 6.6-mile circuit was won by an alcoholic Philadelphia Main Line millionaire named Frank T. Griswold Jr. at the wheel of his own prewar supercharged Alfa Romeo coupe. Argetsinger finished ninth in the race he created. In coming decades, the best professional drivers in the world would compete at Watkins Glen, but in the early years the racing was strictly amateur and based on the English model of clubby, gentlemanly competition unsullied by filthy lucre.

The races were an immediate success, even following the death of Samuel Carnes Collier, the heir to a Manhattan advertising fortune, in a 1950 crash that received front-page coverage in the New York press. Unlike the majority of men dying on the nation's dirt tracks and at Indianapolis, Collier was well-born, a pure sportsman who engaged in a civilized expression of motor sports that rarely led to death.

The ruling body at Watkins Glen was the Sports Car Club of America. Like many WASP-based private organizations of the day, it did not admit Jews. This caused a major upset in 1951, when a wealthy Jewish businessman from New York named Erwin Goldschmidt broke the anti-Semitic barrier and won the Grand Prix with his Cadillac-Allard. Goldschmidt, who had endured Nazi persecution in his native Germany, won a victory that ultimately broke down the racial policy of the SCCA. Ironically, the Indianapolis 500 had already been won three times—in 1941, 1947, and 1948—by a Jewish engineer named Mauri Rose. But it was not until the 1960s that Jews and other minorities who had been excluded from many enclaves of American society were finally given proper admission.

Competition having been outlawed on state roads following the death of the young child in 1952, the Watkins Glen organizers—composed of village businessmen and area enthusiasts—moved the races to a network of Town of Dix and Schuyler County roads on a hill above the village. The course was laid out on barren farmland in a rough rectangle of narrow, rudely paved roads totaling four miles in length. The paddock, such as it was, had been created out of a mown hayfield, topped by a crude timing stand on the edge of Townsend Corner Road. To the north lay the long, blue slit of Lake Seneca.

The paddock was full of rare and strange automobiles. All were European, with names like Lagonda, Aston-Martin, Hispano-Suiza, Mercedes-Benz, Frazier-Nash, Nash-Healy, Triumph, and Riley, in addition to the more popular marques like Jaguar, MG, and Porsche, all of which were appearing in increasing numbers in upscale suburbs from coast to coast.

A large contingent of New York socialites had made the drive upstate. They had become involved with the sport when the Bridgehampton road races had been started on eastern Long Island in 1949. Thanks to their exposure in the chic Hamptons, sports cars had become a fashion item in Manhattan. Former French star driver Rene Dreyfus and his brother had opened the Chanticlair Restaurant on East Forty-Ninth Street. The international racing crowd and major automobile executives used it as their regular watering hole. Henry Austin Clark, an heir to the Singer sewing machine fortune and a major car collector and historian, had started the Madison Avenue Sports Car and Chowder Society, which met monthly at amateur racer Vincent Sardi's famed restaurant on Forty-Fourth Street.

Mingling in the pits on that late summer weekend were such notables as CBS announcer Walter Cronkite, *Today* show host Dave Garroway, and former child star Jackie Cooper, who would compete enthusiastically—if not quickly—in his own Austin-Healy 100S sports car.

Unlike in Syracuse and Indianapolis, here women were everywhere. Some lounged by the cars, while others prepared tailgate lunches. Some helped their husbands, polishing wheels and checking tire pressures. A few even donned helmets and goggles and raced with the men. Sports car racing, with its social exclusivity and high-minded sense of separating itself from the dirt-track rabble, was an example of sexual egalitarianism. To outsiders, the women lent an air of casual frivolity to the scene, as opposed to the hard-edged chauvinism of the professionals.

Most of the cars were marginally set up for racing, which meant that the headlights had been taped over and crude numbers pasted on the doors. There were no special tires, rollover protection, or other safety considerations. Most, like Harris's Cadillac-Allard, which had ripped past us on Route 14 at 110 mph as we headed south from Geneva, had been driven to the race. And presuming there would be no accidents or mechanical failures, they would be driven home again at the end of the day.

Some of the more serious competitors had transported their cars on open trailers, hauled behind station wagons and standard American sedans. And then there was the Cunningham equipe, which had elevated the sport to a higher, more professional level.

Briggs Swift Cunningham, of Greens Farms, Connecticut, was the heir to a meat-packing fortune and had been smitten with fast cars for his entire life. Being relieved of such mundane chores as earning a living, he had grown up preoccupied with yachting (he later won the America's Cup) and motor sports. Several prewar trips to Europe had instilled in him the desire to win the great 24-hour race held each June at Le Mans, in France.

By 1951 he was building his own special Cunningham sports cars, powered by the newly developed Chrysler "hemi" engines. The cars, designed and fabricated in a new factory outside West Palm Beach, Florida, were the equal of any Ferrari or Mercedes-Benz sports car of the day, and with a team of closet professionals including John Fitch, Cunningham nearly won the great race on several occasions. His lead driver was a brilliant ex–World War II glider pilot named Phil

Walters. Also well-born, Walters had returned to Manhassett, Long Island, from the war with a restlessness for action that attracted him to motor racing. His first involvement was in the rough-and-tumble midget racing circuit, which his socially active family felt was beneath his station. In deference to them, he raced under the non de plume of Ted Tappett until he joined the Cunningham team. This kind of racing was considered sufficiently civilized that he could use his given name.

Walters was the number-one Cunningham driver now that Fitch had moved to Europe, taking up residence in Switzerland to work as a double for Kirk Douglas in a 20th Century Fox production about Grand Prix racing called *The Racers*. His driving skills and gentlemanly demeanor had led to a place on the Mercedes-Benz team, which was competing in both the Grand Prix circuit and in world-class sports car competition.

While Fitch had been uncomfortable at Indianapolis, he was fearless at tracks like Le Mans, where the tree-lined, four-mile Muslanne straight had to be driven at 150 mph throughout the dark of night, often probing through fog that obscured the circuit. So too for Walters, who never tried Indianapolis but appeared to posses sufficient courage and skill to drive any kind of race car at any level of competition.

The Cunningham team arrived at Watkins Glen like an army of conquerors. The three cars, painted white with blue stripes—the international American racing colors—were hauled in a giant semi-transporter. A crew of mechanics led by Alfred Momo, a genius Italian émigré, tended to the cars while onlookers gaped at the entourage.

As a series of minor races involving slower MGs, Porsches, Triumphs, and the like buzzed around the course, the Cunninghams—to be driven by Walters, Cunningham himself, and a well-known eastern amateur named Sherwood Johnston—were given a final warm-up as their big V-8s were brought up to operating temperature.

The only serious competition would come from a brace of potent Ferraris to be driven by Jim Kimberly, the scion of Chicago's

Kimberly-Clark Kleenex fortune, and Bill Spear, a hulking, bespectacled sportsman from southern Connecticut.

Lining the snow fences on the outside of the circuit were tens of thousands of spectators, most of whom had driven their own sports cars to the Glen. Many had camped out. Rude tents and smoky campfires still dotted the woods behind them. A few had built scaffolding from which to get a better view of the action, giving the scene the air of a medieval battleground.

The day being chilly, with a sprightly north wind blowing off the lake, Walters and others suited up in leather flight jackets for the main event. It would be one hundred miles in length, or twenty-five laps around the circuit, which featured a long downhill straightaway ending with a sharp right-hander. Since the Glen races aped European events, the course was run clockwise; all other track racing in America was run counterclockwise.

Compared to the wheel-rubbing duels carried out at Syracuse the week before, the Grand Prix was a gentlemanly affair. After a brief contest for the lead by Kimberly, Walters took command and drove away from the field for an easy victory. Kimberly came in second in his screeching red Ferrari; Johnston and owner Cunningham trailed home in third and fourth.

A few spins and a low-speed tumble into a bordering ditch broke the monotony of Walters' smooth and rapid country drive. The event was essentially a high-speed parade of rare and exotic machinery rather than a classic motor race in the American idiom.

Far to the west in California, and virtually unnoticed among the aficionados at Watkins Glen, but soon to be celebrated as a rising superstar in the wider world of entertainment, was a sullen, heavy-lidded actor from rural Indiana named James Dean. After a brief career on Broadway, the young actor was completing a starring role in an adaptation of John Steinbeck's novel *East of Eden* while working on a new picture titled *Rebel Without a Cause*. The buzz in

Hollywood claimed that Dean, with his simmering good looks, subtle acting range, and raw, overpowering sexuality, would become an instant box office hit. That Dean had grown up fascinated with the nearby Indianapolis Motor Speedway and was already known as a skilled and daring motorcycle rider with ambitions to race sports cars was a component of his life unmentioned in the barrage of publicity. But this diversion would cap his pyrotechnic explosion onto the world scene and be inextricably linked to his immortality.

As I headed north to Geneva in a line of sports cars chugging through a phalanx of New York State Police, who had begun savaging the Glen crowds after they took the blame for the young spectator's death two years earlier, I could not help but wonder about the power and speed that new technologies were unleashing across the world. In Europe, Juan Manuel Fangio was about to win his second world championship at the wheel of a revolutionary Mercedes-Benz Grand Prix car that featured a featherlight alloy frame, a powerful eight-cylinder fuel-injected engine, and streamlined bodywork that was light years ahead of the competition.

Seemingly every major automobile manufacturer was now engaged in some form of motor sports, with hordes of talented engineers armed with the quantum leaps in technology developed during the recent wars. Speeds were climbing like the fleets of jet-powered fighter planes now ruling the skies. One wondered where it would all end?

CHAPTER FIVE

THE DANGER
ACCELERATES

WHILE HE HAD ABANDONED AAA CHAMPIONSHIP competition completely—save for defending his Indianapolis 500 title—Bill Vukovich could not remain isolated from the sport that had made him a household name in America and a modestly wealthy man. Despite Esther's urgings that he retire and concentrate on running his two Fresno gas stations, Vukovich agreed late in 1954 to return to Mexico for a second try at winning the Carrera PanAmericana de Mexico. More commonly known in the motor racing world as the "Mexican Road Race," it was started in 1950 by the Mexican government to promote tourism and to develop the new Pan-American highway that had been completed in the late 1940s. The road, rising to elevations of over eleven thousand feet in the Sierra Madre Mountains, ran between the border town of Ciudad

Juárez, south of El Paso, and Tuxtla Gutiérrez, the fly-blown capital of Chiapas, Mexico's southernmost state.

Run south to north over 1,900 miles, the race was held in eight daily stages varying in length from 100 to 300 miles. It attracted hundreds of entries, ranging from rank Mexican amateurs to top professionals in cars entered by major manufacturers like Mercedes-Benz, Porsche, Ferrari, Lancia, and Alfa Romeo from Europe, and Chrysler and Lincoln from the United States. Vukovich signed on with the latter—Ford's premier luxury division—which had specially prepared five powerful Lincoln Capri hard-top coupes for him and fellow Indy drivers Chuck Stevenson, Jack McGrath, Walt Faulkner, and Johnny Mantz.

Open road races like the PanAmericana had long been popular in Europe and South America. Sicily's Targa Florio and the famed Italian Mille Miglia were still run annually on the Continent. Like the Mexican version, they were fiendishly dangerous, both for the competitors and for the millions of spectators who lined the highways. A car careening into a crowd was common. Hundreds had been killed over the years.

American drivers returning from the PanAmericana told of horrific moments when the road ahead would be jammed with peasants parting like the Red Sea as their cars barreled into their midst. They had been warned not to slow down, because this would confuse the timing of the crowds, who had learned to move in cadence with the approaching automobiles. Others recalled the constant thumping beneath their tires as they ran over dogs, and others the daring young men on the roadside who reached out to touch the speeding automobiles for good luck.

Vukovich had run for Lincoln in 1953, but he encountered mechanical problems at the start and was never a contender. In 1954 he teamed with navigator Vern Houle, a California hot-rodder and expert mechanic who would ride shotgun, reading a detailed map and advising Vukovich of the curves, corners, and hazards that lay ahead. The Lincoln team, like the other professional operations, stationed crews along the route at fuel and tire depots—a massively expensive and complex campaign designed to win the large production car class and perhaps to challenge the lighter, faster Ferraris and Porsches for the overall win.

Vukovich and his teammates tended to view the PanAmericana as a long, high-speed lark, a fast drive on open roads. The race, to be held in the final week of November, offered Vukovich a break in the routine of running his gas stations in Fresno and a chance to socialize with his good friends in professional racing, including his rival, McGrath. The pair, so different in stature and background—one small and swarthy from immigrant stock, the other tall, lean, and fair-skinned from solid Scottish-Irish heritage—were able to compete with near-suicidal intensity on the racetrack and still remain pals.

The prerace parties and endless mariachi bands ended quickly for the Lincoln team. Both the Stevenson and Mantz cars retired within miles of the start at Tuxtla with burned pistons, presumably caused by the low-octane gasoline supplied by the Mexicans. Worse yet, McGrath crashed, but without injury to himself or his co-driver.

That left Vukovich and Faulkner to carry on for the team that had dominated the 1953 race. Clearing the narrow streets of Tuxtla, their dusty verges clogged with cheering crowds, Vukovich began to run flat-out across the open desert. Save for the occasional tumbling sagebrush, the odd stray cow, and a few clusters of peasants dotting side paths leading into the distant hills, the road north was vacant. Far in the distance, shrouded in the hazy inferno of the early-morning sun, lay the foothills of the mountains. The noise and heat inside the Lincoln, its interior gutted, its windows cut out to save weight, was unbearable. But again Vukovich, the tough guy from the blazing Fresno summertime, was impervious. He began broadsliding the big Lincoln through the sweeping corners while occasionally getting it airborne over the humps and hummocks that dotted the cactus-lined highway.

As they powered out of the steaming desert and into the mountains, Houle began urging Vukovich to slow down, yelling over the deafening racket of the engine that the car was about to break under the strain. He cautioned that nearly two thousand miles of hard driving lay ahead. Vukovich, the bit in his teeth, ignored him, charging hard as the Capri, built and designed in faraway Dearborn as a luxury cruiser, was pressed into the unlikely role of pure race car. Somehow Vukovich managed to keep the slewing monster on the road until a few miles south of the backwater city of Petlacingo, when he lost control on a tight bend and the enormous, five thousand-pound Lincoln bucked and bounced into a ravine. It tumbled end over end five times before stopping on its roof, precariously balanced on the edge of a one thousand-foot drop-off. Hanging upside down in their seat belts, the cockpit filled with smoke, Vukovich turned to Houle with a wide smile on his face. "OK smartass, now you drive," he sneered.

The pair eased gingerly out of the car, afraid it would continue its plunge. They crawled up to the roadside, where it was decided that Houle would flag a ride into Petlacingo while Vukovich guarded the car. Local looters were known to descend on wrecks and scavenge the wheels, body parts, and even the engine within minutes.

Poor Houle's adventure was far from over. A Ferrari Monza sports car screeched to a halt. It was driven by the notorious Italian sportsman Giovanni Bracco, the son of a wealthy textile manufacturer from Biella. Bracco was a classic European gentleman daredevil, driving his expensive Ferraris and Maseratis in road races with wild abandon. Two years earlier in the Mille Miglia, his co-driver, Umberto Maglioli—who also became a Ferrari driver of note—lit the mad-driving Bracco 140 cigarettes during the one thousand-mile race around Italy, in addition to feeding him slugs of brandy to keep his brio at full tilt.

A year later, still loaded with tobacco and brandy, he had won the Mille Miglia, beating a factory-entered Mercedes-Benz 300SL driven by German professional Karl Kling. Bracco would later attribute his victory to thinking—as he powered through the rain-swept Futa and Raticosa passes high in the Apennines—about how the German SS had massacred Italian partisans in the recent war and how his victory would help avenge their deaths.

Houle piled in beside Bracco, whose Ferrari had been delayed with mechanical trouble. The Italian rocketed away from the wrecked Lincoln. Running 140 mph with his foot flat on the throttle, Bracco asked Houle to hold the steering wheel while he lit a cigarette. Vukovich had asked poor Houle to drive on a lark. But Giovanni Bracco was serious.

The race ended, minus a shaken Houle, a mildly soused Bracco, and Vukovich, and with a victory for the aforementioned Maglioli. But like the first four Mexican races, the toll had been high. A local driver named Hector Palacios lost both legs in a high-speed crash that killed his navigator, Vincente Solar. Four other drivers, a second co-driver, and two spectators also died. Among them was English expatriate Elliot Forbes-Robinson, a popular sports car driver from Los Angeles who was serving as navigator for Jack McAfee, another top West Coast road racer. They had been competing in a powerful Ferrari entered by multimillionaire playboy John Edgar, whose team of big Italian machines was dominating amateur competition in California.

Unable to control the crowds and the ever-increasing speeds, the government cancelled the Carrera PanAmericana de Mexico. Four decades later it would be revived, in name only, as a rally for vintage cars.

While Vukovich and his Lincoln teammates were escaping various disasters south of the border, Jim Travers and Frank Coon were back in Los Angeles plotting a new assault on the Indianapolis 500. Car owner Howard Keck had decided that the now-aging Fuel-Injection

Kurtis-Kraft had to be replaced. This was fine by Travers, who had secretly called the car the "Toonerville Trolley," referring to what he believed to be builder Frank Kurtis's archaic fabrication techniques. There had been bad blood between Kurtis and Travers from the start, with both claiming to have created the so-called roadster design for Indy cars. While Travers no doubt had a strong influence on the conceptualization of the car, Kurtis had in fact developed two others using the general theme prior to building Keck's. Vukovich continued to call the much-honored race car builder "Cold Roll Kurtis," thanks to the steering failure that had cost him the 1952 race. He and the Keck team called the Kurtis operation the "blacksmith shop," which was unfare, since he employed excellent craftsmen and, say what one might about his overall designs, the detailing and finish on Kurtis products was first-rate.

Kurtis countered that the Keck team had insisted on an unproven, seldom-used Manning steering gear, which was at the root of the 1952 problem. Still, the aged car that had dominated the last three 500s and had revolutionized speedway design remained a bone of contention between its builder and its crew and driver.

Nevertheless, the Kurtis-Kraft Company on Alger Street in Los Angeles was booming with orders. Twenty-one of the thirty-three cars in the 1954 500 had come from his shop, and seven of the top ten finishers, including Vukovich's winner, were fabricated by this brilliant, self-taught son of a Croatian blacksmith. Clearly, until somebody came along with a better idea, Frank Kurtis's roadster concepts were the cars to beat at the Indianapolis 500.

Travers was bound to produce that better idea. Backed by Keck, he sketched out a plan for a fully streamlined car with enclosed bodywork. Early in 1954, Mercedes-Benz had entered international Grand Prix racing with revolutionary streamliners that had helped world champion Juan Manuel Fangio and his young teammate, Stirling Moss, dominate the season. While Mercedes-Benz would eventually abandon the full-bodied cars because of their extra weight, their strange aerodynamic behavior (a mystery in those days), and driver complaints that they could not see the front wheels, the streamliner idea seized the Indianapolis crowd. Several car builders in Los Angeles embarked on plans for just such swoopy machines, including Travers and Coon.

But rather than depend on the time-honored four-cylinder Meyer-Drake—still known as the Offenhauser or "Offy"—Keck underwrote Travers's idea for a radical new power plant. It would require the financial muscle of an oil mogul like Keck to finance such a project. Leo Goossen, the widely respected designer/draftsman for Meyer-Drake, was commissioned to lay down engineering drawings for the radical new engine.

Rather than an in-line four-cylinder like the ultra-rugged "air-compressor" Offy that had been the standard power source at Indianapolis since the mid-1930s, the Keck team planned on a compact three-liter V-8 to be supercharged by a Rootes-type blower. A similar supercharged system had been employed successfully by Wilbur Shaw in his Italian-built Maserati, which had won the 500 in 1939 and 1940.

Sadly, the idea for the engine arose at roughly the same time that the much-respected Shaw, who was then serving as president of the Speedway, died in a plane crash, in late October 1954. He was returning home to Indianapolis from a business meeting in Detroit.

Working with expert designer Norman Timbs, Travers created several experimental body shapes and tested them at the CalTech University wind tunnel to gain maximum efficiency. This was two decades before anyone thought of using "ground effects," wherein the airstream would be used like a reverse wing to literally glue a racing car to the pavement. Timbs and Travers were instead seeking the slipperiest shape possible to permit maximum speed on the straightaways. But Travers added one fillip—a small wing, attached to the tail, that could be used to adjust weight on the suspension as tire wear and fuel load changed during the race. This may have been the first wing of any sort—now standard equipment on all race cars—ever tried. Travers also was the first to attempt so-called weight-jacking, by adjusting the suspension to equalize poundage on all four wheels. He and Coon did this with the Fuel-Injection Special by setting agricultural scales under the wheels, then adjusting the torsion bars and shock absorbers accordingly.

The actual construction of the radical new streamliner was assigned to master fabricator Quinn Epperly, who, following Travers's instructions, worked with lighter chrome-molybdenum tubing to shave 75 pounds from the standard Kurtis-Kraft-style tubular chassis. Another 35 pounds was carved off the car by using a special aluminum differential—a critical pounds amount considering that the full-fendered body work would add an extra 150 pounds to the car.

As 1955 arrived, Travers, Goossen, Coon, and Epperly were racing against time to build both a new car and a new engine from the ground up. They believed they could finish the chassis and body by May, but the vastly more complex issue of creating a completely new engine remained a question.

Meanwhile, the automobile world's attention had turned eastward, where the Detroit industry was making massive strides in performance. Chrysler had introduced its radical new 300, a lovely two-ton coupe carrying a 300 horsepower V-8 engine. Two of these brutes would be turned over to Karl Kiekhaefer, the diminutive, tough-talking Wisconsin industrialist who was manufacturing his highly successful Mercury outboard engines. He then hired former bootleggers "Fonty" Flock and his brother, Tim, to drive his cars in the NASCAR "Grand National" stock car series, which was exploding in popularity. His Chrysler 300s went on to dominate big-time stock car racing, winning twenty-four of thirty-eight Grand Nationals during 1955. The upstart series was being run by "Big Bill" France, who rose out of his modest Daytona Beach gas station operation in 1947 to become one of the richest, most powerful men in worldwide sports. France had been tossed out of the Indianapolis Motor Speedway pits in 1954 by crusty chief steward Harry McQuinn. McQuinn was a leader in the "Chicago Gang" of ex-drivers, promoters, and track officials who maintained de facto control of the American Automobile Association's racing policies. Competition outside the approval of the AAA was branded as "outlaw." Participation in races unsanctioned by the AAA meant instant expulsion, as had happened to the 1948 500 winner, Bill Holland, who had been discovered racing in a Florida stock sprint car race under an assumed name and was banned for two years. He, like many other professionals, felt forced to compete in "outlaw" events to make a living, there simply not being enough AAA-sanctioned events to generate a reasonable income.

McQuinn had tangled with the wrong man in Bill France. Already, France's Grand National stock car series was running successfully up and down the East Coast, and major Detroit manufacturers like Hudson, Oldsmobile, Ford, and Chrysler were heavily involved in supporting teams like that being operated by Kiekhaefer. A whole new cast of ex-bootleggers, including the zany but talented Flock brothers, Curtis Turner, Lee Petty, Junior Johnson, and Herb Thomas, were exploiting skills honed as haulers of "white lightning" to become masters at controlling France's hulking "stock car" sedans and convertibles in his woolly, action-packed races.

France had vowed eternal revenge after being ejected from Gasoline Alley. By the end of the year, he was seeking financing for a giant, 2.5-mile high-banked "super speedway" in Daytona Beach that would ultimately rival Indianapolis as a world-famous motor sports venue. The foundation for the incredible rise of the NASCAR "Winston Cup" (now Nextel) was being laid based in part on McQuinn's arrogance.

As the horsepower race gained speed in Detroit, the once-proud Chevrolet division of General Motors was losing market share to

Ford. Chevrolet was looked upon as an old lady's car, thanks to its tepid, antiquated Blue Flame Six power plant. But in early 1955, an engineering team headed by bright, aggressive Ed Cole—who would rise to the leadership of the corporation—designed and built the ultimate, mass-produced V-8 engine and introduced it on a fresh lineup of Chevy sedans and the Corvette roadster.

The engine, to be known forever as the "small-block Chevy," was lighter, more efficient, and potentially more powerful than anything the industry has seen. Employing a lightened push-rod valve-train and an alloy block, the new 265-cubic-inch "Turbo Fire" 180 hp V-8 version would quickly be embraced by the racing crowd. Within months, hot-rodders would be developing over 300 hp from the engine. Still in production to this day, the "small block" has been sold by the millions and must rank as the most brilliant mass-produced passenger car engine of all time.

While the liberal press was chastising Eisenhower's secretary of defense and former GM chairman "Engine Charlie" Wilson for his crack that "what's good for General Motors is good for the country, and vice-versa," his beloved corporation was about to rise out of its lethargy. By the end of the decade, it would control nearly 70 percent of the domestic car market. This revival could be attributed, at least in part, to the horsepower found by Cole and his Chevrolet engineering team. In an era when postwar optimism and the resulting technology boom had led to demands for high performance on the highways of the nation, the breakout of Chevrolet—and of its equally dowdy partner, Pontiac, with its "wide track" advertising campaign and its ultra-fast Bonneville sedans—led the way to a new world of speed, power—and danger.

In the early months of 1955, Detroit's elite ad agencies— Chevrolet's Campbell-Ewald, Pontiac's McManus, John and Adams, and Chrysler's Young & Rubicam—geared up to force-feed glamour and performance to the American public, the racing season slowly accelerated to full speed. Bill France's fledgling stock cars were competing on a strange rectangle formed by Florida's Highway A1A, south of Daytona Beach, connected to a stretch of Atlantic Ocean beachfront. It would be the scene of major confrontations between factory-supported teams from Chrysler, Ford, Hudson, Oldsmobile, and Chevrolet.

Farther to the north, sprint cars, the smaller, more nimble versions of the AAA championship cars, were beginning to roll. The Offy-powered machines served not only as training vehicles for young men aspiring to Indianapolis, but as income sources for many established professionals. Eastern Pennsylvania was a hotbed of such competition, and tracks like the half-mile at the Williams Grove Amusement Park, south of Harrisburg, and Langhorne near the New Jersey border were favored venues.

Unlike the aged horse tracks that generally served as battlegrounds for the championship cars, both Williams Grove and Langhorne were built for automobile racing. Langhorne was the older of the two, having been constructed in 1926 on a plot of sloping swampland. In contrast to the conventional rectangular shape of most American speedways, Langhorne was a perfect one-mile circle. Sixty feet wide, with a surface of dirt soaked black with used engine oil, drivers either loved or hated the "Horn." Some praised the fact that one could circulate in constant, 100-mph powerslides. Others cited the dangers of the downhill section beyond the starting line, called "puke hollow." There, the swampy moisture wicked up through the dirt, causing immense ruts to form under spinning wheels. A poor entry into "puke hollow" could send a race car tumbling high over the wooden fence and into the copse of trees bordering the track.

Langhorne stood as the ultimate test of bravery—the Eiger face of motor racing. While some avoided it and others drove it with trepidation, men like Jimmy Bryan and "Iron Mike" Nazaruk embraced its demand for raw, unbridled cojones.

When the racers came to the "Horn," the Howard Johnson's motel and restaurant in nearby Bordentown, New Jersey, was the center of the action. The parking lot filled up with big sedans and station wagons hauling race cars. It was not uncommon to see crewmen and drivers working on the race cars outdoors, their aluminum bodywork spread out on the macadam.

In the evening, the crews gathered at local bars to share war stories and, more importantly, to hook up with the young women who inevitably appeared. Life on the road was long and lonely, rolling from track to track, from cheap tourist home and motel to rooming house. While many of the vagabonds were married, it was often in name only, their wives left back home in distant isolation. Their replacements were the same women who chased football and baseball players, seeking the thrill of a night with an alpha male.

Early in March, Langhorne bit one of the brave ones. Larry "Crash" Crockett was a burly kid from rural Indiana who had been named Rookie of the Year at the 500 the year before. Presuming his wild streak could be tamed, many believed him to have a bright future. But on March 20, Crash Crockett's sprint car hooked a rut in "puke hollow" and pinwheeled out of the park. By the time safety crews scrambled through the trees to the wrecked car, the young driver was dead.

Two weeks later in Italy, a brilliant young prospect for the Maserati Grand Prix equipe, Sergio Mantovani, had his leg severed in a crash at Turin. He never raced again.

As March gave way to the steady rains of April, it was clear to Travers and Coon that Goossen's V-8 engine could not be completed in time. They suggested to Keck that perhaps a conventional Offenhauser could serve as a replacement. Keck refused. He was beginning to devote his attention to thoroughbred horse racing. His stallion Ferdinand would win the Kentucky Derby in 1986, thereby making him the only man in history with victories in the most prestigious automobile and horse races in the world.

Keck said that unless the new car was completed in time, it would have to wait until next year before appearing at the track. He then called a friend, Coca-Cola millionaire Lindsey Hopkins, and offered his entire team—Travers, Coon, and, most important, Vukovich—to him. Realizing his good fortune, Hopkins instantly accepted, and turned over his year-old Kurtis-Kraft 500C roadster to the dream team. The car would carry the number 4 on its metallic blue tail and Hopkins's well-known rabbit in a top hat logo on its long hood. The Hopkins Kurtis would hardly be a breakthrough vehicle like the aborted Keck V-8, but it would still be a first-class machine once whiz kids Travers and Coon had finished their immaculate preparations. Vukovich, a man who seemed comfortable behind the wheel of any race car, was pleased with the change and spent extended periods in Travers's Los Angeles shop helping to ready the car.

His two chief rivals, Bryan and McGrath, were also reloading. Bryan's car's owner, Al Dean, had commissioned master craftsman Eddie "Zazoom" Kuzma to build a new Offy-powered roadster. It would carry a distinctive flat tail, devoid of the standard streamlined headrest. In its place would be a small metal hoop—the first known roll bar to appear at the Speedway. Still, it was too flimsy to offer much protection for the hulking Bryan. McGrath would return with the Hinkle Kurtis, much improved thanks to Jack the Bear's skills as an engine tuner and mechanic.

As the teams rolled into Indianapolis on the first week of May, little attention was paid to a stunning drive across Italy just completed by the dazzling English star Stirling Moss. Running for the Mercedes-Benz factory team with his friend and navigator, English journalist Dennis Jenkinson, Moss won the Mille Miglia open-road race in just over ten hours, averaging a stunning 97 mph over the 997-mile lap of the Italian boot.

From the perspective of a half-century later, Moss's drive borders on the unbelievable. The Mille Miglia was both Italy's greatest sporting event and a national holiday. Schools, banks, and government offices closed. Millions lined the route, which led from the northern starting point in Brescia, south along the Adriatic coast, through the holiday beach town of Rimini, to Pescara. From there it was a vault over the spine of the Apennine Mountains to Rome, back north through Siena, across the Arno at Florence, and over the perilous mountain pass at Futa into Bologna. Then home to Brescia.

Uncounted corners and blind hills demanded sheer brilliance behind the wheel. On the straights along the Adriatic coast, Moss let the sleek Mercedes 300SLR roadster have its head, often reaching 180 miles an hour. Working from a scrolling roll of route notes, Jenkinson hand-signaled Moss about upcoming course changes as the young Englishman snaked through the Italian countryside, leaving his Italian and German rivals far behind. He completed the arduous run in just seven minutes over ten hours, establishing him as the fastest open-road driver in history. Never again would such a drive be accomplished—nor would the 300SLR ever again attain such an honor, considering the tragedy that lay ahead for the brilliant machine.

But European competitions like the Mille Miglia were faraway thoughts to the drivers and crews who rolled into Indianapolis. Several European champions had recently tried the Speedway, the last being the likable Alberto Ascari, who had competed, without success, in 1952. But "sporty car" racing, as it was called, was generally discounted by the Indy crowd—until they were overwhelmed by its technology a decade later.

Then came word from Langhorne. "Iron Mike" Nazaruk, the nail-tough veteran of Guadalcanal, Iwo Jima, and Bougainville, had run one last warm-up for Indy in a sprint car event at the "Horn." Fighting for the lead in the twenty lap feature race, Nazaruk slid high in "puke hollow." The tail of his Nyquist Offy slapped the fence and fishtailed as

Nazaruk fought for control. Snap-rolling high into the air, the impact against a bordering tree was so pulverizing that Nazaruk's helmet was ripped off and his driving suit torn from his body. Big-time racing had claimed its second victim in a month.

It was just the beginning.

CHAPTER SIX

THE UN-MERRY MONTH OF MAY

CROSS-COUNTRY ROAD TRIPS IN 1955 WERE STILL something of an adventure. Interstate 40 lurked only in the minds of road planners and legislators formulating President Eisenhower's dream of an immense, 42,500-mile highway network. It was intended not only to meet the nation's growing automobile population, which was edging toward 100 million vehicles, but for national defense. Ike, who was headed for an easy second term, advocated such a system following his exposure to Germany's brilliant autobahns during World War II. Those superbly designed four lanes had served not only to rapidly transport troops and supplies for the Wehrmacht, but had been adopted as Luftwaffe fighter bases late in the fighting.

Eisenhower's plan was to invest $33.5 billion over the next sixteen years to complete the vast project. That was an optimistic projection; the Interstates would not reach their planned mileage until the late 1980s.

I decided to drive my MG back east for the Indianapolis 500, having received an assignment from *Liberty* to do a profile on Vukovich, who was expected to win an unprecedented third straight race. The trip, over rough, two-lane Route 66, the "Mother Road," took me east to Kingman on the Arizona border after a slow, heat-ravaged climb by my wheezing MG over the Cajon Pass. From there it was a top-down run to Lordsburg, the famed destination of John Wayne, Claire Trevor, and company in John Ford's classic 1939 film *Stagecoach*. Down off the Continental Divide, the MG regained its breath on the Texas panhandle flatlands and into dusty Amarillo for an overnight.

Angling north, I rolled through Oklahoma City and past Tulsa, where up ahead I spotted the unmistakable shape of a race car's tail on a trailer. Pushing the MG to its maximum, which nudged near 80 mph, I caught up with a dazzling pink-and-white Kurtis-Kraft roadster being towed by a heavily laden Ford station wagon. The race car was open, mounted on a trailer manufactured in Burbank, California, that featured a distinctive third dolly wheel on its fork. The car itself was exposed to the elements, save for a small leather tonneau cover over the cockpit. On its long nose were painted the large letters "JZ." This was a car belonging to Tulsa millionaire John Zink, and no doubt headed for Indianapolis. I instantly recognized the driver of the station wagon, a lean, sharp-nosed young man with a military crew cut. His name was A. J.—for Abraham Joseph—Watson, an Ohio native living in Glendale, California, who was viewed as a rising star among Indianapolis mechanics and car builders.

Watson had first appeared on the Speedway scene in 1950, when he and his friend Jud Phillips, another talented mechanic and hot-rodder, fashioned a car in Watson's Glendale garage. Using parts cadged from other race shops and donations from neighbors and local businesses, their "City of Glendale Special" became known among the racing fraternity as the "Pots and Pans Special." It joined another home-built car of the day, "Basement Bessie," which had been fabricated by race mechanic Ray Nichols in the cellar of his northern Indiana home. In an era when money was tight and race car design pretty basic, numerous race cars with equally humble beginnings appeared at the Speedway.

This was hardly the case with John "Jack" Zink, the son of a wealthy industrial-furnace-and-heating baron who had built his own three-quarter-mile test track on the family's sprawling ranch twenty miles west of Tulsa. No doubt his pink car on the trailer—a color quickly dubbed "Zink Pink"—had been inspired by the pastel fashions now embraced by both men and women, and in particular the pink button-down shirts being favored on elite college campuses from coast to coast.

I had heard through the Los Angeles grapevine that Frank Kurtis was building a new 500D roadster for Zink, with Bob Sweikert assigned to the seat. With Watson "twisting the wrenches," as it was phrased, and audacious young Sweikert at the wheel, the Zink Pink number 6 would be a strong contender at the Speedway.

I cruised beside the rig, gaping at the car's lacquered flanks and chrome fittings, which shimmered in the Oklahoma sunshine. Watson gave me a perfunctory wave as I spotted a wink of yellow in my rearview mirror. Rushing up was a new Cadillac Coupe de Ville Model 62, its enormous, egg-crate grille and its "Dagmar" bumper gnawing at my taillights. I quickly moved right to let the monster through. Drawing alongside, the hulking Caddy nose-dived from 100 mph, its front tires smoking and its driver, a large man in a Stetson, sawing at the wheel for control. He had obviously seen the race car trailer and wanted a closer look.

As our trio puttered along two-lane Route 66, a fourth machine appeared, again rolling up at high speeds, then slowing to a crawl to join the caravan. It was a 1932 high-boy roadster, a fenderless hot rod being driven by a gaunt young man in a T-shirt and sunglasses.

This was a classic American hot rod, powered by a modified flat-head Ford V-8—Henry's revolutionary, affordable, breakthrough engine, which became the biggest factor in his company's domination of the American market for over twenty years.

We dawdled along, my MG, the Cadillac, and the Ford roadster representing totally divergent aspects of domestic automobile enthusiasm—a powerful, flashy, be-finned Detroit mega-machine, a spindly English sports car, and a pure, home-built hot rod.

The Cadillac represented the latest advances in luxury passenger car technology—automatic transmission; power windows, seats, and steering; all packaged in so much chrome it looked like a Wurlitzer juke box on wheels. The other 2 vehicles—the hot rod and my MG—were simple cars compared to the Cadillac—at the time the undisputed king of the American road. Like its smaller, lower-priced General Motors sisters, Buick and Oldsmobile, Cadillac's sales were booming. It had far out-paced rival Lincoln, while the once-haughty Packard had descended to a point so low that the company had made a desperate alliance with the equally weakened Studebaker.

In fact, General Motors and Ford were on the verge of driving all other domestic brands off the market. Even Chrysler, the traditional third arm of the so-called Big Three, was struggling. Its Plymouth brand, long the third-best-selling marque in America, behind Ford and Chevrolet, had dropped to fifth in sales, now passed by both Buick and Oldsmobile. Hudson and Nash, two aged and much-honored makes, were united in a final, futile bid for survival, while upstart Kaiser-Fraser and Willys, the maker of the world-famous and beloved Jeep, were both on the edge of bankruptcy.

With its impudent tail fins, the Caddy represented quintessential American optimism; it was bold, oversized, overweight, and overtly flashy. It was a perfect and proud representative of what one critic denounced as "insolent chariots."

The Zink Kurtis-Kraft riding on Watson's trailer, its outrageous "tropical rose" paintwork blossoming for all to see, was itself a classic American race car. While the first known rearview mirror was believed to have been used on Ray Harrouh's 1911 Marmon Wasp in the first 500, the Zink, like all American race cars, carried no such device. At some point, long since forgotten, rearview mirrors were removed from American race cars and were never reinstalled. Whether it was for streamlining, or based on an unspoken policy that left all passing responsibility to the car behind, with none on the leading driver, was not unknown. The Zink, like all its brethren, was an elemental machine, bereft of top, headlights, turn signals, mirrors, brake lights, windows, fenders, doors, and all other standard automobile accessories. Its gearbox, a simple two-speed unit, was used only for acceleration out of the pits. Even the starter was missing. The Offenhauser engine was activated by a portable unit to save weight. While powersteering was being adopted for passenger cars, the extra weight and presumed power loss made such devices undesirable at Indianapolis. With its driver on board and its sixty-gallon tank loaded with methanol-alcohol fuel, the steel, aluminum, and magnesium Zink weighed in at about one ton—a brutish, basic hunk that had to be kept under rein at up to 180 miles an hour, for 500 miles.

I could not help but muse upon the contrast between the Zink and my tiny MG. The little English roadster was widely used in amateur sports car races both here and in Great Britain, but the two vehicles were light years apart in design and intent.

Road racing cars—be they tiny MGs or ultra-powerful Mercedes-Benz or Ferraris that competed in Grand Prix races or in open-road contests like the Mille Miglia—depended on four- and five-speed gearboxes and giant brakes to give them maximum performance over a wide range of speeds and differing track conditions. In contrast, the Kurtis-Kraft was designed for constant high velocities exclusively on sweeping left turns. Brakes and gearboxes were a relatively low priority for their designers.

The big Cadillac with the Oklahoma cowboy was yet another breed. Its home was the Great Plains, where endless, flat roads ran to the horizon permitted 100-mph cruising speeds with the air conditioning running full blast and the radio trilling Hank Williams classics. The kid's hot rod, on the other hand, was intended only for spotlight bursts and occasional runs on the quarter-mile drag strips that were springing up across the nation. Like the Indy car, its priorities lay in light weight, high power, and one-dimensional performance.

By the time I reached the Missouri border and stopped for the night in a tourist home outside Joplin, the foursome of strange automobiles had long since dispersed. Watson had moved on with the Zink, no doubt planning a nonstop run all the way to Indianapolis.

Less pressed for time, I didn't reach the city until a day later, whereupon I settled into my new quarters. The Manifold rooming house was full, and I had found other, nicer lodgings even closer to the track. Ray Newsome, a retired tool-and-die maker from the long-defunct Marmon Automobile Works, owned a pristine bungalow on Georgetown Road. His property, set back in a grove of tall Elms with a neatly manicured yard, bordered the fourth turn of the Speedway.

A quiet man, Newsome and his younger brother, Elton, had accommodations for five guests in two double rooms and a single—that was mine. In the others were two Buick salesmen from Philadelphia, who proudly parked their Roadmaster sedan close to the house, and a Firestone tire dealer from Des Moines with his wife. The Newsome brothers were Baptists, but they nevertheless joined the Buick men and the Firestone dealer when they gathered late each day in the backyard to share stories and drink Old Grand-Dad bourbon in water glasses borrowed from the kitchen.

In a corner of the yard, well back from the street, was the Speedway's gray cement retaining wall, mounted high on a dirt embankment. One evening, after Elton had had his second glass of bourbon, he told the story of how, in 1935, a driver named Stubby Stubblefield and his riding mechanic, Leo Whittaker, had tumbled over that wall in their Miller special and landed in Newsome's yard.

"Lemme see," said Elton, pulling on the strap of the Oshkosh "Can't Bust-em" overalls that appeared to be his entire wardrobe, "I was about twenty-three at the time. Always stayed around for the big race because our daddy, who owned the place, took in guests and parked cars in the yard. Just like me and Ray do to this day. It was one of them qualifying days when all of a sudden I'm standing on the porch and I hear a terrible screeching of tires and a big boom. Here comes these two guys and then a big orange car a-flying over the wall. Like birds, ya see. Damned if they didn't land right by that juniper over there, which was just a sapling in those days.

"Scared the hell out of me. I ran over to 'em. They were still as stones. Bloodied up and everything. Then here come a bunch of guys jumpin' over the wall with fire extinguishers and medical kits and they shoved me back. Never did see a thing after that. The ambulance came and hauled 'em away, but that wrecked race car laid in our yard for a whole day.

"For years after that the family of poor ol' Stubblefield came all the way from Oregon or some damn place out west. Of course we give 'em permission to lay some flowers on the spot. I ain't the superstitious kind, but I was near thirty before I'd go back there and mow that part of the lawn. That I'll be honest about."

"Ain't the half of it," said Ray, his face ashen gray. "Thirty-five was a terrible year. They brought in this hot-shot kid from the eastern circuit named Johnny Hannon. He gets in some guy's Miller and damned if he don't make a lap. Not even one. Pitched over the wall down yonder. At least beyond our property, thank God. So he's dead, but the car owner gets the car repaired in time for the race. He sticks in another rookie kid named Clay Weatherly. In those days they had to carry a riding mechanic for some damn fool reason. You won't believe it, but on the ninth lap of the race Weatherly has a wreck in about the same spot, and he's killed too.

"The poor guy riding with him gets a broken back. When that month was over, four of 'em were dead, all within a stone's throw of here." Ray Newsome took a long slug of bourbon, then looked at the wall. "Sometimes in May this place can be hell on earth," he said quietly.

The Buick men listened in silence. Then the older one, with a red face and a heavy belly who wheezed when he talked and sported enormous gold cufflinks on his French-cuffed white shirt, took another swig of bourbon. He said, "You gotta wonder if that's what folks come to see. Do they want to see some racing or do they want to see guys get killed?"

"You gotta wonder," repeated the younger Buick man, slouching in his chair and gazing at the wall.

"You see it once and you don't wanna see it again. I'll tell you that," said Elton.

"I think the essence of racing is watching men at the edge," I chimed in. "People want to see 'em take big risks but survive. I think they vicariously ride with the drivers and do brave acts in their minds. When a driver dies, it means failure. I think the crowd dies with him."

"Damn, I never thought of it that way," said Ray.

"But I can remember one year, maybe five or six races ago when Duke Nalon whacked the wall with the Novi." Newsome pointed toward the short straightaway connecting the third and fourth corner, now shielded by a stand of elms.

"Duke hit hard and the car caught fire. . ."

"Hell, you see the smoke all the way to Terre Haute," interrupted Elton.

". . . But then Duke rolled over the wall, right into our backyard," Ray continued. His coveralls were on fire, and my cousin Bert, who was down from South Bend for the race, rolled him in the dirt and put out the fire. When the public address system announced Duke was all right, you could hear a giant cheer go up." He paused, then looked at me. "Maybe you're right with your theory. They die. We die. They live. We live."

Somebody passed the bottle of Old Grand-Dad.

Thanks to my connections with *Liberty*, the director of press relations at the Speedway, a former *Indianapolis Star* reporter named Al Bloemaker, gave me a "99" press pass. With it pinned to my shirt, I was free to move almost anywhere. When practice opened on the first day of the month, I spent most of my time in Gasoline Alley or in the adjacent little cafeteria, where news and gossip was shared by the mobs of mechanics, car owners, journalists, and drivers.

The center of my world was the Vukovich garage, where Travers and Coon allowed me entry, even when the large green-and-white wooden doors were closed. Vukovich was pleasant enough, but always distant, feeling as he did that members of the press were needlessly nosy and bound to misquote him.

Lindsey Hopkins, the car owner, was a soft-spoken Georgian, mannerly and reserved in that special way of Southern gentlemen. He was part of a friendly alliance of wealthy car owners with a connection to Coca-Cola. The track owner, Tony Hulman, owned the franchise for the entire state of Indiana. Chapman Root, who regularly entered cars at the Speedway, was the grandson of C. J. Root, who had started the Root Glass Company, which still held the patents on the famed pinch-waisted Coca-Cola bottle and was the primary bottler for the world's most famous soft drink. Joining this group was Hopkins, who was a major stockholder in Coca-Cola while owning large parcels of real estate in Miami Beach—a boomtown that had been created out of the mangrove swamps by entrepreneur Carl Fisher, who had also been the prime mover in building the Indianapolis Motor Speedway. Behind the fastest race cars in the garage were immensely wealthy men like Root and Hopkins, who engaged in big-time automobile racing for the pure sport of it.

It became clear during the first week of practice that three major players were in the game to win the 500. Of course there was Vukovich, who, many felt, was a sure thing to win his third straight—even with a different car, albeit a first-class machine from the Hopkins stable. There was McGrath, of course, whose Hinkle held the outright lap record at over 141 mph, and who was the fastest driver in the place. Following the 1954 500, McGrath had taken the Hinkle to the new Chrysler Proving Grounds at Chelsea, Michigan, for a demonstration run. On a sunny day in June he had blazed around the 4.7 mile test track at a wink under 180 mph, to set a world's closed-course speed record. He and the same yellow Kurtis-Kraft were back to up the ante at Indianapolis. The third favorite was Jimmy Bryan, his fresh new Kuzma roadster carrying a blue number 1 on its tail, signifying his national AAA championship. While there were others who might challenge, including Sweikert's Zink-Pink Kurtis, the trio of Vukovich, Bryan, and McGrath was considered by the rail-birds to be in a class by itself.

Back-markers, strokers and struggling rookies were on hand as well, ready to nibble at the leftovers, happy simply to make the thirty-three-car starting field. Many were in ancient, battered automobiles that had seen better days. Al Keller, a thirty-five-year-old veteran of jalopies, midgets, and stock cars, was taking his first shot at Indianapolis in a six-year old-Kurtis-Kraft dirt track car, the former "Wolfe Special," which had carried the immortal Rex Mays to his death at Del Mar, California, in 1949. Like many of the cars in Gasoline Alley, the Keller car had a bloody past—now forgotten— and was repainted with a new owner and revived hope.

Rodger Ward, the tough guy with the edgy reputation, was also back, with another veteran machine—albeit with a more positive heritage. His Aristo-Blue Special was the former Agajanian dirt-track car that had carried young Troy Ruttman to victory in 1952. After four seasons of combat, the aging car was now owned in part by an

Indiana automobile dealer and in part by Hoot Gibson, the retired cowboy movie star of the 1930s.

The Chevrolet division of General Motors had descended on the Speedway with a full contingent of sales and public relations types. A new convertible would serve as the race's pace car, while Mauri Rose, three-time winner of the 500 and now a Chevrolet engineer, was on hand to give press demonstrations with a V-8-powered Corvette. The latter was intended to energize the flagging model in the face of Ford's vigorous new Thunderbird challenge. The fleet of Chevrolets that supported the campaign, as well as all of the handouts and sales brochures, were lavished with the division's ivory and red theme colors.

Dinah Shore would present the winner with the four-foot-tall silver Borg-Warner trophy. She was the hostess of a wildly popular Chevrolet-sponsored Sunday evening television variety show. Her theme song, "See the USA in Your Chevrolet," was one of the most successful musical numbers in the history of advertising. Her planned presence on race day would lend an air of big-time glamour seldom seen in a city that some New York and Los Angeles cynics referred to as "Indian-no-place." Dinah's wardrobe would, as expected, be red and ivory.

Practice leading up to the first day of qualifying was thankfully uneventful, aside from a few spins and some damaged egos. As expected, McGrath was easily the quickest; once more, an argument flared between Vukovich and Travers about the use of nitro. With his friend McGrath running almost two miles an hour faster, Vukovich wanted the extra boost of "pop" to narrow the gap. Travers stood firm as his star driver stomped around the garage demanding that the volatile stuff be loaded into his fuel tank. "McGrath will be quick in qualifying," Travers kept saying, his angry eyes shielded behind his ever-present aviator's Ray-Bans. "But I'm telling you, an engine with that junk in it won't last five hundred miles. So what do you want, the track record or some kissy-face with Dinah Shore at the end?"

The grumbling between the pair, usually good-natured, went on in fits and starts until the first day of qualifying, the so-called pole day, when the coveted pole position—and its bonus money—would be determined.

As I finished my scrambled eggs at Newsome's, the skies darkened and my walk down Georgetown Road took place under a spattering of rain. By the time I reached the garage area, the shower had cleared, but a brisk, chill wind began to stiffen the flags and send hats sailing.

By noon, heavy nimbus clouds hung over the track. Yet the giant, double-decker grandstands had filled with fans, each of whom had paid a dollar to watch qualifying and intermittent practice. No car moved. The track was buffeted by 30-mph gusts. A crewman from Chapman Root's Sumar team ducked into the garage and gathered up Vukovich and Travers. "The teams have all gotten together. We're saying, if you don't go, we won't go. Too damn windy."

Vukovich watched him leave. "Fuck 'em," he mumbled. "I'll go when I'm ready. Not when they tell me."

Still, the Hopkins stayed in the garage. So did McGrath's Hinkle and Bryan's Dean Van Lines, as well as every other serious contender. The giant track remained empty and silent. An occasional angry shout from inside the grandstand echoed into Gasoline Alley. The crowd was getting restless. Still there was no movement.

A small, spare, balding man in a gray suit bustled into the garage. He had a pinched, humorless face. The treasurer of the Speedway, Joe Cloutier, he pulled Travers aside. "Look, somebody's got to get out there and make some laps," he said with his squeaky Hoosier twang. "I've got sixty thousand of 'em sitting in the grandstands at a buck apiece. Unless somebody does some qualifying I'm in the tank for refunds. The last thing I need—and you guys need—is me passing out sixty thousand rain checks."

Travers shrugged and said nothing. Vukovich walked away and then turned. "Look, Joe. I ain't gonna take a chance of stuffing this thing in the wall so I can save you and Tony a few bucks. If the wind dies down, I go. If not, we go another day. Maybe you can get some other poor sucker to try it."

He did. Jerry Hoyt was a twenty-six-year-old Chicago native who had grown up around the business. At age nine, he was the mascot for Lucky Teeter's traveling automobile thrill show, where his father worked. He began racing midgets and sprint cars as a teenager. Three previous tries at Indianapolis had resulted in dry holes, although Hoyt was considered a solid player on the sprint car circuit and had teamed with Sweikert to run the half-miles for the remainder of the season. His Speedway car was an aged Myron Stevens creation owned by Detroit sportsman Jim Robbins that had done yeoman service over the years but had never been considered a serious contender.

With less than half an hour left before qualifying officially ended at six o'clock, a whoop rose up from the remaining loyalists in the grandstand. The Offenhauser in Hoyt's Robbins Special rumbled into life on pit lane. Pulling on his driving gloves, he set out to brave the breezes in a wild charge for the pole position. As other crews, including Vukovich and Travers, sprinted to the pits, Hoyt took the green flag to begin his four-lap run against the clock. Dodging the gusts and driving perhaps beyond his skill, he ran a shocking average speed of 140.045 mph to win the number-one starting position. Two others then tried before the gun went off ending the day, with only former national champion Tony Bettenhausen joining Hoyt in the field, at a disappointing 138 mph. But Cloutier's precious money had remained in the bank. Surely higher speeds would come as the serious players faced the timing clocks the following day.

We slogged back to the garage area. In the distance, the impatient honking of horns rose up. The giant crowd had headed for the gates. Now Sixteenth Street and Georgetown Road had become a sea of fuming iron. "You gotta give it to Hoyt," said Travers. "The guy has some balls." Vukovich stalked ahead, saying nothing. A reporter from the *Chicago Tribune* came up. "Ol' Hoyt kinda snookered you hot guys. Whaddya say to that?"

"Nothing. Last I heard the race ain't till Memorial Day," snapped Vukovich.

Back at Newsome's, the Buick men cracked open another bottle of Old Grand-Dad and watched the sun set.

"Tomorrow oughta be good," said the cuff-linked one. "All the hot-shots will be ready. Weather is supposed to improve. We'll see some serious speed."

"Not so fast that somebody ends up in my yard," said Eldon Newsome.

The Buick man was right. The next day, calm winds and sunny skies produced big speed. Vukovich put the Hopkins in fifth place at 141 mph while, as expected, McGrath was far and away the fastest, at nearly 143 mph. He would start third. Bryan was a wink off the pace and would be eleventh on the grid. The long day involved all manner of qualifying attempts, both fast and slow, with Keller surprising everyone by manhandling his antique Kurtis-Kraft around at 139 mph.

One who never left the garage was Manny Ayulo. He was a friend of Jack McGrath's who drove for Peter Schmidt, whose family owned a large St. Louis brewery. Manny, as he was known in the fraternity, both drove and served as chief mechanic on Schmidt's bright red roadster. The son of a Peruvian diplomat who had been raised in Los Angeles, Ayulo stubbornly refused help when the car's Offenhauser developed endless lubrication problems. The tiny, balding driver labored so furiously over the engine in search of the ailment that his friends urged him to get some sleep before testing the car. Ayulo shrugged them off and worked through the night to get the engine right.

Even his close friend Wayne "Fat Boy" Ewing couldn't dissuade him. Fat Boy was a metalworking genius. Armed with only a copper hammer, a pair of tin snips, and a bag of sand, he could form stunning, complexly curved race car noses and tails out of sheet aluminum. He was one of several such unique craftsmen in the sport, a hard-drinking drifter who often lived in the back of his beat-up station wagon as he rolled from racetrack to racetrack, "stooging" for various race teams. Fat Boy employed his mystical skills with aluminum and steel until the early 1960s when fiberglass and other synthetics began to replace his beloved metals. At that point he disappeared from the tracks and was never seen again.

"Manny's got a hair in his ass," grumbled Fat Boy as he left the Schmidt garage. "He's gonna do it by himself or not do it at all. He's in some kind of a zone. No sleep. Might as well leave him alone," he said, shrugging his wide shoulders and walking away.

Late in the afternoon, during a lull in qualifying, the Offy was fired up. After loosely strapping on his seat belt, Ayulo surged onto the Speedway. Blazing down the front straightaway to complete the first test lap, the Schmidt never turned. Ayulo smacked the wall head on. As the car bounced away from the freshly whitewashed concrete and pinwheeled to a stop, it was obvious that survival of such impact was impossible. Still, the wiry little man who had banged his way to Indianapolis via a hundred other crashes lived out the night at Methodist Hospital.

Some claimed that in his haste to get on the track, Ayulo had failed to properly connect the steering linkage. Others were convinced that his reflexes had failed and his timing was off as he barreled into the corner. A millisecond's misjudgment in correctly finding a proper entry line at 175–180 mph, and the car might have augured into the wall.

Either way, on Monday his young wife, Bonnie, was on an American flight to Los Angeles, taking Manny Ayulo home for burial.

The two weeks of terror had begun.

On May 22, with qualifying for the race completed, word came via the Associated Press that Alberto Ascari, the former two-time world driving champion and well-liked personality among the Indy crowd, had suffered a strange accident in Monaco. While running the Grand Prix through the streets of the tiny principality and fighting for the lead, Ascari's D50 Lancia had locked up a brake entering a chicane in a section of the course that bordered the harbor. In an instant the Lancia mounted the low stone wall and pitched into the Bay of Hercules. For a moment Ascari was trapped—until skin divers, posted for exactly such an incident, hauled him to the surface. Although he spent a night in the hospital, the plump man known among his friends as "Ciccio," returned to his Milan home without apparent injury, other than a stiff back.

Ascari had run the Indianapolis 500 in 1952 with a factory-entered Ferrari. While he spoke no English, his easy manner and ribald sense of humor had won him many friends among the Americans. His car was ill-suited to the big track, and he retired after forty laps when a wheel fractured and he spun harmlessly. But it was clear that he had enjoyed his sojourn into the heartland and spoke of returning with a more competitive car.

Then Ascari's long relationship with Enzo Ferrari, the powerful, tyrannical capo of Scuderia Ferrari, broke up in a dispute over money and Ascari moved on to drive for the newly formed Lancia team. With that, further plans for a return to Indianapolis ended.

Little was said about Ascari's plunge into Monaco's harbor, other than the typical spate of gallows humor that followed all accidents in the sport. In the 1930s several drivers had ended up upside down in a now-filled creek that bordered the Speedway's first turn, but a muddy face was small potatoes to a salt-water dunking in a deep Mediterranean harbor.

Then, four days later, during a lull in practice, came the stunning news that Alberto Ascari was dead. How could this be? He had survived his Monaco crash, only to be killed at the giant Monza Autodome, located on a former royal park in a suburb of Milan.

The mad coincidence of his demise haunts the sport to this day.

Ascari left his Milan apartment on a warm May day to visit some fellow drivers who were participating in the upcoming Super-cortemaggiore 1,000-kilometer sports car race set for the Monza track on the coming weekend. After a quiet lunch with his longtime Ferrari teammate Luigi Villoresi, who had run well at Indianapolis in 1947, Ascari visited the pit of Eugenio Castellotti, a darkly handsome Florentine who was considered a major talent. On a whim, Ascari asked Castellotti if he might take a few slow laps in his 750 Monza Ferrari to "work some kinks out of my back." After removing his tailored sports coat and tucking his tie into his pima cotton shirt, Ascari climbed into the car. He was handed a borrowed helmet, having forgotten his own favorite robin's egg blue one, which he considered a good luck talisman. Strapping it in place, he eased out of the pits and, per his promise, made three easy laps around the sprawling, tree-lined circuit. But passing the pits, he punched the throttle of the powerful Ferrari sports car and disappeared down the long straight, its V-12 growling like a deranged cat.

Then silence. Shouts of alarm echoed through the forest from a single witness. Ascari had crashed on a left-hand curve known as Vialone. It was an easy section of the track that an expert like Ascari would hardly acknowledge. Castellotti, Villoresi, and the car's crew rushed to the scene. Ascari had been flung from the tumbling car—it having no seat belts, as was the accepted practice in Europe at the time. Gravely injured, he died in Villoresi's arms in the back of an ambulance.

Italy was plunged into mourning. Ascari was a national hero, equaled only by a few soccer players and a handful of movie stars.

Telegrams of sympathy poured in from industrial and political leaders across Europe. The Church of San Carlo al Corso draped its giant front columns in black, with the huge inscription: "On the last finish line, O Lord, meet the soul of Alberto Ascari." His funeral was held at the immense Piazza del Duomo in the center of Milan. Thousands jammed the area while traffic stopped. The normal buzz of motor scooters and the incessant honking of horns fell silent, only the ringing of a telephone in one of the houses bordering the piazza broke the reverent silence.

Then came the numerologists and mystics, who began to reveal the bizarre coincidences that surrounded his death.

Alberto Ascari was the son of Antonio Ascari, a brilliant race driver for the Fiat Grand Prix team in the 1920s. While leading the French Grand Prix at Linas-Montlhery outside Paris, Antonio Ascari crashed to his death. The date was June 26, 1925. In memory of his father, Alberto had refused to race on the twenty-sixth day of any month—except on the day of his own death, May 26, 1955. Both Ascaris, as well as Alberto's patron saint, Antonio of Padua, were thirty-six years old at the time. Both Saint Antonio and Alberto had been born on June 13. Both Ascaris had died on the twenty-sixth day of the month, or twice thirteen. Antonio had lived for 13,463 days. His son had lived for 13,466 days. Some in the Italian press noted that both father and son had crashed on left-hand bends on circuits with predominantly right-hand corners.

Whatever the mystery, if any, the harsh fact remained that one of the world's most accomplished drivers was dead. The season was not halfway through, and Crockett, Nazaruk, Ayulo, and Ascari were gone, with another, young Sergio Mantovani, permanently disabled. Surely, this madness could not last.

Or could it?

CHAPTER SEVEN

DEATH IN THE MORNING

THE BOMB'S DETONATION SHOOK ME OUT OF MY cot. It was still dark. I looked at my watch. Four in the morning. I thought of Korea. Shaking myself awake, I heard the distant honking of horns. As I lay there it began to make sense. At this ungodly hour on race day, the Speedway management traditionally set off a charge of dynamite signaling that the infield gates would be opened. This triggered a mini–Oklahoma land rush as fans poured into the immense acreage, seeking the best locations along the backstretch fence. As the tumult continued, I crawled out of bed to wash up. Through the tiny window over the sink, I could see that Georgetown Road was already packed with cars, all seeking entry into the track. While I was shaving, dawn broke, dark and threatening, with banks of low nimbus clouds scudding in from the west.

The Newsomes cooked up breakfast for their guests. The Buick men had box seats for the race, facing the pits, while the Firestone dealer and his wife would be guests of the company in a special section in the first turn. I was silently envied as the privileged one, sporting as I did the "99" pass pinned to my blue blazer.

"Tell that crazy bastard Vukovich to take it easy," said the older Buick man as I left the breakfast table.

"He won't beat McGrath this year," said his partner. "That boy's too slick for ol' Billy this time."

"Don't bet on either one of 'em," said Eldon, wiping a crumb of toast from his freshly laundered bib overalls. "This place don't play no favorites."

I walked into the yard. In the gloom, Ray Newsome was parking cars, fender by fender, taking two dollars each from the drivers. Soon the entire plot of Newsome's land would be a sea of automobiles. I walked down Georgetown Road, paralleling the jammed traffic. I passed a modest house on the opposite side of the road, where twelve-year-old Wilbur Brink had been playing in his yard on Memorial Day in 1931. When race leader Billy Arnold crashed in the fourth turn, a wire wheel and tire shorn loose by the impact bounced crazily over the Speedway grandstands and killed the child. When the race cars ran at Indianapolis, nobody was safe.

I entered the track through a gate that permitted pre-race pedestrians to cross the main straightaway. The brick surface, having weathered forty-four Indiana winters and the pounding of thousands of cars during thirty-eight 500s, was shockingly rough, even to a new pair of Bass Weejun loafers. I could not imagine how it punished a human body in a cart-sprung race car at 180 miles an hour.

I squeezed past a blue-shirted Speedway guard, with his standard-issue yellow pith helmet, into Gasoline Alley, and spotted big Ed Keating, the general manager of Chevrolet. He was the prototypical auto exec, well-tanned, his perfectly coiffed hair graying at the temples. His bright red blazer and ivory silk shirt were in Chevrolet theme and would match the convertible he would drive to pace the start. He was without his star, Dinah Shore, who, despite her celebrity, was not allowed into the all-male precincts of the garage area.

I eased into the Vukovich garage, which had been roped off. The royal blue Hopkins with its red number 4 and the owner's rabbit-in-a-hat symbol on its cowl, was ready. Coon nodded, silently acknowledging my entry as Travers gapped a spare set of spark plugs on the bench. "How ya doing, Smokey?" asked Vukovich, "Smokey" being his catch-all nickname for everybody. "Look at this." He handed me a piece of blue-lined note paper. On it was a child's neatly printed message: "Dear Daddy. Be sure and smoke these guys today. Love Billy." Vukovich took the paper back.

"My kid. Little bastard. He's something. Little fucker is only ten years old. Already he wants to race. Maybe I'll make enough money to get him into another line of work." He began to frantically work on his hand grip.

"Esther wants me to quit. She's on my ass worse than ever. For her and the kids, she keeps saying—he began to mimic a female voice—"'Come home to Fresno and run your gas stations. Be a family man like real people.' She's right. If I win this son-of-a-bitch, you've seen the last of me."

"Cut the shit," said Travers. "You're too fucking crazy to quit. Some smart-ass kid comes along and people start to say, 'Hey, that guy could beat Vukie,' and you'd be back."

"Don't bet on it. I win and you've seen the last of Vukovich at Indianapolis."

This would not be the case. Bill Vukovich Jr. would become a fine race driver in his own right. Between 1968 and 1980 he would compete in twelve 500-mile races, finishing second in 1973 and third a year later.

McGrath walked in as Vukovich pumped up his ever-present hand exerciser. McGrath, a head taller than his friend, leaned against the bench. "Gotta watch that wind," he said.

"It's a shit day," said Vukovich.

"Whatya going to do about it?" asked Travers rhetorically.

"Nothing. The weather is the fuckin' weather. I didn't come here for my health in the first place," he said.

"Jerry says he'll move over," said McGrath. He was referring to Jerry Hoyt, who had won the pole on a fluke.

"He better, or I'll drive over his fuckin' ass," said Vukovich. Then a giant gap-toothed smile spread across his face. "And that goes for you too, asshole," he said, laughing at McGrath.

Vukovich grabbed McGrath by the arm. His vise grip tightened, making McGrath wince with pain. "How can a skinny fucker like this expect to run with me?" he asked no one in particular. Laughing, McGrath pulled free. He pointed to his head. "Up here, you dumb Russian. Here's where I beat you."

"Oh, yeah," smiled Vukovich. "Here's where I beat you." He raised his right foot.

Both men laughed. McGrath walked to the door. Then he turned. "Watch your ass with the wind, Vuke. I'll see you later."

"You gotta like that McGrath," said Vukovich.

"He's the one you gotta beat," said Travers, never looking up. "The rest of those guys you can handle. But that son-of-a-bitch can get around this place."

"If you fuckers would let me use that pop he's runnin' there'd be no problem."

"Here we go again with that shit," said Coon. You wait and see how long he runs before he scatters his engine."

Vukovich rolled his eyes, knowing the argument was futile and went back to working his hand exerciser. I walked outside. A writer for *Speed Age* magazine named Bob Russo was talking to McGrath. Russo knew everybody in the business. It was believed that he had coined the term "championship trail."

As I walked by, I heard McGrath say, "Vuke is a helluva driver, but I just won't take the chances he does. It isn't worth it in the end."

As the cars were rolled onto the starting grid, the usual prerace festivities had ended. The Purdue University band, chilled to the bone, had played their usual rendition of "On the Banks of the Wabash" and the national anthem. A few celebrities eased through the crowd, including singer Mel Torme and General Curtis LeMay, who had opened up his strategic Air Force bases for sports car racing until Congress shut him down.

The big guest star was Dinah Shore, who did a lap of the Speedway in a Chevy convertible, riding in the backseat with an unlikely companion, the four-foot-high silver Borg-Warner trophy reserved for the winner.

Vukovich barged out of his garage, smoking a small cigar. He was headed toward the track when his friend and fellow driver Freddy Agabashian moved in beside him. Agabashian was an old pro, having raced in the Bay Area with Vukovich since the 1930s and having run at Indy since 1947. He had won the pole position in 1952 aboard the strange and wonderful Cummins Diesel, and was considered one of the brightest and wisest of the drivers. He was also haunted by superstition. When asked to test-drive a green-painted Cummins car in 1951, he refused, until every last trace of the hue had been buffed and sanded away.

As the slight, handsome Agabashian stepped closer to Vukovich, a bystander brushed against them, causing Vukovich to drop his helmet. As he reached down to pick it up, Agabashian reeled in horror. This was to him the ultimate curse. The mark of death. Helmets were sacred talismans to many drivers, as Ascari's had been to him. Dropping it was, to Agabashian, akin to riding with a black cat in a car numbered 13 (a taboo number never used in big-time American racing).

Agabashian, his face stiff, pulled away from Vukovich and slipped into the crowd. Thinking little of the incident, Vukovich shrugged and headed toward his car.

Along pit row, Dinah Shore, dressed in a bright red suit, began singing the traditional "Back Home in Indiana," which had in the past been the job of opera star James Melton. This time, in deference to Mitch Miller's popular sing-along TV show, the lilting star requested that the grandstand audience join her in the second verse. The response among the chilled crowd was limited at best.

Back in the fifth row of starters, Bob Sweikert made a final check of his pink Kurtis-Kraft before climbing into the cockpit. A week before, word had come from Glendale that chief mechanic A. J. Watson's young son had died. He had rushed home to be with his wife. Sweikert, an expert mechanic in his own right, had taken over the final preparations of the car.

Shielding the microphone against the wind that blustered out of the west, track president Tony Hulman gave the traditional call to arms, "Gentlemen, start your engines."

Thirty-three raucous, blatting Offenhausers bombarded the grandstands with noise and methanol fumes. Travers pulled the portable starter from the snout of the Hopkins as Vukovich pulled on his helmet and driving gloves. Coon stood behind the tail of the car, ready to push it away on the starter's signal. Holding his ears against the thunder around him, Travers went to the cockpit and brushed Vukovich's shoulder in a rough gesture of good luck. Vukovich returned it with a cursory nod. He had entered another zone.

The Chevrolet convertible pace car, driven by Keating with Tony Hulman beside him, rolled out of the pit lane. The thirty-three race cars lumbered slowly in its wake. They disappeared around the first turn and out of sight as the crews scuttled back to their positions in the pits bordering the straightaway.

Two pace laps. The massive crowd was on its feet. A deafening bomb exploded and an immense cluster of multicolored balloons blossomed over the infield and quickly scattered in the breeze. The field reappeared, gaining speed. The grandstands became a sea of waving hats, hands, and handkerchiefs. The drivers returned the salute with their gloved hands.

By then most of the establishment press, the big-city reporters, and a few Associated Press and UPI staffers and magazine writers had adjourned to the press box, a long row of seats hung high under the eaves of the grandstand from which pit action could be observed. Standings were unknown during the race, save for the teletyped bulletins passed around every ten laps by Eagle Scouts selected for the honor. Rather than sit there in splendid isolation, I chose to stay trackside, standing directly behind the Vukovich pits, where I could observe Coon and Travers as the race unfolded a few feet away.

One more pace lap and the Chevrolet scurried into pit lane. Bill Vandewater, the starter standing at the edge of the track, whipped out a giant green flag and began waving it at the wildly hued clot of mechanical bulls charging toward him. Accelerating hard, they rumbled past, briefly enveloping him in a cloud of dust that had lain dormant in the grout of the bricks.

Distant thunder. The backstretch. "Jack's got the lead. Vuke's in second, right on his ass," yelled Travers over the din, somehow in receipt of information unseen by others. It was the beginning of a long, desperate, raggedly insane battle for the lead between McGrath and Vukovich. The others were left behind to fight for the pickings as the pair dueled wheel to wheel, passing and re-passing, sometimes two and three times a lap. Never in the history of the Speedway had two men struggled with such mechanical intensity. Generally, such tiffs lasted no more than a lap or two before one driver or the other established supremacy, through either sheer will or superior horsepower. But this time, McGrath and Vukovich each refused to give, slicing into the corners abreast and wailing down the long back straight side by side. The crowd was on its feet, its cheers faint and squeaky against the din of the engines.

The war went on for forty laps before smoke began to ooze from McGrath's exhaust pipe. I walked to Travers, who was holding a pit board that said, "P1 137." It signaled Vukovich that he was first, running a record-setting 137 mph, a phenomenal speed considering his heavy fuel load and the gusting wind. Travers shouted, "McGrath's gonna blow. Just like I told Vuke. That pop is death on an engine." He turned and held up the pit board as Vukovich passed.

A yellow flag was waved by Vandewater. Agabashian had spun, gyrating into the infield grass without injury. I thought of the helmet.

A slit in the clouds produced a suggestion of sunlight. Perhaps the weather was clearing. Things were back in order. Vukovich was leading. McGrath was faltering. The rest of the field was straggling, far behind. I began to compose the lead for my story. On the fifty-third lap, McGrath coasted into the pits and climbed out. He opened the hood of the Hinkle as he was handed a spark plug wrench. After extracting the plug, he examined it and shrugged his shoulders. Clearly the plug had told his trained eye that the engine was mortally wounded. Yanking off his helmet, he turned and stalked toward the garage area.

Back at the Vukovich pit, Travers and Coon were preparing for their driver's first stop for fuel and tires. Four fresh Firestones were laid at the pit wall while Travers checked the valve on the immense tank of methanol fuel mounted at the back of the pit. The movements were routine, measured, almost laconic by the perfectly trained crew.

Another yellow flag. This time Vandewater was at the edge of the track, waving frantically. The cars slowed as they passed. Several drivers were gesturing toward the backstretch. Others were tapping the tops of their helmets, indicating that somebody was upside down. I looked for the blue Hopkins. It did not come by. Travers looked worried. He stared at the stopwatch in his hand. The pace car was out on the track, leading a pack of cars now lumbering by at 50 mph. The stands were silent. Someone gestured behind me. I spotted a pall of smoke rising in the distance, apparently near the exit of the second turn.

A man in a suit with an AAA armband came up to Travers. He was obviously an official. He moved close to Travers and whispered in his ear. Travers reeled back, clearly disturbed. He moved to Coon and spoke softly. Coon dropped his head, then looked back at the rising smoke.

A man came up and said, to no one in particular, "Four cars. Vuke's upside down, outside the track. Car's on fire. Looks bad." Bryan came by, ugly smoke pouring out of his exhaust. Clearly his car was in trouble, but at least it was still moving. Vandewater kept the yellow flag waving. I turned to see Travers and Coon leaving the pits. I followed them back to the garage area in silence. Several reporters came up, but they brushed them off and kept moving. They reached the garage. Before I could catch up, they went in and closed the door. I dared not follow.

Tom Medley came up. I hadn't seen him in two years. There was no greeting. His face was dark, absent his usual joviality. "Real bad," he said grimly. "I heard Vuke's had it. Went out of the park trying to miss some other cars. Maybe Ward. Boyd. Keller, too."

"Where?" I asked.

"Out there on the back, right near the pedestrian bridge," he said. "A guard with a walkie-talkie told me Vuke got into a bunch of spinners. Couldn't get through. Boom. Flipped and landed upside down. He's still in the car."

"Any chance he made it?" I asked.

"Naw. He's a goner," said Tom, walking away.

The rumble of cars on the track was subdued, meaning they were still running slowly, under caution. This meant the wreck was large and complex and would take a long time to clear up. Suddenly the whole insane world around me was repellent. More men walked past, heads down, mumbling about Vukovich. All confirmed he was dead. I looked again at the closed doors of the garage, filled with joviality and hope such a short time ago. My watch read a few minutes until noon. Medley came back. "They just announced it on the PA system. Vuke is dead. The three other guys, Ward, Boyd, and Keller, are OK, I guess. Looks like he won't win his third in a row."

The entire Speedway was hushed, even the muffled growl of the cars running at low speeds. I thought of the Buick man and his speculation that bad accidents somehow stimulated and energized the crowd. Not on that blustery day at Indianapolis. The crowd was wounded—if not dead—as they watched the wispy smoke still rising from the backstretch.

Enough of this, I thought. My story was ended. My subject was dead. I had to get out of the place. Elbowing through the silent masses, I made my way to the tunnel under the front straight, a narrow, dank tube leading to Sixteenth Street. Once there, I drifted for a moment, seeking my bearings. Then it came to me. It was two blocks away. Walking quickly, I made my way to the little malt shop where Vukovich had celebrated his first victory. It seemed right. I ordered a vanilla milk shake and sat down, silently toasting the Mad Russian, the Fresno Flash, Vukie, Vuke, or whoever, who had so dominated the bravest of the brave. In the distance I heard the thunder again. The cars were at full throttle. Racing had resumed. Speeds were up. The wreck was forgotten. A small radio on the counter carried the race. Sid Collins, "the voice of the 500," was chattering away as if nothing had happened. Sweikert was leading in the Zink Pink Kurtis. He seemed headed for victory, but I didn't care.

Leaving half of the shake, I began the long walk down Georgetown Road to Newsome's place. The roar of the cars beyond the high barrier of the grandstands was menacing—and vaguely frightening. By the time I reached Ray's house, the yard was half empty. In place of the cars were empty beer bottles, rumpled newspapers, and other effluvia of a large, absent crowd. The big Roadmaster was gone. The Buick men had left, headed back to Philadelphia, where they would recount the moment when they had witnessed history and the demise of a legend.

CHAPTER EIGHT

RISK AND REWARD

THE DAY AFTER THE RACE DAWNED SUNNY AND calm. The storm had passed. I ate breakfast with Eldon, who once again rattled on about the crashes in his backyard, as if to exorcise the demons that haunted the track beyond his juniper tree. Trying to salvage something for a story so that my whole trip wouldn't be wasted, I walked back to Gasoline Alley. It was deserted, save for the crews loading up the battered, grease-and-rubber-stained cars that had survived the race. They would head to Milwaukee, where next weekend it would all start again.

The Vukovich garage was still closed, no doubt housing the charred hulk of the Hopkins. I wondered what would be done with such a wreck, having been the vessel of death for such a man as Bill Vukovich. I later learned that the car was repaired, repainted, and revived to carry young Jim Rathmann to the second starting position the next year before falling out with engine trouble. The old warrior would appear twice more at the Speedway, its role in the horrific incident on the backstretch three years earlier long forgotten—or purposely ignored.

As I'd expected, the primary subject among the men in Gasoline Alley was the Vukovich crash. It had apparently begun when Rodger Ward, driving the old Kuzma dirt-track car, caught a gust of wind while exiting the second turn. Before he could regain control, the car slapped the wall and tumbled in front of Al Keller, in his even older Kurtis, which was equipped with only a hand-brake hung on the outside of the cockpit. Keller apparently yanked too hard and locked up the wheels, sending his car into a slide in front of Johnny Boyd, a racing buddy of Vukovich's from Fresno. Boyd hit the spinning Keller as Vukovich—running perhaps 100 mph faster than all three—blazed off the turn and into the melee. With nowhere to go, he clipped Boyd's rear wheel, sending both cars tumbling. Vukovich's Hopkins slammed against the base of the footbridge crossing the track and sailed upside down over the retaining wall, landing on a security patrol Jeep. It then flipped crazily to end upside down, on fire.

As Boyd's car tumbled down the track, he ducked deep into the cockpit—which saved him, other than some badly scuffed knuckles. In the middle of the madness, with his car bouncing like a berserk beach ball, he later recalled seeing his wristwatch coming loose in the impact. "Oh shit, I'm gonna lose my watch," he thought to himself. The car slid to a stop upside down, with Boyd trapped inside. He heard a voice yell, "Oh no, he's really had it!"

"Bullshit," yelled Boyd from inside the wreck. "Get this son-of-a-bitch off me!"

Two men helped him escape. Once clear of the wreck, he spotted Keller, one of his rescuers, but also, perhaps, partly of the cause. In a fit of rage, Boyd grabbed him and began cursing and pounding him on the chest. At that point Ward came up and grabbed them both.

"Get off the track, you idiots, before some other dummy comes through here and gets all of us."

The dazed, confused trio staggered into the infield as another race car slid to a halt. Out jumped Ed Elisian, a Northern Californian from an Armenian family whose admiration for Vukovich bordered on hero worship. Hysterical, he tried to cross the track until he was subdued by guards. Elisian was trying to reach the smoking wreck of his fallen idol, a futile and irrational act that, ironically, would win him a sportsmanship award following the race.

It was later determined that Vukovich had died from a basal fracture of the skull, probably suffered in the first millisecond of the first flip. The gruesome photos carried the following day in newspapers around the world—of the burning car with Vukovich's gloved hand probing out of the bodywork—added a ghoulish touch to the accident.

Old-timers at the Speedway talked endlessly about the coincidence of the 1939 crash, at the same spot, that had killed Floyd Roberts. Like Vukovich, Roberts had won the previous year. When exiting the second turn on the 107th lap, he had run into the spinning car of Bob Swanson and also crashed over the outside fence to die of a broken neck.

Anger over who had caused the crash surged through Gasoline Alley like an evil wind. Much of the blame was directed at Ward, whose profligate lifestyle left him, in the minds of many, too physically debilitated to run the full distance without losing concentration. Whether or not this was the case, Ward was to use the incident to transform his life. Soon after, Ward married a staunch Baptist woman, stopped drinking and gambling, and would go on to win two 500-mile races and become a stellar spokesman for the sport. Others, like Boyd, laid the blame on Keller, a rookie in an ancient car who panicked and locked up his brakes. This in turn had left Boyd no room to maneuver, and blocked the way for the surging Vukovich. But while an automobile is traveling almost three miles a minute, decisions at close quarters are often beyond human capability. In the end, the crash was laid off on "racing luck," the catch-all repository for all such disasters, when the victim is in the wrong place at the wrong time.

While Sweikert was headed for his Indianapolis victory, the pain and misery had not ended. As the final laps unfolded, Cal Niday, a thirty-nine-year-old midget racing champion who had already lost a leg in a motorcycle crash, was riding in fourth place in his locally owned D.A. Lubricants Kurtis roadster when he lost control in the fourth turn. The car slammed the wall, then caromed across the track into an infield ditch. He was hauled off to the infield hospital, where chief doctor C. B. Bonner discovered a frontal skull fracture, a crushed chest, and third-degree burns on his right leg. Niday was taken to Methodist Hospital, where he started to recover. Nine days later, he suffered a hemorrhage of his pleural cavity, a collapse of his right lung, paralysis of his bowels, and severe jaundice possibly caused by a bad blood transfusion or a ruptured liver. A team of surgeons opened Niday's chest cavity to make repairs and miraculously, he survived. But like his cohorts, he could not stay away from fast cars. In his seventies, he was killed running in a race for vintage midgets in California.

The nightmare of the 500 behind me, I drove back to Los Angeles in three hard days. Still hoping to salvage a story on Vukovich, I headed north to Fresno for his funeral. It was huge. Perhaps three thousand mourners appeared as the Mad Russian was laid to rest. The Fresno Junior Chamber of Commerce announced the establishment of a scholarship fund in the Manual Arts Department of Fresno State College, a fitting memorial to a man who lived and died with machinery of the highest form.

A week later, in Milwaukee, a young charger from Massachusetts named Johnny Thomson won the 100-miler on the ancient oval, beating Sweikert in a close race. A new generation of drivers were ready to

Dick Wallen Productions

The Mad Russian ready for war. Bill Vukovich prepares for a 100-mile championship race protected only by a thin leather helmet, goggles, and a pair of driving gloves. Note the absence of a roll-bar or protective cage or insulation from the red-hot exhaust pipe within a few inches of his right elbow.

Two racing pals Manuel Ayulo (l) and Jack McGrath (r) share a victorious moment following the 1953 Milwaukee, Wisconsin 100-mile championship race. Both men grew up in Los Angeles and raced midgets and hot rods together before gaining success in the major leagues of AAA competition. Sadly, both men would die in the brutal 1955 season.

Dick Wallen Productions

Brave men at play. Sacramento, CA 1954 prior to a AAA 100-mile race. Left to right: Jerry Hoyt, Jimmy Bryan (with his omnipresent cigar), Bob Sweikert, Jimmy Reece, Rodger Ward, Johnny Boyd, and Edgar Elder. Standing behind Reece and Ward is Sam Hanks. The four men on the left would all die in racing accidents within six years. Bryan, Sweikert, and Hanks would be future Indianapolis 500 winners. Ward would win the big race twice. (Dick Wallen Productions)

Bill Vukovich works to build hand strength prior to the 1955 Indianapolis 500. Crewman Frank Coon works on the Hopkins Special's Meyer-Drake engine.

Dick Wallen Productions

Dick Wallen Productions

Bill Vukovich poses for a publicity shot at his Fresno home with his wife Esther and children Billy, Jr., and daughter Marlene. Billy, Jr. would go on to compete at Indianapolis from 1968–83 finishing 2nd in 1973 and 3rd in 1974. Vukovich's grandson, Billy III, ran at Indianapolis from 1988–1990.

War at 120 miles an hour. Don Freeland (number 38 M.A. Walker Special) and Rodger Ward battle for position during the 1953 Milwaukee 100-mile championship race. Both men battle for control on the rutted, slippery dirt surface, struggling with their heavy machines without power steering or protection from the flying stones and dirt. Freeland is "rim-riding" against the outer rail, seeking better traction on the cushion of dirt flung outward by the spinning tires. The races were flat out, with no pit stops or relief, forcing the drivers to near exhaustion. Ward can be seen wearing a plastic visor and two pairs of goggles to help keep his vision clear. Note the absence of any rollover protection. The drivers sat in front of seventy gallons of volatile methanol fuel carried in easily punctured fuel tanks. (Dick Wallen Productions)

Dick Wallen Productions

Rodger Ward in the car that would trigger the Vukovich crash. A broken front axle and a gust of wind would send the car out of control. This is the same machine that Troy Ruttman had driven to victory in 1952—ironically after Vukovich's steering failed while in a dominant lead a mere eight laps from the finish. Coincidentally, this machine was involved in two Vukovich crashes at Indianapolis—the second one costing him his life.

Dick Wallen Productions

Two of northern California's finest race drivers confer prior to the 1955 Indianapolis 500. Johnny Boyd of Fresno (in car) would be involved in the Vukovich crash while his friend, Bob Sweikert (standing) would drive on to victory.

Dick Wallen Productions

Bill Vukovich celebrates after his incredible rain-soaked qualifying run prior to the 1953 Indianapolis 500. The windshield and bodywork of the car are water-spattered indicating the severity of the rainstorm that he somehow managed to navigate despite the fact that his Firestone tires were totally unsuited for running on anything but dry pavement.

The cocky, brilliant Bob Sweikert often admitted, "I'll never live to grow old." He was right, dying at age 30 in early 1956 during a sprint car race at Salem, Indiana.

Dick Wallen Productions

The end of a champion. The shattered, burning Hopkins Special that Bill Vukovich rode to his death is hauled away from the crash site. The car would be repainted and run in two more 500-mile races.

The moment before the disaster. Rodger Ward's car (in a cloud of dust near a pedestrian crossover bridge) smacks the retaining wall after breaking its front axle. Approaching are Al Keller (on left) and Johnny Boyd (right). Race leader Bill Vukovich brings up rear, preparing to lap all three down the 4000-foot back straightaway. It appears that Vukovich is looking down to his left. Some observers believe he was reaching for a rag to clean his goggles. If this was the case, the split second his vision was away from the incident ahead might have prevented him from taking evasive action. Vukovich is traveling about 140 MPH, meaning that he was less than a second away from entering the melee about to unfold in front of him. Vukovich's car ended up outside the track, well beyond the bridge, after hitting several parked cars and miraculously missing a cluster of spectators. (Dick Wallen Productions)

Dick Wallen Productions

Jack McGrath buckles up for his last ride at Phoenix, Arizona 1955. Always concerned with safety, McGrath wears a new, aircraft-style plastic helmet in place of the aged leather units favored by most drivers and uses four-point seat and shoulder harness. But the lack of rollover protection was the cause of death for this popular driver during a series of violent flips following a front axle failure.

Phil Waters in the Cunningham C4R drives to victory in the 1953 Watkins Glen Grand Prix. The crude 4.6-mile network of paved Town of Dix roads was adapted after a major spectator crash on the original course through the Upstate New York village. Note the lack of guardrails on a circuit that was the antithesis of the super-tracks to be designed and built around the world within the next half-century. Walters averaged 83.3 MPH on this primitive course.

William Green Motor Racing Library

William Green Motor Racing Library

Phil Walters celebrates his 1953 Watkins Glen victory. This brilliant driver raced midgets and stock cars under the name "Ted Tappet" in deference to his high family who considered professional automobile racing below his station. Walters was a decorated WWII glider pilot who, following the 1955 LeMans race, was headed to the Ferrari Grand Prix team. But after witnessing the carnage of the Levegh accident, Walters quit racing in his prime and opened a Volkswagen agency on Long Island, never to race again.

Sports car racing in the 1950s was elemental at best. Smalley's Garage in downtown Watkins Glen served as the technical inspection station for cars competing in the amateur sports car races. In the foreground is the Italian-built Bandini of Roger Merrill, Jr., while number 94 (with its top still up, implying that it was to be driven to the races) is the MG TD of William Bastrup. Under the tent in the right background, a volunteer committee performed the technical inspection, checking brakes, tires, lights, etc. A Jaguar XK120 and MGTD can be seen at the left. (William Green Motor Library)

One of the greatest duels in Indianapolis history unfolds in the opening stages of the 1955 '500.' Bill Vukovich dives below the white line in turn one to pass Jack McGrath, nearly driving on the grass apron. The pair passed and re-passed each other before. McGrath's engine failed and Vukovich drove to his death.

IMS Photo

© Bettmann/CORBIS

French Gendarmes and rescue workers attempt to treat the survivors following Pierre Levegh's crash. While his Mercedes-Benz 300SLR race car never reached the crowd, its engine and front suspension assembly scythed through the throng, initially killing 81 and injuring another 75-100. The final death toll has never been officially determined, but many believe it ultimately exceeded 100.

© Bettmann/CORBIS

James Dean prepares to leave a Los Angeles gas station after filling the tank of his new Porsche 550 Spyder. He will then head north for his rendezvous with eternity at Cholame, California later that day. Behind him is parked the Ford station wagon with Dean's race car trailer. It will be driven to the race at Salinas by studio photographer Sanford Roth and friend Bill Hickman. It was planned to haul the Porsche home with this rig.

The shattered wreckage of the so-called "little Bastard" lies at the roadside near Cholame, California. The primary impact was directly behind the left front wheel, meaning Dean's body was protected only by a thin layer of aluminum bodywork. The fate of this automobile—one of the most notorious in history—remains unknown to this day.

© John Springer Collection/CORBIS

© Bettmann/CORBIS

The skeletal remains of Pierre Levegh's Mercedes-Benz 300 SLR smolders atop the earthen barrier intended to protect the crowd from the speeding cars at LeMans. The deaths were caused not by the automobile, but from its engine and suspension bits that flailed through the packed crowd. Levegh was thrown clear of the wreck and died on the track surface. In the background are the pits mobbed with curious onlookers. Race officials made the decision to continue with the competition so that emergency vehicles would be able to leave the crash site unimpeded by the giant crowd departing the track following an immediate cancellation.

© Bettmann/CORBIS

Pierre Levegh at the wheel of the ill-fated 300SLR Mercedes-Benz prior to his death at LeMans. The impact of the accident sent the engine and Front suspension assembly into the crowd while Levegh, wearing no seat belt, as was the practice in those days, was pitched from the cockpit and killed.

John Fitch Collection

John Fitch celebrates a 1953 victory while driving for the Cunningham sports car team. With him is his wife, Elizabeth. During the 1955 LeMans race she stayed in Switzerland and heard a report on U.S. Armed Forces radio that it was her husband, not his co-driver Pierre Levegh, who had been involved in the catastrophic crash.

Dick Wallen Productions

Bill Vukovich in the revolutionary Kurtis-Kraft 500A fuel-injection special that carried him to victory at Indianapolis in 1953 and 1954 with a near miss in 1952.

take the place of the dead king. Thomson was driving for Peter Schmidt, who only two weeks before had lost his driver, Manny Ayulo. But in the sport of AAA championship racing in the mid-1950s, fourteen days was ancient history.

Who in God's name were these people, who dealt with death so casually? Were they all insane? All obsessed with a death wish? "Motorized Lemmings?"—as *Newsweek* columnist John Lardner denounced them following the Vukovich crash. Surely some of them had come home from the war restless for action, bored with the Ike and Mamie good life that had overwhelmed the prosperous, vinyl- and dacron-coated nation with its Barcaloungers, its drip-dry fashions, its automatic everything, and its nightly dose of network feel-good. Others, like Jack Kerouac and his fellow beatniks, were rebelling in the coffeehouses of Greenwich Village and Haight-Ashbury, while some, wilder and more lethal, were forming motorcycle gangs like the Hells Angels, Booze-Fighters, Satan's Sinners, and Outlaws.

An Englishman once observed that at some point, all sane young men in their late teens or early twenties will attempt to kill themselves in a looney, risk-taking adventure. The poet Richard Hugo, who, before being cursed with alcohol and depression, was a pilot in World War II, confirmed the suspicion. Following V-E day, his squadron was stationed in Sicily, training for future combat. Their aircraft, P-47 fighters with giant radial engines, were claimed to be unditchable in water. Flight engineers warned all the pilots that landing in water meant certain death. In the summer of 1945 a fellow pilot and friend of Hugo's was returning from a training flight over the Bay of Naples when, on a whim, he decided to try a water landing with the gear up. He was killed instantly. Hugo would later ponder the possibility that deep in the psyche of all young men lies a hatred of peace and safety and an irresistable urge to flout all rules and conventions. He suggested that his friend might have chosen the risk as opposed to the prospect of returning home to the cushy domesticity of postwar

America. His choice was to play Russian roulette with his airplane and his own mortality in the cauldron of war.

Years later, Michael Cimino would have one of the characters in his classic film *The Deer Hunter* play the same game with his own .45 automatic, when there was no gambling involved. This urge to walk the edge seemed particularly tied to war, whereas conventional thinking presumed that human nature would be to seek to preserve one's life rather than waste it. Yet following the American Civil War, young men rushed west to face the dangers of savage Indians, cattle stampedes, rustlers, fierce weather, and drunken gunfighters rather than languish in the tranquility of the East. So too for the World War I vets who migrated to Paris as the Lost Generation, there to booze and bar-fight themselves insensate. Looked at in this light, the men who unleashed their passions in race cars and on motorcycles in the late 1940s and the 1950s were hardly breaking new ground in terms of mad, self-absorbed risks to life and limb.

Ironically, the technology that rose out of the industrial creativity energized by the war effort on all sides offered even more macabre opportunity for self-imposed danger. The cars competing at places like Indianapolis and in European road racing were light years more advanced than those of the prewar years, thanks to quantum leaps in metallurgy, fuels, bearing surfaces, lightweight alloys, and synthetic materials of all kinds. But regardless of the fevered increases in performance, the men riding inside those incredible capsules remained as fragile and physically vulnerable as ever.

Bill Vukovich's death caused a short, frantic outcry in the national press and among a few politicians who denounced the sport of automobile racing as barbaric madness appealing to only the basest, most ghoulish human instincts. Several bills to ban racing totally were introduced in Congress, but were ignored. Homer Capehart, the powerful Republican senator from Indiana, was sure to roadblock any such legislation, which meant certain death in the Upper House.

The danger and carnage at Indianapolis seemed to trace a course in American society that ran in direct opposition to the pallid, pastel-hued lifestyle now recalled from the 1950s. In the midst of the saccharine sweetness that engulfed daily living and that enraged Kerouac and his ilk, automobile racing stood as a steaming fissure of violence and death on an otherwise tranquil landscape.

Of the thirty-three men who climbed into race cars at the start of the 1955 Indianapolis 500, *eighteen* of them would die violent deaths in races—three of them before the year was ended. *All of the top five* finishers were doomed, as were Keller, Elisian, and McGrath, while two others would suffer horrific injuries that would end their careers. Half a century later, when two major wars were fought in Iraq and American casualties barely reached the triple digits, the notion of a sporting activity that consumed the lives of over half its participants borders on the demented. Such levels of danger would simply not be tolerated today. Life has become too precious and too easily preserved to accept the idea that death and injury are realistic components of war, much less of a sport. Lawmakers, insurance underwriters, social activists, safety groups, editorialists, and moralists of all stripes would be at full cry at the first hint of such potential carnage. Risk-taking, once an accepted component of life, has in the past few decades been relegated to the closet with other antisocial activities, leaving the men who knowingly faced destruction in 1955 among the more bizarre and perverted of humankind.

Returning to Los Angeles, I received word, as expected, from the editors of the *Saturday Evening Post* that my story had been cancelled. I was settling back into my little apartment to devise another project when I received a call from a friend who edited a small, struggling sports car magazine based in New York titled *Sports Cars Illustrated.* His European correspondent had met a lovely girl while on vacation in Monte Carlo and, being a wealthy Italian who didn't need the work, had quit on the spot. The editor needed someone to cover the upcoming

Le Mans 24-Hour race in France in less than two weeks. If I was available, a free plane ticket, modest expenses, and $500 would be mine. Having no real prospects for work and figuring a week or two in Paris and environs might be good for the soul, I jumped at the offer.

As I readied myself for the trip to France, updating my passport, packing, and arranging airline reservations, I couldn't resist making one more trip to Travers and Coon's shop to fathom their reaction to Vuke's death. Jim Travers was alone when I arrived early one morning. The Keck streamliner was in its customary spot on jack-stands in the middle of the shop floor, surrounded by spare parts. Travers was seated at his small desk, littered as always with blueprints, work orders, and invoices. "Look at this," he said, a hint of bitterness in his voice. He handed me a sheet of paper from the Speedway listing the finishing order and the prize money. Vukovich was placed twenty-fifth, with winnings of $10,833.64, a total inflated by the bonus money he received for leading so many laps before crashing. "At least he's ahead of McGrath. They've got him listed twenty-sixth. I hope Vuke understood that the nitro shit Jack was using didn't work. That ain't much solace, but at least it's something."

Travers reached into the pile on his desk and pulled out an eight-by-ten photo. It was a shot taken from behind the second turn facing down the long back straight. Ward's car could be seen scuffing the wall in a cloud of dust, with Keller and Boyd close behind. In the foreground, headed into the chaos that was about to commence, was Vukovich. "Take a close look at that," said Travers, handing me the picture.

I examined it closely, then handed it back. "It looks like what everybody described, basically," I shrugged.

"Except for one thing. Look closely at Vuke's head. It's tilted downward. I think he was reaching into his lap, looking for the cloth he always carried to wipe his goggles. In the second he took his eyes off the track, that may have been enough for him to get into Boyd. Maybe, just maybe, if he'd had that extra second, he might have missed the whole thing."

"That close, huh?" I asked.

"That close. That much difference. Right at that point on the track he's hard on the throttle, coming off the corner at maybe 140, 150. One second makes a world of difference at that speed."

Travers took the photo back and laid it on the rubble covering his desk. He turned to look out the window at a typically warm Southern California morning. "Either way, it doesn't make any difference now."

"What now?" I asked.

"I dunno."

Hopkins says he's gonna repair his car and keep going. But Frank and I are out. I don't want to see that thing again. And Keck. He's got a new babe who's into horse racing. The new car just sits there. I guess he'll want us to finish it. But with rich guys like that, who knows? Their money makes 'em different. I wouldn't be surprised if he didn't drop the whole project."

Travers was right. While the Keck streamliner car was entered in the 1956 race, without a driver assigned, a call came in late December from Superior Oil. It was Howard Keck's private secretary. She announced coldly that the racing team was dissolved. Without ever speaking to their boss, Travers and Coon picked up their tools and walked out, leaving the streamliner, the winning Fuel-Injection Special, a mass of spare parts and engines and several midget race cars in the dark shop.

Puzzling over what was no doubt the last photo taken of Bill Vukovich alive, I left Travers and headed back home to make my final trip preparations. Surely the more civilized atmosphere permeating the European-style motor sports I had seen at Watkins Glen would help cleanse the memory of Indianapolis. Or so I naively believed.

CHAPTER NINE

LE MANS: THE NIGHTMARE PEAKS

TO GET TO PARIS FROM LOS ANGELES IN THE SUMMER of 1955 was a serious journey. Intercontinental jet travel awaited the development of the Boeing 707, which meant a series of hops via a Pan Am Douglas DC-8B. With its four Pratt & Whitney radial engines humming away, these 300-mph giants took me from Burbank airport to New York's Idlewild, then to Gander, Newfoundland, and finally into Paris's Orly airport. The trip, including an overnight stop in New York, consumed the better part of two days—which still stood as a massive gain in time over earlier travel by transcontinental train and ocean liner between New York and Cherbourg.

After a day spent working the kinks out of my body in Paris, I took a train to Le Mans, a bustling trading center lying to the south and west of the capital that had served as Eisenhower's headquarters in the latter stages of World War II. Like all major French towns, its history dated back to Gaul and the Roman occupation. It had been the scene of endless sieges and massacres during the Hundred Years War and was said to be the favorite haunt of Henry II and the birthplace of Jean Bon, the first Plantagenet king. It had suffered heavily in the Franco-Prussian war and in World War I. It spread out from its shell-pitted fortress walls housing a twelvth century cathedral that towered high above the River Sarthe.

The city had hosted automobile racing since the early 1920s. The only victory by an American driver in an American-built car in a major European Grand Prix race came at Le Mans in 1921, when Californian Jimmy Murphy drove a Duesenberg in a win notable because the Indiana-built race car carried four-wheel hydraulic brakes, a revolutionary breakthrough in an era when even the most exotic automobiles employed crude, cable-operated units based on technology dating to horse-drawn buggies.

Since 1923, Le Mans had been the site of the world's longest and most difficult endurance race. The local Automobile Club D'Ouest organized, each June, a twenty-four-Hour race for production-based automobiles to test both speed and endurance. At that time of the year, in that northern latitude, the night lasted little more than six hours. Over the decades, the great European marques Alfa Romeo, Bentley, Bugatti, Jaguar, Talbot, Ferrari, and Mercedes-Benz had dominated the event and, like Italy's Mille Miglia, the race had become a major national holiday. Run over an 8.4-mile circuit through the provincial countryside on a rough rectangle of public roads closed for the occasion, the great race attracted hundreds of thousands of spectators who spent the day jammed fifty deep on the perimeters of the track or in the amusement park that carnival operators erected for the occasion. Aside from a large grandstand on the main straightaway, there were no provisions for the spectators, who crushed together like subway riders around the course. The privileged few were offered food and drink at the Café de Hippodrome on the edge of the three-mile-long Mulsanne straight.

The magazine had arranged lodging for me at the small Hôtel Moderne in the center of the city, near the Place de la Republique, were the Café Gruber was located. This was the main hangout for English-speaking race teams and notables, meaning that interviews and informal chats with drivers and team managers might be carried out away from the noise and frenzied atmosphere of the racetrack.

Unlike at Indianapolis, where the entered cars were housed in Gasoline Alley, there were no such centralized accommodations at Le Mans. Cars were prepared for practice and the race at rented garages and car dealerships scattered around the city, and driven daily to the track on public roads. Indy machines were Spartan single-seaters, but the sports cars set for Le Mans carried full road equipment—lights, fenders, two seats, spare tires, and even horns—according to the fiendishly complex regulations that governed the race.

While the large teams entered by the Mercedes-Benz and Jaguar factories rented warehouses and factory annexes and filled them with mountains of spare parts and legions of expert mechanics—all clothed in the coveralls that were the fashion of the day—smaller operations were left to prepare their cars in private garages and in the open courtyards of small hotels.

The Moderne was no exception. Below my window in the small courtyard, two independent English teams, one with an MG, the other with a Triumph, labored into the night, the rattle of their spanners and the garble of Cockney mechanics echoing off the stone walls of the little canyon. Everywhere in the city, the rumble and whine of racing engines being tuned up for the race added to the chatter of the crowds, the clatter of the street traffic, and the cries of vendors hawking souvenirs.

Having arrived at Le Mans before official practice began, I spent the days at Gruber's Curbside café. It was alive with beautiful people decked out in the latest fashions. Men in Lacoste shirts, tailored slacks, and Gucci loafers were everywhere, while an endless parade of Pucci- and Chanel-draped women battled for my attention. The square swarmed with all manner of Ferraris, Porsches, and other svelte roadsters, all vying for space and adoration.

Early in the going, I met an American journalist named Peter Coltrin. He was a scrawny man in his early thirties with a receding chin and wispy reddish hair. A Kansan by birth, he had left the heartland as a private in Patton's Third Army—and never returned. He had begun photographing motor races for several obscure British magazines and had taken up residence in Modena, Italy, near the fabled Scuderia Ferrari, a place that was becoming increasingly important in international motor sports circles.

Embittered about what he considered to be the excess and hubris of his homeland, Coltrin was a classic expatriate whose forerunners had convened in Paris in the twenties following World War I and again in the forties and fifties following the collapse of Germany. Coltrin was given to rages on subjects ranging from President Eisenhower's middle-class obsession with golf to the brinksmanship of John Foster Dulles to the dreadful state of American car engineering. He was a Europhile, a midwestern émigré who ardently rejected American culture and technology. Yet Coltrin was a fountain of information about the European racing scene and I therefore tolerated his tirades in hopes of gathering valuable inside gossip.

Late in the afternoon, as we drank Camparis and sodas, Coltrin smiled and said, "Oh god, here they come. The guys from Cunningham."

I turned in my chair to see two clean-cut men in sports shirts ease under the blue canopy of the restaurant and seat themselves at a small table near the curb.

I recognized them from Watkins Glen. The older one, with a

square jaw and a sandy wad of curly hair, was Briggs Cunningham. The other, leaner, and with a level stare of faint defiance, was Phil Walters, the superb driver who had won at the Glen with ease.

"Briggs keeps showing up here trying to beat the Europeans," Coltrin said. "Got to admire him. At least this time he was smart enough to give up on his giant Chrysler-powered lumps and buy a Jaguar. But his second car is powered by an Offenhauser, one of those silly dirt-track engines from Indianapolis."

"Like the one that dominated the 500 with Vukovich?" I mused.

"Yeah, they do allright with that roundy-round stuff, but not here where real performance counts," countered Coltrin.

"Why do you have such a hard-on for your own country?" I asked.

"A lot of us do. We're tired of being linked to a nation of small-town Babbitts. Like Gertrude Stein said, 'There's no there there.'"

"Cunningham is an heir to a meat-packing fortune," I countered. "His middle name is Swift, like in the meat-packing business. He's a very wealthy Yale man. He can afford to build his own sports cars. He doesn't look like a small-town Babbitt to me."

"Maybe not. But he's out of his league here," said Coltrin, waving at the waiter for another drink. "Briggs is a pure gentleman amateur. A sportsman loaded with money who surrounds himself with real talent. Like Walters. Glider pilot in the war. Ran midgets and stock cars professionally under the nom de plume 'Ted Tappet' because his family thought racing as a professional was beneath his station. Began to use his given name when he hooked up with Briggs. Now he's got a shot with Ferrari. He's headed to Modena right after this. Wants to run Formula One. No more of this sports car stuff. Walters wants to go head-to-head with guys like Fangio and Moss."

"Is he good enough?" I asked.

"Probably. But you never know. It takes more than the physical things—reflexes, eyesight, endurance. All that. It's a head thing. You either have it or you don't. We'll have to see with Walters."

"Vukovich had it. And see what it got him," I said.

"Braver than Dick Tracy. That I'll give him."

"So who's gonna win this thing?" I asked.

"Jaguar has to be the favorite. Won it the last two years. Hawthorn's their lead driver. Very quick. Then there's Mercedes-Benz. Three new super cars. They carry air brakes—big panels that flip out of the rear deck to help them slow down at the end of the Mulsanne straight. Three flat-out miles that end with a forty-mile-an-hour right-hander. They've got Juan Manuel Fangio, the world champion, teamed up with Stirling Moss. Two of the best drivers in the world." Coltrin paused and lit a cigarette, a foul-smelling Gauloise. "But one of their cars is a bit of a joke. Very political, those Germans."

"Meaning what?" I asked.

"Meaning they've teamed John Fitch with a Frenchman, Pierre Levegh. Mercedes picked a Frenchman and an American to gain a few points with the French public. He's over fifty years old. Maybe fifty-five, for god's sake. They call him the 'Bishop.' Weird man. Stony and distant. Two years ago he tried to run the whole damn twenty-fours hours solo. Insanity. He got in a fugue state. Delirious. Round and round like an automoton. With less than an hour to go, he had a lead of twenty-five miles. Three goddamn laps on the second-place Mercedes. Then he missed a shift and broke the engine. All of France went insane. He hid out in Paris for two weeks. Real name is Bouillion. His Uncle, Louis Levegh, drove for the French Mors team back around the turn of the century. Bouillion legally changed his name in honor of his uncle.

"He got the ride with Mercedes when another Frenchman, Paul Frère, a very good driver and a journalist, turned down the seat because he had already signed with Aston Martin. So the Krauts thought they could score a few public relations points with the Frogs by signing poor old Levegh."

"His teammate is John Fitch. He ran with Cunningham, didn't he? Now he's with Mercedes?"

"Yeah, the guy is really good. Won the grand touring class for Mercedes at the Mille Miglia. Finished fifth overall in a basically stock gullwing coupe. That got him the ride here." Coltrin took a long drag on the cigarette, exhaling the smoke through his nose. "Fitch ran the Millie with a guy named Kurt Gessel as his so-called navigator. A reporter for some Hamburg newspaper. Never even been to a race before, and they stuck him in a car for a thousand miles of the wildest driving in the world. Scared the shit out of him, but it got Mercedes some good press. They were lucky Fitch was good enough so he didn't crash and kill the poor bastard. Mercedes' little public relations game would have backfired then."

"It doesn't sound like you've got a whole lot of love for the Germans or the French."

"You spend time in Italy and you'll know why."

"Ferrari?" I asked.

"Yeah, Ferrari. The food. The women. The sense of humor. No place like it on earth. You come to Modena and I'll show you what I mean." Coltrin continued to grump about practically everything in sight as I left him and introduced myself to Cunningham and Walters. They were both reserved easterners, endowed with that subtle élan that radiates from old money and privilege. They invited me to sit down, and the conversation turned quickly to the event at hand and Walters' future.

"Phil will be leaving us, and we'll miss him," said Cunningham. "From here he's headed to Modena. Ferrari wants him to drive for the Scuderia. No American has ever run Formula One, so we're hoping Phil gets a fair shot," said Cunningham. "They say that Rex Mays was invited to join the Alfa Romeo team after he ran so well at the Vanderbilt Cup on Long Island in '37. But when Rex heard that you had to dress for dinner and be very social, he said 'to hell with it' and stayed in California."

"So I guess you've brought along your tux," I said to Walters.

"It's in my luggage, right next to my helmet," he said, smiling.

"What do you think about running for a European team?" I asked.

"It'll be different. Old man Ferrari is a real character. Pretty much a tyrant. But running Formula One will be a kick. Going against Fangio and Moss and Hawthorn will be a real challenge. Right after this I'm going down there to test. Phil tells me the politics are pretty tricky at the factory."

Walters was referring to young Phil Hill, a talented Californian who was already on the Ferrari team as junior sports car driver and was running his first race for the Scuderia at Le Mans. He would be teamed as the second driver with Umberto Maglioli, although his chances to compete in the more challenging Formula One cars seemed dim, at least for the near future.

"We'll just have to wait and see how the Italians treat us," Walters mused.

"At least you'll make a little money," said Cunningham.

"I won't be rich. Tavoni, the team manager, says I'll get 40 percent of any appearance money they wangle out the of the promoters—which won't be much, considering that I'm unknown in Europe—and 50 percent of my winnings. Whatever that might be."

"The Europeans all think Americans are rolling in money. So they get us to race for nickels and dimes. And we're so eager we'll take anything. There are ten Americans running here and not one of us will make enough to buy a new suit. I suppose that's our fault," Cunningham shrugged.

A lanky man with a wide smile walked up and sat down. John Fitch was taller and thinner than I had expected, once again affirming that race car drivers come in all sizes and shapes. Yet they seem to share one characteristic. It was the eyes. Someone had once described them as "gunfighter's eyes," even and clear, deeply penetrating, unblinking, laser-like at their target. Eyesight was one of the most important elements in fast driving, and Fitch was not only accomplished in all conditions, day and night, but had been a trained P-51 fighter pilot in the recent World War.

After some light banter between the three about how their old teammate had deserted Cunningham for a ride with the vaunted Mercedes-Benz, the conversation turned to the upcoming race.

Between them, the trio had dominated American sports car racing for three years, and it was Fitch and Walters who had driven a Cunningham to third overall in 1953 at Le Mans. It was to be the highest finish for the team in the legendary contest. The same year, the pair won the Sebring 12-Hour, thereby becoming the first all-American team in history to win an international championship endurance race. Because of the long bond between the three, the conversation flowed freely, even though Fitch now belonged to a major rival.

"Your Merc looks damned good," said Walters.

"The thing is amazing. Rock solid. The engine's unbelievably responsive. Fuel-injected. Magnesium bodywork. The air brake is like an anchor at the end of the Mulsanne."

"Is the team as good as they say?" asked Cunningham, referring to the legendary organization led by Mercedes-Benz chief engineer Rudolph Uhlenhaut and team manager Alfred Neubauer, both veterans of over twenty years of competition.

"You can't believe it. Every detail is attended to. Like an army. I thought we were pretty good when we ran together, but these people are amazing."

I watched the exchange with interest, recalling the banter between Vukovich and McGrath prior to the 500. It had been profane and hard-edged, full of good-natured threats and rough talk. But now the chat was civilized and understated. Fitch, dressed in a tailored tweed jacket and perfectly creased slacks, appeared to have stepped out from a Brooks Brothers store window, the epitome of country chic. When the waiter asked for his drink order, he spoke in French.

"What about Levegh?" asked Cunningham, referring to Fitch's co-driver.

"A good fellow. I had dinner with him and his wife a few nights ago. A bit morose. Still haunted by his failure to win here a couple of years ago. Has mixed feelings about the Germans, of course, like a lot of Frenchmen. They're the ones who beat him when his Talbot broke and now they're giving him a chance to win again. That seems to gnaw at him."

"He's at least fifty years old. Maybe more," said Walters.

"Yes, but he can find his way around here blindfolded. He probably has more miles under his belt at Le Mans than anybody. And this time no one-man heroics. He'll follow team orders. He's going to run the first four hours. Kind of a salute to his devotion to the race over the years."

"Still, he's damned old for this sort of stuff," said Walters.

"This will be his last race if he wins it, you can be sure of that," said Fitch. "But Le Mans rules his entire life. A bit intense for me, but a decent teammate. Our plan is to run easily for the first half of the race, then up the pace. Levegh isn't particularly comfortable with the car. Hates driving on the left side for some reason and maintains that the circuit—especially the front straight—is too narrow for the current cars.

"He's probably right. I'd be hell trying to run three abreast. In the old days with skinny-tired Alfas and Bentleys, maybe. But not today," said Walters.

"The car looks fantastic," said Cunningham, referring to Fitch's Mercedes.

"About perfect. We tested at Hokckenheim for twenty-four hours last month. The whole track was pitch-black at night, except for some tiny lanterns they'd placed on the tops of the corners. The headlights were a bit weak, which made for some bad moments. But they've fixes that with a big pair of extra lights in the grille. I think we're ready."

"You've moved," said Cunningham, changing the subject.

"Yes, to Lugano. Lovely place. Elizabeth is pregnant, you know. So she's staying there until the baby. Sometime later this summer, we expect."

Again I was struck by the civility of it all. Living in a beautiful Swiss resort, staying in the best hotels, dining in the finest restaurants, and driving with a bunch of gentlemen in exotic sports cars. Cunningham, a man of great wealth and social stature, heir to uncounted millions—able to race cars and yachts as his mission in life. I thought of Vukovich's family, now struggling to survive, his legacy amounting to little more than a pair of gas stations, a small house, and two Ford convertibles.

Were these gentlemen as hard-edged and courageous as the flinty professionals who risked everything at Indianapolis? Was this form of sport as elemental, as fiercely challenging and physically demanding as that which I had witnessed at Indianapolis and Syracuse? My exposure to sports car racing at Watkins Glen had indicated otherwise. A thin layer of artifice and faintly feminine gentility had pervaded the atmosphere, counterbalanced only by the professionalism of the Cunningham team.

"Was doing the movie fun?" asked Cunningham, referring to Fitch's work on the soon-to-be-released *The Racers* starring Kirk Douglas and Belle Darvi. He had been critical to the production, arranging for three faux Grand Prix cars to be created from old Maseratis and doing extensive driving as Douglas's double in various European locations.

"Good fun. Hard work. The Hollywood types are very professional. Everything on schedule. Like the Germans."

"What was Kirk Douglas like?" asked Walters. "A good guy?"

Fitch laughed. "Douglas? Never met him. He never came to Europe. Stayed back in Los Angeles and shot all that footage in the cars at the studio. The magic of motion pictures. They call it rear-screen projection. He just sat there, sawing the wheel back and forth, looking fierce, while the scenery was rolled in behind him." Fitch stood up to leave. "Got to run. Another meeting. The Germans love meetings."

He turned to me. I had remained silent during the conversation. "I enjoy your magazine," he said. "We get it by airmail in Lugano." He reached into his coat, pulled out a small leather packet, and withdrew an engraved business cards. "If you ever get to Lugano, don't hesitate to call. Elizabeth and I enjoy entertaining our American friends involved in the sport." Fitch handed me the card, which read: "John Cooper Fitch. Via Seminario 2, Lugano, Switzerland."

"Thank you sir. Perhaps the next time I'm in Europe," I responded, blithely implying that I was a regular traveler to the Continent.

"Perhaps," said Fitch politely.

"If you see me in your rearview mirrors, make sure you get out of the way," said Walters, smiling widely.

"Of course I will," returned Fitch, laughing. "Because that will mean I'll be slowing down to make a pit stop."

With that good-natured jab, Fitch drifted back into the crowd.

After a few more perfunctory exchanges, I thanked the men and returned to Coltrin. "Maybe I'll take you up on that offer to go to Modena," I said.

"You can drive down with me. I'll get you a room at the Albergo Real, the hotel where all the action is. And I mean real action."

Thanks to Coltrin, who could speak reasonable French, I was able to work my way through the Byzantine madness of gaining proper press credentials from the track officials, a maddening process of furious paper shuffling, endless signatures and jackhammer rubber stamping on a pile of duplicate forms. Irascible, as he was, Coltrin knew the right moves in the middle of the shouting, arguing, and pandemonium as journalists from all over the world fumed and raged with the officials, who icily stood their ground behind their littered desks.

I rode with Coltrin to the track in his tiny Fiat, thinking twice if this was the vehicle I would choose to take over the Alps to Italy. We rattled and wheezed into a press parking compound and went to the paddock behind the pit area, a long, low building linking the front straight. Unlike at Indianapolis, the Le Mans pits were enclosed on three sides—open-faced boxes with a second story housing officials and guests in open galleries rented by the teams for hospitality during the long hours of the race. Entrance to the pits was through a guarded door at the back. Squeezing through the piles of tires, spare parts, and toolboxes was difficult. Following Coltrin, I edged my way into one of the Ferrari pits, where a swarm of mechanics in greasy coveralls worked on a shimmering red sports racing car to be driven by the star of the team, Eugenio Castellotti, and his co-driver, Giannino Marzotto, a wealthy textile manufacturer who had won the 1953 Mille-Miglia for Ferrari.

Coltrin, who spoke Italian fluently, moved easily through the crowd and went up to a small, well-built young man lounging in a corner. He was darkly handsome with a proud, aquiline nose and a pair of goggles draped around his neck. They spoke quickly in Italian before the man smiled, gave Coltrin a gentle cuff on the cheek, and walked away.

"That's Castellotti," said Coltrin, returning. "He's hot stuff with the babes in Italy. They call him "Il Bello," the beautiful one. Now that Ascari's gone, he's Italy's best. He told me that he got a quick time in practice. If anybody can run with Hawthorn in the Jaguar and Fangio in the Mercedes, it's Castellotti."

"Where's Enzo Ferrari?" I asked.

Coltrin laughed. "Are you crazy? The old man never comes to

the races. Never, except sometimes to the Italian Grand Prix at Monza. He stays home in Modena and runs the whole show by telephone. They say he's only been out of Italy once or twice in his whole life. The general never visits the front line. And believe me, this is a war."

I looked down the pit lane. The race cars were parked along the narrow straightaway, a strip of macadam that seemed only half as wide as that at Indianapolis. I could see the Jaguars and Austin-Healys from England, all painted in British racing green. The Mercedes and Porsches were muted silver, while the French cars scattered among them were light blue. The Italian Ferraris and Maseratis were all bright, bloody red. The cars carried no sponsor decals or identifying logos other than large numbers painted in white roundels for easy identification by the scoring teams at night. The cars represented not only their manufacturers, but more importantly, their nations of origin. Car colors at Le Mans were based on nationality and not on the styling whims of individual owners like those at Indianapolis. No Zink Pinks here.

A slight, sharp-featured young man came up. He seemed edgy and growled to Coltrin in tense, truncated sentences about the narrowness of the track, then jittered back into the crowd.

"Who's that?" I asked.

"Phil Hill. California guy. First shot at the big time. Nervous as a cat on Benzedrine. Like that all the time. But he calms down in the race car. Very bright. Maybe too bright for this business. Thinking too much is not good. Stab it and steer it. Anything more and you're asking for trouble." Coltrin was permitted into the Scuderia Ferrari pits, but the doors to the major teams' boxes remained closed. Thankfully he had access to the Scuderia's hospitality suite, above the Ferrari pits—where a wide view of the action was available. Better yet, a small bar in the corner offered wine and cheese during the race. Coltrin was a hard man to know, but without him I was doomed to a distant back seat for the upcoming drama.

The Indianapolis 500 had started on a cloudy Indiana morning, but Le Mans, the *phenomène de Mans* as the French called it, was launched at four o'clock on a Saturday afternoon, to then run twice around the clock for a Sunday afternoon finish. Coltrin and I arrived at the circuit early, hoping to beat the crowd, estimated to expand to more than three hundred thousand. We parked in the press lot behind the pits, and, displaying our leather armband press credentials, were allowed access to almost anywhere on the property. We had both decided to stay in the paddock area behind the Ferrari, Mercedes-Benz, and Jaguar pit boxes rather than take seats in the giant press-tribune grandstands across the track, the same as I had done at Indianapolis.

The place was awash in the aromas of crepes, frying bacon, hot pastries, and pungent cheeses—a sharp contrast to the heady odors of hot dogs and French fries that permeated the air at Indianapolis. Wine rather than beer was the drink of choice. In the distance, the tinkle of a merry-go-round calliope drifted over the chatter of the crowds while, towering above the track in the distance, a giant Ferris wheel rotated majestically, making me think of the State Fair at Syracuse.

Beyond the pits, on both sides of the circuit, an immense camping area called the *enceintes popularies* had been laid out. The area was littered with tents of all sizes and shapes, offering the campers access to the track, which split the area in a series of ess-bands. Adjacent was the honky-tonk carnival compound, where everything from belly dancers to trained-dog-and-pony acts to boxing exhibitions went on for the duration of the race. A small, temporary Catholic chapel had been erected in the midst of the place— here Mass was said several times during the early Sunday hours. Offsetting the piety were tents housing teams of hookers who had migrated from their customary Parisian haunts to service the predominantly male crowd.

I was overwhelmed. In less than two weeks I had moved from the essence of the American heartland to what seemed not just another continent, but another time altogether. Following Coltrin, I made my way past two credential checkpoints and into the inner sanctums of the paddock, now piled high with spare tires and extra parts for quick repairs during the race. Among the clutter were small trailers to be employed by the drivers for snippets of sleep during their off-duty hours. The cars would be manned by two-drivers each, each running four-hour shifts, or twelve full hours behind the wheel. During the twenty-four hours, 2,500 miles of driving would be unwound, both in the Sarthe sunshine and in the nighttime hours, when ground fog haunted the long Muslanne straight.

My notebook and small Kodak in hand, I stepped out with Coltrin onto the main straightaway, where the cars were parked diagonally along the pit counters. At Indianapolis, the start was made at speed, with the cars following a pace car. At Le Mans, by contrast, the race began on foot. The drivers lined up across the track, then sprinted to their silent cars, leapt aboard to start their engines, and powered away in a mad dash toward the giant Dunlop pedestrian bridge that arched over the track.

Drivers, crews, important guests, and legions of journalists lingered among the all-green Jaguars. Lined up with them was the Cunningham, D-type, painted in traditional American racing colors— stark white with two wide, blue stripes running down its spine. Nearby were the three red Ferrari and the trio of silver 300SLR Mercedes-Benzes, all contenders for victory.

High above the grandstand a small Esso blimp floated into the light breeze, reminding me that while I was in a foreign land, the long arm of the Standard Oil was omnipresent. I spotted Fangio, the reigning world champion Mercedes team engineer, speaking intently with Uhlenhaut, no doubt over opening race strategies.

There was little doubt that world champion Fangio would start the race, with his teammate, Moss, taking the second four-hour shift. Fangio would play the rabbit for Mercedes, goading the fastest Jaguar—surely to be driven by Mike Hawthorn—and Castellotti's Ferrari into a furious race for the lead, possibly causing them to break under the strain. The Ferrari and Jaguar teams were planning the same tactics for the opening laps, which assured us of a wild race between the three. The plan was simple: to send one of the three cars out at top speed, while the other two maintained slower, more reliable paces. If the "rabbit" held up, all the better. But if it failed under its lashing, a pair of backup machines was ready to move into contention.

The team of Fangio and Moss had to be considered the favorite. But the Jaguar of Hawthorn, with his co-driver Ivor Bueb, and the lead Ferrari of Castellotti and Marzotto, were no doubt quick enough to keep pace. In the second tier were cars like the Mercedes of Fitch and Levegh, who would run steadily and be ready to take up the fight should the lead car fail. So too for the second Jaguar team, to be driven by A. P. R. "Tony" Rolt and Duncan Hamilton, a hard-drinking man known among the British motor sports press as "Drunken Duncan." These two well-born amateurs had won the race for Jaguar in 1953, while Rolt had run second with another driver, Peter Whitehead, the following year. As we sidled down the track, scanning the contending cars, Rolt was chatting with a collection of English journalists. Suddenly he dropped one of his leather driving gloves. He quickly stooped down to pick it up.

"Oh shit," growled Coltrin. "That's all we need."

I thought of Agabashian and Vukovich's dropped helmet. "Bad luck?" I asked.

"Yeah, bad. Drivers are spooked about gloves and helmets. Ascari didn't wear his own helmet at Monza, and look what happened."

"You know that Vukovich dropped his before the race? I saw it happen."

"I didn't know," said Coltrin, his face tightening with concern. "That only adds to it."

"What do you think about all that superstition?"

"Hell, who's to know? I guess when you operate on the edge, you don't mess with the fates," he said grimly.

Whistles began a shrill chorus as a battery of gendarmes began clearing the track. I looked at my watch. Half an hour until the start. Waggling their batons and tooting their whistles, the police herded the crowds off the track, leaving only the crews and the drivers to make final preparations for the start.

Coltrin led me through a maze of corridors and up a rickety set of stairs to the Ferrari hospitality box above the Scuderia's pits. The space was jammed with Italian journalists and elite Ferrari customers, all stacked around a tiny bar where a white-jacketed bartender frantically served drinks. A corner table was piled with breads, cheese, and sausages. I thought of the grubby little cafeteria in Gasoline Alley and understood why the Europeans tended to view our form of motor sports as marginally barbaric. A band appeared on the track and began playing a series of national anthems, beginning with "La Marsellaise" and ending with the "The Star Spangled Banner." By then, the drivers, all fifty-two of them, had lined up across the track from their cars, helmets strapped in place. Some stretched and limbered up, as if readying for a hundred-yard dash. The sprint to the cars was little more than fifty feet long, but a quick run meant a chance to leave the pits before the mob scene of iron, aluminum, steel, and rubber clogged the narrow stretch of macadam. Behind the drivers, the crowd, hundreds deep, jammed shoulder to shoulder beyond the low earthen fence that formed the outer barrier of the track. They craned their heads for a better look, forming a sea of faces within spitting distance of the cars and drivers.

An enormous Rolex clock cantilevered over the pits served as the official timepiece for the race. All eyes turned to its stark white face as the minute hand clicked toward the start. The drivers tensed, all hunched forward. They were a strange collection, all sizes and shapes. Rolt tall and gangly, Castellotti lean and muscular. Fangio, who was forty-four years old and the most senior driver in the field next to Levegh, looked stubby and bandy-legged in contrast to the blond, barrel-chested Hawthorn, who was dressed in his trademark Eisenhower field jacket, white shirt, and bow tie that served as his fashion nod to the days of yore, when true gentlemen went motor racing.

The minute hand clicked into position. Four o'clock. A wild cheer surged through the crowd. The public address system announcer screamed in French as the drivers sprinted across the track and plunged into their cockpits. The younger, more athletic ones vaulted over the closed doors, while the older men, like Fangio, oozed into their seats deliberately, understanding that the saving of a few seconds at the start meant nothing in the course of twenty-four hours. As a stout man at the start-finish line furiously waved a blanket-sized French tri-color, the first engines exploded into life and a gaggle of cars squirted away, leaving ugly scars of rubber on the pavement.

"Look at Rolt," Coltrin shouted. "He's having trouble." I thought of the glove. Were they real, these superstitions? After the field cleared, the Jaguar engine finally caught and Rolt was off, a few miles behind.

Over the din of the cheering crowd, the chatter of an Italian radio broadcast that had been piped into the box escalated to the edge of apoplexy. "The broadcast says Castellotti has the lead. This place will go crazy when he comes by," said Coltrin.

Heads craned down the track toward a small kink, at a corner called Maison Blanc a kilometer away. A blink of red. The scream of a high-revving engine. Mad cheers around me. Wine and champagne were poured as the clot of Ferraristas went wild. Castellotti powered past the pits to lead the first lap. It meant nothing in the long term, but for an Italian driver in an Italian car to lead the opening round meant a celebration in the little box that lasted for three more laps. Then the relentless pursuers—in the form of Hawthorn's green Jaguar and Fangio's silver Mercedes—hunted down the Italian and passed him.

With the field strung out around the massive circuit, the smaller machined buzzing fecklessly among the more powerful cars, the race quickly centered on a vicious battle between Fangio and Hawthorn, with Castellotti driving with his typically feverish style to keep up. Two hours into the race, the lead between the Argentinian and the Englishman had been swapped countless times, reminding me of the mad duel between McGrath and Vukovich only two weeks earlier. I fervently hoped that this one would end with less violence.

I was wrong.

Peering down pit row from the Ferrari box, I could see a Jaguar mechanic holding up a large board with a chalked message that read, "fuel-in." The Ferrari crowd was more subdued and the screaming of the radio broadcaster had descended into dispassionate muttering. Castellotti had spun entering the Mulsanne corner, and had fallen back to a distant third. "Hawthorn is getting ready to stop," said Coltrin. "One more lap. About time, considering the way he's running."

The Englishman was averaging over 122 miles an hour, a record pace, and had squeezed out an eight-second advantage over Fangio. Thirty-five laps—280 miles—around the circuit had been completed by the leaders, and fuel stops were in order.

A buzz of excitement ran through the crowd as they pressed closer to the earthen barrier across from the pits for a better look as the leader's crew set to changing tires and adding fuel in a matter of a few critical minutes. The public address announcer blared in French that Hawthorn might stop on the next lap.

Ivor Bueb, Hawthorn's co-driver, who was running his first race for the Jaguar team, stood on the pit counter, helmet on, hands gloved, in case his partner wanted relief. This seemed unlikely. It would be a rapid stop, then back to the war. It was expected that Fangio would also come in shortly.

I looked at my watch. It was 6:26 in the afternoon. Two and half hours had gone by, and had been almost entirely consumed in a desperate battle between Fangio and Hawthorn.

A hint of dark green arrowed toward us from Maison Blanc. Hawthorn on the inside of the narrow track. He was presumably slowing for his pit stop. A wink of silver to his left was coming at 150 mph. Was it Fangio? No. The number 20 sister car—Levegh. Suddenly another speck of green. A smaller car that had been hidden behind Hawthorn's onrushing Jaguar popped into view. Lance Macklin's Austin-Healy. It veered into the path of Levegh's Mercedes, which didn't seem to alter course.

In one mad moment, the silver car vaulted up the back of the little green roadster. Its nose pointed high in the air, the Mercedes slammed down atop the outside barrier, and then, in a crazed, blurred second, a pair of shattering explosions, and the Mercedes disintegrated, flinging two enormous hunks of metal into the massed crowd. Macklin's Austin-Healey gyrated crazily down the narrow straight before shuddering to a stop. Then Fangio came through the smoke, angling toward the pits and maneuvering through the madness. He barely missed Hawthorn as the Jaguar rolled to a stop.

Pandemonium. Sirens screeching. Men waving yellow flags. Screams of agony from the crowded gallery. Macklin scrambled out of his wrecked car and staggered into the pits. Gendarmes and track officials rushed to the wrecked Mercedes, burning fiercely atop the barrier. Levegh lay face down on the track beside the smoking hulk. Black clouds poured into the darkening sky. Then the place fell strangely silent, save for the distant, confused rumble of cars on the back part of the course, the incessant cacophony of the carnival, and the shriek of ambulance sirens.

"Holy shit," said Coltrin. "Levegh's Mercedes launched like a fucking rocket off the back of Macklin's Healey. Never seen anything like it."

"The crowd. They must have gotten hit by all the flying debris," I said.

The Italians were gaping and drinking hard. The radio was chattering in the background. Coltrin listened. "They're saying Fitch was driving. That can't be right. It was Levegh who started the car. It had to be him. Either way, they say the driver was killed."

We watched in silence as a near-riot broke out across the track. It was a fair distance away, and difficult to see through the pall of smoke, but it was apparent that thousands were trying to flee the scene—now a gaping hole filled with what appeared to be bodies and smoking bits of car.

"Let's get out of here. To the paddock. They'll know more down there." Said Coltrin. He claimed that crewmen, drivers, and team managers would know more than what we could witness from our distant vantage point.

The area behind the pits was swarming with journalists, crewmen, and officials. I was reminded of Gasoline Alley following the Vukovich disaster. Then Fitch elbowed through the crowd, looking frantic. He had lost his suave composure. A pair of driving goggles wobbled around his neck as he rushed up. He said to Coltrin, "I must get to a phone. The Italians are saying on the radio that it was me in the car. I've got to call Elizabeth in Lugano and tell her I'm allright."

"Try the press tribune. There's a bank of phones there. That's the best place," said Coltrin.

Fitch's face darkened. "I was having a coffee in the Mercedes trailer with his wife when it happened. I left her to help get some of the injured people out of the pits. When Macklin spun, he hit some crewmen and journalists. At first we thought it was Fangio. His wife was hysterical. Then someone said that it was my car. Then I found

Levegh's wife. Before I could speak, she looked at me and said, 'I know, Fitch. It was Levegh. He is dead. I know he is dead.' I tried to tell her that he might have been thrown clear, but she'd have none of it. She just kept repeating, 'I know he is dead.' She was right."

He turned away from us and rushed into the crowd.

A large man with a stone-bald head staggered out of the confusion. A battery of Leicas was draped over his shoulders. He was wearing the khaki vest with multiple pockets favored by professional photographers. It was spattered with blood.

I had seen him before at Indianapolis. Dan Rubin was a top photographer for *Time* and *Life* and other major periodicals.

"Are you all right?" I asked.

"No. Not after what I just saw. I had just crossed over on the Dunlop bridge and was walking through the crowd. I planned to shoot the Hawthorn pit stop from across the track. I was checking my F-stops when I heard this terrible explosion off to my right. I looked up to see Levegh's car carom onto the barrier. Then these giant hunks of steel pinwheeled into the crowd. It was awful. Then suddenly people were rushing toward me, all of them screaming. Most of them were covered with blood. Some were holding gaping wounds on their faces, arms, and upper bodies. An old man collapsed in front of me. I knelt down to help him and was nearly crushed. I covered Korea and I never saw anything like this."

"They say some people were killed."

"Some? You've got to be kidding. There has to be a hundred dead over there. Maybe more. I need a drink."

"The Ferrari box. All you need up there. Tell 'em I sent you," said Coltrin.

Rubin reeled off.

"You think they'll stop the race?" I asked.

"They bloody well ought to," said an English journalist. "This is a bloody catastrophe."

"They're still running out there. You can hear 'em," said Coltrin. "Like nothing even happened."

"Same at Indy," I said. "They cleaned up the Vukovich crash and the race went on. Within minutes it was forgotten."

Fitch reappeared. "Thank God I got through to her," he said. "Elizabeth had just heard on Armed Forces radio about the crash. They were saying that it might have been me."

"What now?" I asked.

"I've told Uhlenhaut and Neubauer that we ought to retire. Quit right now. Pull out the cars. There's enough bad blood between these two countries. We don't need this."

"The French are saying that three or four people are dead," I said.

"Good God! There are dozens dead. Maybe hundreds. What's the matter with them? That's nonsense," said the Englishman.

"So will Mercedes withdraw?"

"I doubt it. Fangio wants to run. He's very tough-minded. Moss is ready to keep going as well. But for the sake of the company's reputation, Mercedes ought to drop out."

"They ought to stop the whole bloody show," said the little Englishman. "Enough is enough."

Another man with a scrawny beard and wire-rimmed glasses butted in. "No way they'll stop. They've decided that stopping the race would clog the road, and the emergency vehicles would be stranded. No way to get the injured out. So they'll keep it going." I recognized the face. Dennis Jenkinson was perhaps the best-known British motor sports journalist, a regular for the venerable *Motorsport* monthly magazine and having recently won fame as the navigator for Stirling Moss on his epic, record-shattering victory drive in the Mille Miglia. "Jenks" was not only a vertitable encyclopedia of racing knowledge, but a three-time world champion—with Eric Oliver—in the insanely dangerous sport of motorcycle sidecar racing.

"That's a shitty excuse," said Coltrin.

"Maybe. Maybe not," I said. "They've got to get people t hospitals. Jamming the highways with traffic won't help. I can see their reasoning."

"That's ridiculous," snapped Coltrin. "Stop it now. Respect the dead. Worse yet, the car is German. They've already stirred up the old Franco-German antagonisms. It's in Mercedes' best interest to retire to affirm the Company's basic humanity and reputation."

"That's bloody nonsense," growled Jenks, rising to his full five-foot-four-inches. "Thousands of people die each day for one reason or another. It would be bloody sentimentality for Mercedes to withdraw someone because some people died here. One death is the same as a hundred."

"The press will report that the ruthless German drove to victory over the dead bodies of Frenchmen. Neubauer wants to keep going. So do Moss and Fangio. But Uhlenhaut is on the phone trying to reach the board of directors in Suttgart. They'll be the ones to decide, said Coltrin.

The argument going nowhere, Jenkinson stalked away.

The place had devolved into madness. The screech and roar of the cars continued, mixed with the cacophony of the carnival and the end-less wailing of ambulances and fire trucks. As darkness fell, the giant Esso blimp hung dolefully on its flagstaff, seemingly losing air. A bright neon Mobil Flying Red Horse sign and the garishly lit press tribune and grandstand were the only hints of color on the gray landscape as the brightly hued cars blended into the oncoming night.

Rumors flew about the carnage. It had been officially announced that Levegh was dead, although the track press office remained cir-cumspect about the civilian casualties. Coltrin spoke with crewmen and other journalists and all agreed that the toll would be high, per-haps over one hundred dead, with scores more injured.

The Fangio and Moss Mercedes had now established supremacy over the Jaguar, which had fallen two laps in arrears. The team Ferraris had broken, leaving the little hospitality box dark and empty, save for a chilled bartender and a few Scuderia loyalists. The floor was littered with empty champagne and wine bottles. The food platters were picked clean.

Tired and depressed, I sat on the tongue of a small trailer behind the pits, trying to decide what to do. Surely hard news of the crash would be forthcoming, although there seemed to be an official reluctance to deal with the reality, perhaps out of fear that more of the massive crowd would flee the track and further clog the adjacent highways. Coltrin reported that intense phone calls were being exchanged between team manager Uhlenhaut and the Daimler-Benz board of directors in Stuttgart. The sentiment seemed to be leaning toward an official withdrawal.

It came shortly after two o'clock in the morning, 10 hours after the start of the race and eight hours following the disaster. An official statement from Stuttgart claimed that in deference to the dead and injured, the two remaining Mercedes-Benz 300SLR cars would be retired. The statement also noted that all of the team cars had operated within the rules of the event and could not be held responsible for the crash.

I sensed that this would be the opening volley in an ugly, protracted effort by drivers, teams, and even nations to fix the blame on anyone but themselves.

With the Hawthorn/Bueb Jaguar now far ahead in an uncontested lead and the major competition from both Ferrari and Mercedes-Benz gone, the drama had been drained from the race. The night was dark and cold. It was time for bed. I found Coltrin dragging on one of his countless cigarettes and sharing a bottle of Scotch with an English journalist behind the pits.

He agreed to leave, and we trooped to his Fiat in the nearly vacant press parking lot and weaved back to the city. He dropped me off at the Moderne with an agreement to meet for a late breakfast at the Continental Hotel.

My room was pulsing with heat. I opened the window. The whine of the race cars at the faraway track drifted in, along with the faint glow of dawn in the east. As I lay there my mind fixed on the image of Levegh's car's nose pointed into the air, then pancaking onto the fence, followed by two sharp detonations and the burst of fire and flying metal. If anything, the crash resembled wartime newsreels of a fighter plane crash. Thankfully, the smoke and the high earthen barrier that was supposed to protect the crowd had at least shielded me from the awful carnage that ensued. I finally drifted off to sleep while trying to compose the lead to my story, which I knew would have to center on the greatest disaster in motor racing history.

Coltrin was at a table in the Continental dining room when I arrived, unshaven and wearing the same rumpled shirt as the day before. He was drinking champagne and reading several French and English newspapers, along with the international edition of the *Herald Tribune*. He handed me the front page of *Le Monde* and said, "It's all in there. Just as bad as we thought it." The picture accompanying the story showed the Mercedes tumbling over the fence toward the crowd, and a second shot of a pile of dead and injured amid a jumble of upturned chairs, scattered knapsacks and purses, and shredded clothing.

"The car itself never got into the crowd," he said. "The engine and the front axle assembly tore loose. That's what did the killing. That and the spilled fuel that caught fire. Most of the papers are saying eighty were killed. Plus Levegh. But a few of 'em are claiming the death toll is over one hundred. I doubt the frogs will ever tell us. A friend of mine who works for Renault says official count will only include French citizens. The rest will be ignored."

"Why is that?" I asked.

"National pride. The effect on their tourism industry. The fact that some of the critically injured will also croak. Who knows how many in the end? So they'll keep the number at a minimum."

"Whose fault do you think it was?"

"Fangio and Macklin are saying it was Hawthorn's. That he cut in front of Macklin and caused Lance to spike the brakes. Levegh had no room and nailed him in the back. Fangio says in one of the papers that Levegh raised his hand—warning him—just before he hit Macklin. That's the German version."

"Are there others?"

"Hell, yes," said Coltrin as he rustled through the pile of papers beside his chair. He pulled up the *London Telegraph* and pointed to a page-one story. "The Brits are blaming Levegh. The Jaguar team manager, Lofty England, is claiming that the Frenchman was so worried about being overtaken by Fangio on the main straightaway in front of all his countrymen that he was glued to his rearview mirror and paying no attention to Macklin and Hawthorn. England says he has photos to prove that Levegh never changed course when Macklin veered in front of him. Others are saying it was Macklin's fault, because he panicked when Hawthorn braked in front of him and headed for the pits. That's hard to believe. Lance had six Le Mans under his belt and is a good, steady driver."

"So everybody is blaming everybody," I said.

"Except the French for running a race where cars will go over 180 on a road about as narrow as a country lane. That's the problem. There is just no damn room for cars that fast to maneuver. It was only dumb luck that Fangio didn't get into the pits and kill a few dozen more. They are saying that when he weaved through the mess, his Mercedes scuffed some paint off Hawthorn's Jaguar. It was that close."

"What do you think will happen? Some politicians in America are already screaming about banning racing," I said.

"Same thing in Europe. The Swiss government is saying it will ban all racing immediately and the French and Germans are talking about at least a hiatus until the investigations are completed. It will raise a shit storm, I'll guarantee you that."

Briggs Cunningham and Phil Walters came in for breakfast. With them was a rotund man wearing glasses. It was Bill Spear, the skilled amateur who had co-driven with Walters until their Jaguar expired. There was no joy at the table. Walters looked particularly morose, sipping a cup of dark coffee and saying nothing.

When we finished, Coltrin gathered up his armload of newspapers and stopped at the Cunningham table.

"A shitty way to run a motor race," cracked Coltrin.

"Cunningham shook his head and exhaled heavily. "This is the worst that could happen."

"Will I see you in Modena, Phil? When do you plan to get there?" Coltrin asked.

Without looking up from his coffee, Walters said firmly, "Never."

"Never?" said Coltrin. "Your contract with Ferrari—what about that?"

Walters looked up, his clear blue eyes glinting with anger. "Look, Coltrin, I've been racing for over ten years. I've seen a lot of guys buy it, especially in the midgets. That was OK. They knew what they were facing. But this? Those people in the grandstands didn't come here to risk death. They came to have a good time in the French countryside. Dying wasn't part of their deal. I can stand guys like me getting killed, but innocent spectators—that's bullshit. If that's the way it's gonna be, count me out."

"So no Ferrari?" Coltrin asked, shocked.

"No Ferrari. No Cunningham. No nothing. I just told Briggs I'm through. Kaput. *Finito.* I used to love the sport. But after what I saw yesterday, I don't even want to have anything to do with it."

"So you're quitting."

"Right now. On the spot."

"You could have run with the best of 'em," mused Coltrin.

"Maybe. Maybe not. That we'll never know."

"So what are your plans?" I asked.

"Tomorrow I'm driving to Wolfsburg, Germany, just across the border. The Volkswagen plant. It's a hot little car. It's starting to sell pretty good in the United States. If I can get a dealership or a distributionship, I'm in the car business."

"What do you think about losing your star driver?" Coltrin asked Cunningham.

"That's Phil's call. He's proved his point in a race car. If he feels this way, we're behind him 100 percent."

We moved away, stunned at the news that one of America's most accomplished and honored road racing drivers was suddenly retiring, in turn giving up a chance to drive with one of the greatest Grand Prix teams in the world.

"That's got to be a kick in the ass for Briggs," said Coltrin. "First he loses Fitch to Mercedes-Benz, now Walters quits, and the government is shutting down his car-building operation for tax reasons. Maybe he ought to try something else." (Cunningham did. While he continued to race Jaguars, Listers, and Corvettes until the mid-1960s, he also diverted his talents to ocean racing and skippered the America's Cup twelve-meter *Columbia* to victory in 1958.)

We stepped into the square. Traffic was moving routinely. The faint hum of the race could still be heard. "Sweet Jesus, will they ever stop that fucking race?" I asked in frustration.

"Three more hours and it's over," said Coltrin, looking at his watch. Hawthorn and Bueb have it. They're just cruising around hoping the car doesn't break."

"What are your plans?"

"I'll go back to the track and pick up the press clippings and final interviews. Then a drive back to Modena." He paused, then said, "You still want to come with me? A lot of laughs. It'll help you forget all this madness."

"I dunno. . ."

"Come on. Italy is a gas."

I thought about my alternative. A train to Paris, packed flights to

Los Angeles, and back to work. On the other hand, how could a few days in Italy hurt? A tour of the Ferrari factory and possibly hooking up with the Commendatore himself might generate more stories. I was more than halfway there already. Why turn back now?

"What the hell," I said, stepping back from the curb as a leggy blonde oozed from a Porsche cabriolet that had skidded to a stop. "I'll pack my stuff and meet you here in twenty minutes."

With a Le Mans victory in hand, Hawthorn's initial remorse over the crash disappeared and was replaced by a noisy conviction that the crash had been caused by Levegh's poor judgment and his preoccupation with being overtaken by Fangio and Kling. A year later he met John Fitch in London, where the American told him he was on his way to Stuttgart for a meeting with Mercedes-Benz. "Take along a bomb for me," Hawthorn said bitterly.

Mike Hawthorn raced for thee more seasons, concentrating on the Formula One Grand Prix competition. In 1958 he won the world championship by a single point over arch-rival Stirling Moss, yet was devastated by the death of two of his Scuderia Ferrari teammates, close friend Peter Collins and the fiery Luigi Musso. Having reached the pinnacle of international motor racing, Hawthorn abruptly announced at age thirty that he was retiring to concentrate on his thriving automobile business and occasional forays into vintage racing.

On January 22, 1959, he left his home in Surrey for a trip into London. On the way he met his old friend Rob Walker, gentleman, sportsman, race car owner, sometime journalist, and heir to the Johnny Walker liquor fortune. After lunch at a pub, the two began a casual, high-speed duel between Hawthorn's 3.8 Jaguar-sedan and Walker's Mercedes-Benz 300SL gullwing coupe. A Jaguar-Mercedes rematch. This time the results were reversed. On a bypass around the village of Guildford, Hawthorn's Jaguar skated on a patch of standing water, and then caromed off an oncoming truck and into a stout English oak. He was killed instantly.

CHAPTER TEN

DISTRACTION, ITALIAN-STYLE

GROUSING ABOUT THE CHATTERING GEARBOX IN his road-weary Fiat, Coltrin headed east across France's superb network of Routes Nationales. Two days earlier, we had witnessed the terrible carnage at Le Mans, and I was happy to be fleeing the morbid scene. Despite my driver's steady complaining, I could not help liking him. He insisted the blame for the crash lay with the French for having failed to modernize and widen the Le Mans circuit and for placing the crowds so close to the track that any sort of flying debris would cause a catastrophe.

The French, Spanish, and German governments had cancelled all motor sports until further evaluations of safety conditions could be made. The Swiss had simply outlawed all forms of racing. The Swiss Grand Prix would never be run again. The Vatican was at full cry about the savagery of the sport. Meanwhile, Coltrin had spoken with friends at *Road & Track* magazine in Los Angeles and had been told that the American Automobile Association, which sanctioned all major racing in the United States, was considering leaving the sport entirely. The AAA had edged toward the decision following Vukovich's death; now the Le Mans disaster seemed to have tipped the scale. The world of automobile racing was in chaos, with rumors now filtering out of Stuttgart that Mercedes-Benz, which had been involved in the sport for half a century, would also drop out at the end of the season.

Richard Neuberger, a liberal Democratic senator from Oregon, demanded that President Eisenhower ban automobile racing. In an impassioned speech before the Senate, he ended his denouncement of the sport with the following statement: "I believe the time has come for the United States to be a civilized nation and stop the carnage on the racetracks, which are a stage for profits and for the delight of thousands of screeching spectators." *The New York Daily News* followed with an editorial dealing with the AAA's rumored plans to leave the sport, claiming that "auto racing in these times attracts a lot of people who morbidly expect to see somebody killed or injured—and often do. Why should the AAA cater to that morbidity any longer?"

The sole defender of the sport was NASCAR's Bill France. He sidestepped the fact that three drivers—Larry Mann, Frank Arford, and Lou Figaro—had died in recent stock car races, and persuaded a number of southern senators that those "screeching spectators" would vote the following year. His claim that auto racing actually improved highway safety through better automotive design helped to defuse Neuberger and other critics, and no anti-racing legislation ever reached Congress.

Napoleon's epic program of military road building in the late eighteenth century made highway travel relatively easy, although France was yet to seriously invest in four-lane superhighways of the type that already crisscrossed Germany and were about to spread over the United States under President Eisenhower's massive Interstate and Defense Highway Act of 1956. But the poplar-lined two-lanes were fast and smooth, even for Coltrin's Fiat, and we made the city of Nevers for lunch after crossing the Loire River.

The small roadside café was a favorite stop of his, due in part to a wonderful local Cabernet that Coltrin consumed with amazing relish. As we sat on a sun-drenched patio, an immense red Fiat truck rumbled past. Hunkered down in its special two-deck storage racks were the three battle-scarred factory Ferrari sports cars that had competed at Le Mans. The truck bore the familiar yellow and black prancing horse of Maranello crest of the Scuderia on its door, and the driver, spotting Coltrin's Fiat on the verge, honked wildly and waved as he sped past. The transporter, with its cargo of brutish machinery, was headed back to the factory, where the race cars would be torn apart and refurbished for more competition, presuming all motor racing on the Continent was not ended forever.

"They're good boys," said Coltrin as he watched the big Fiat trundle into the distance. "They work their asses off for the Commendatore. Loyal as hell. The cars are practically a religion to the Italians. When Ferrari wins, the nation cheers. When they lose, the nation weeps. It's like no other place on earth."

We heard another engine in the distance—high-pitched and angry. Then another red vehicle burst out of a tunnel of trees and arrowed toward us. A Ferrari 375 Mexico coupe. Its snout sank under hard braking as the driver expertly downshifted through the gears. The Ferrari skidded to a stop next to Coltrin's Fiat. It was squat, with the traditional Ferrari egg-crate grille and a hand-built aluminum body designed by coach builder Giovanni Michelotti and built by the Carrozzeria of Alfredo Vignale. A 4.1-liter V-12 developing 280 horsepower was tucked underneath its low hood.

The Mexico's door swung open and a svelte young woman stepped out. She was wearing Ray-Ban sunglasses. Her hair was combed back until she reached up and unpinned it, letting a cascade the color of an angry sunset tumble onto her black leather jacket. Yanking off her glasses with a dramatic sweep, she approached with feline grace. I watched, slack-jawed.

"Peter, just in time for lunch," she said, smiling. "I couldn't miss that clapped-out Fiat of yours in the car park and thought I'd join you." Before I had a chance to rise from my chair, she held out her hand. "Hi, I'm Diana Logan. Peter and I have known each other for years. Seems like we meet at almost every Grand Prix race. What fun. Have you ordered?"

Diana Logan, the daughter of a senior production executive at Warner Brothers, had become a motor sports groupie, drifting around Europe, mingling with the drivers, team owners, and other elites on the Grand Prix circuit. She was twenty-four years old, with the devastating good looks of a screen star. As I stumbled through my lunch, I fought the urge to stare at this lovely creature dominating the conversation.

"I was so thankful Gino wasn't involved in that awful mess," she said, referring to Eugenio Castellotti.

"Lucky he was well back when it happened," Coltrin said.

"They have to do something about that track," she said, lighting a gold-tipped cigarette. She turned to me, her azure-blue eyes curious and unthreatening. "What are your plans in Modena?"

"Uh, well, I guess I'm going with Peter. Never been there. The Ferrari scene sounds interesting." Diana looked at Coltrin and the pair exchanged knowing smiles. "Oh yes, you could say that. Where are you staying?"

"I made him a reservation at the Albergo Real. In the middle of the action," said Coltrin.

"Perfect. I'm there too. We'll have to get together."

"Sounds good to me. But I'll need a translator. I know about three words in Italian and they're all dirty."

Diana laughed. "In that crowd, you'll be in good shape."

As we finished lunch, she stood up and swept a mop of hair from her face and put on her sunglasses. "I've got to run. I'd like to get over the St. Bernard before dark."

"Great meeting you," I said. "I look forward to seeing more of you in Modena."

"Me, too. And don't let Peter kill you in that shit-box." She spun to leave, then turned. "In fact, if you want to come with me, I'll guarantee you'll get there a lot faster than riding with him."

I looked at Coltrin, seeking his response. He shrugged in defeat. "Lemme see," he puzzled. "Ride with me in that junker of mine or in a Ferrari with a beautiful woman. I give up."

Diana grabbed my hand and hauled me toward the Ferrari. Pitching my small leather bag and portable typewriter in the tiny trunk, I wedged in beside her. The interior of the Ferrari smelled of rich leather and Chanel. The V-12 came awake with a lusty crackle from its exhaust and a cacophony of gear whines. Diana powered onto the highway, leaving a shower of stones and a desolate Coltrin in her wake.

She drove across western France like a fugitive from the furies. Rushing toward the Swiss border, we skimmed a farmer and his horse-drawn wagon at 120 miles an hour. The Ferrari lurched sideways in a long slide under hard braking. She laughed hard as we regained speed.

The St. Bernard Pass over the Alps was a sickening maze of serpentine curves and switchbacks that probed through the craggy peaks. Traffic was light, which meant that Diana had a clear shot with the Ferrari, unimpeded by slower vehicles that might have served to ease her pace. And my mind. We plunged off the mountains with the car's outer wheels gnawing at the edge of the pavement and within inches of 1,000 foot drop-offs. "Your knuckles are getting white," she mused, glancing down at my hand gripping the dashboard. "Not to worry, I've made this trip a hundred times. The car practically steers itself."

Once on the flats of the Aosta Valley, the long legs of the Ferrari unlimbered and we sped south with the tachometer floating at around 6,000 rpm. With the gear lever jammed in fourth gear, I was unable to see the speedometer, but I reckoned the Ferrari was touching speeds of 160 mph.

She short-cut around Milan and headed east on the ancient Via Emilia, a Roman road that had served the empire since three hundred years before the birth of Christ. It remained an engineering wonder, with one 163-mile stretch from Rimini on the Adriatic Coast to Piacenza on the banks of the Po River an almost perfectly straight line, with barely the suggestion of a hill or a curve. There being no speed limits in Italy and virtually no traffic enforcement, we blazed across the northern part of the country like a low-flying airplane, reaching the outskirts of Modena as the sun dipped into the horizon to the west, reflecting off the shimmering thirteenth century Duomo and the various campaniles scattered around the city.

Modena, once known as Mutina to the Romans, had been a center of commerce on the vast Padana plain since Etruscan prehistory. Controlled by the powerful Este family during the Renaissance, Modena—a center of metal crafts, porcelain works, and machine-tool industries—was the thriving capital of Emilia-Romagna known for its heavy Lambrusco red wine, its "Zamponi," stuffed pigs' feet, and swarms of summer mosquitoes that bred in the marshes of the Panaro River. The uncrowned king of the city was Commendatore Enzo Ferrari, at the height of his powers, running the Scuderia Ferrari racing stable and producing the most exotic, powerful, and expensive cars in the world. But, unknown at the time, a challenger to his throne was on the rise. A young, robust twenty-year-old schoolteacher was refining his stunning tenor voice, hoping someday to leave school and enter the opera. Six years later, he would shake the music world with his power and range, when he debuted in La Scala's *La Bohème*. This Modenese teacher and aspiring singer was named Luciano Pavarotti.

The Albergo Real, owned by an ex-madame, was set on the Via Emilia, which sliced through the center of the city, bordering the edge of the elegant Garibaldi Square. Diana pointed to a cross-street as we eased toward the hotel. "Ferrari and his family live down there. Eleven Viale e Trieste. An apartment on the second floor over the old race shop. The main factory is a few miles out of town on the Abetone Road. Down there about a mile is Maserati. Owned by the Orsi family. Ferrari and the Orsis hate each other. Bad blood."

We entered the lobby, a slightly threadbare example of provincial Italian baroque. The staff, with typically grand gestures, hauled off our luggage. As we headed to the elevator, Diana spun away and rushed into the arms of a slight handsome man. I immediately recognized Eugenio Castellotti.

The Albergo bar was crowded with a cacophony of chatter in Italian, English, French, and German by the time Coltrin wandered in. He was still growling about the evil behavior of his Fiat.

"Was your ride with Diana OK?" he asked, knocking back a second Scotch.

"The woman can drive, I'll say that."

"She's something. Half the guys on the Grand Prix circuit are in love with her. But she's elusive."

"Not with Castellotti. She was all over him like a cheap suit when we got here."

"And that shot your dreams in the ass, right?"

"My mama didn't raise no fool."

"Relax. She may have the hots for ol' Gino, but he's all hooked up with an Italian movie star, Delia Scala. The two are Italy's heartthrobs. He's from Lodi. Old Italian aristocracy. Ego the size of the Coliseum. A little self-conscious about his height, so he wears elevator shoes. But now that Ascari is dead, he's the great hope of Italy to run with Fangio and Moss. If Ferrari lets him live long enough, he might have a shot."

161

"Meaning what?"

"Meaning the old man—that's what we call Ferrari—plays crazy mind games with his drivers. Keeps them on the edge, tweaking them to go faster. They call him an 'agitator of men.'"

"Americans have the idea that he's this towering genius and a kind of benign father figure."

"Yeah, like Mussolini. He's one crafty old son-of-a-bitch and a small-town Paisano. You'll see later."

"He's coming in here?"

"Regular as clockwork. About eight. His home life is a nightmare. His wife, Laura, is an ex-*putana* from Torino and his mother is an old shrew who lives with them. His only son, Dino, is twenty-three and dying of something—maybe muscular dystrophy and nephritis, who knows? Although some claim he contracted incurable syphilis in his mother's womb."

"Man, what a mess."

"That's only the half of it. He's got a mistress named Linda Lardi who lives in a little village, Castelvitro, near here, and she's got Enzo's ten-year-old bastard son, Piero. Laura knows about the kid and keeps Enzo's feet to the fire. He comes over here—it's just around the corner from his house—to get away from her."

"Can you blame him?"

"The best part of it is that he's maybe the biggest ass man in northern Italy. Hard to figure, but he always has women, including a few of his customer's wives. The Rasputin of automobiles. He's amazing. I think the only thing he likes better than his cars is pussy."

Diana's fierce red head eased through the crowd. She came up, dressed in an elegant silk blouse and tight-fitting leather pants, riding on four-inch stiletto heels. Slick-haired Italian heads swiveled in her wake.

"Are you all settled in?" she asked.

"My little home away from home," I said.

"Sorry we left you, Peter. But I guess you made it all right," she said, turning to Coltrin.

"Better late than never," he answered.

"We should get some dinner. There's a little trattoria around the corner."

"I figured you'd be eating with Gino," I said.

"Don't be silly. We're just old friends. Tomorrow he's testing the Grand Prix car at the Autodrome. I'll see him there. Are you going, Peter?"

"Wouldn't miss it for the world. And I'll bring my American cousin here." He gestured to me.

Coltrin had settled in with a sweet, slightly round Italian woman in a small apartment, but seemed to spend his waking hours either at the Albergo bar or haunting the various car businesses scattered around Modena. He joined us for dinner—heaping portions of tortellini, the favored local pasta, and endless glasses of Lambrusco.

"What is it about this world of motor racing that so intrigues you?" I asked Diana. "I mean, you were raised in the movie industry. Hollywood. All that glamour. Why this?"

"The people. The joie di vivre. Living on the edge, I guess. Hollywood is so plastic. So filled with *poseurs*. This is real."

"Yeah, real. Like maybe a hundred dead in Le Mans. I was there when Vukovich got it. And Chet Miller. Then Ascari. Maybe that's too real."

"Oh, I know. Sometimes it's terrible. But the rest of it—alive, vibrant. Packed with fascinating people. Like tomorrow. Gino trying out a new car. The noise. The power. The fumes. To me it's haunting."

Outside the restaurant, a Maserati roadster fired up, its blatting six-cylinder instantly recognizable compared to the V-12 shriek of a Ferrari. Its driver powered away, the roar of the engine echoing off the shuttered buildings lining the narrow street.

"You don't hear a sound like that on Wilshire Boulevard," said Diana.

"Hot rods and fatso Cadillacs," sneered Coltrin. "The whole damn

Los Angeles basin is a nightmare. I was there last year—never again. The politicians are talking about building thousands of miles of their so-called freeways and it's 'drive-in' everything—hamburger joints, movie theaters, shopping centers. Even a drive-in church in Garden Grove."

Coltrin raged on about the decadence of Southern California until Diana forcibly changed the subject.

"I suppose you guys have been so locked up with automobile racing that you haven't been paying any attention to what's going on in the rest of the world. Like maybe the movies?"

"The last one I saw was *Birth of a Nation*," grumped Coltrin.

"That's what I thought. But maybe I can give you a scoop. There's this young actor my father says is going to set the world on fire. A super-talent. His first movie opened in March. The Steinbeck novel *East of Eden* directed by Elia Kazan. Then he shot a picture for Warner's called *Rebel Without a Cause* and after that he's in an adaptation of Edna Ferber's *Giant*. Then Rocky Graziano bio-pic *Somebody Up There Likes Me*. His name is James Dean. Remember that."

"Another flash-in-the-pan movie hero. Who cares?" sniffed Coltrin.

"You'll care because he's also a major racing talent. When he got to Hollywood from Broadway, he bought an MG, then a Porsche Speedster, and won his first race at Palm Springs. He ran very quickly again at Bakersfield and then at Santa Barbara over the Memorial Day weekend. He just finished *Rebel* and now he's in Marfa, Texas, with Liz Taylor and Rock Hudson shooting *Giant*. The studio has made him stop racing until production finishes in September, but everybody says he's a terrific talent on the race-track."

"Seems like he'll have run to more than three amateur sports car races before anyone would recognize it," I said.

"Bill Hickman, his pal and the stunt driver on *Rebel*, says Jimmy is a natural. He grew up in a little Indiana town. Loved the Indy 500. It's in his blood," she replied.

"Yeah, Diana, I've seen a million of these playboy racers come and go," said Coltrin. "They buy a fast car, run against some wankers in a few minor races, and when they get with the big boys they fade like watercolors in the noonday sun." Said Coltrin.

"OK but they say he's the master of Mulholland. Nobody beats him there," she snapped.

Mulholland. Coltrin's head jerked up at the word. Mulholland Drive was a legendary serpentine road that ran along the rim of the Santa Monica Mountains connecting Laurel Canyon in Hollywood to Topanga Canyon in Woodland Hills. Nineteen miles of endless tight corners and switchbacks that demanded maximum skill to negotiate at speed. "He's quick there?" Coltrin asked.

"The best, they say. Unbeatable. So he's got to have talent."

"We'll see. You can run like a raped ape on the public roads and still be a back-marker."

"Remember that name. James Dean," Diana said firmly.

"OK, OK," said Coltrin. "I'm installing his name in my memory bank right now. The future world champion, Mr. James Dean." Smiling, he pointed his index finger at his frontal lobe with a screwing motion and knocked back another glass of wine.

After I had doled out a wad of inflation-bloated lire for dinner, we drifted back to the Albergo Real bar, where a crowd had gathered around Enzo Ferrari. He was nearly a head taller than his admirers, instantly identifiable with his shock of white hair and huge aquiline nose. He spoke in grand gestures in a Modenese dialect that might as well have been Swahili to me. Finishing off a glass of Lambrusco, he yelled "*andiamo!*" and headed for the front door.

"It's race time," said Diana. "This will be fun."

"The Biella Club is going to have a race," said Coltrin.

"The Biella Club?"

"A little social group of Ferrari and his cronies. Members of the Scuderia. Tavoni, Ugolini, Amarotti, Giberti. They eat, drink, and whore around together."

The little crowd burst onto the street, where a stack of bicycles leaned against the Hotel Fascia. Ferrari was the first to haul his huge frame aboard.

"Get on!" yelled Diana over the din, kicking off her high heels. "Five laps around the square," she said, pedaling into the swarm.

Not having ridden a bicycle since my college days, I threw a leg over and fell in near the back of the riders, now numbering nearly thirty. I had read that Italians were mad for cycling and that several of their greatest race drivers, including the immortal Tazio Nuvolari and Giuseppe Campari, had begun their competition careers on bicycles.

Pedaling hard, I swept into the first corner around the square. Traffic was mercifully light. A few bystanders began cheering as the field huffed and puffed down the wide avenue. Breathing hard, my stomach full of pasta, my bladder bulging with wine, I tried to keep up. After two laps I saw Diana glide to a stop in front of the hotel. Up front, half a lap ahead, Ferrari and a few lean young men pedaled mightily for the lead. I could see Coltrin, his skinny frame leaning into the handlebars, flailing to keep up.

As we slanted around a corner, Coltrin's bike clipped the curb and he took a wild tumble onto the hard, lumpy bricks of the Via Amelia. Taking advantage of his accident as an excuse to stop before my heart failed completely, I jerked up beside him. He lay groaning and holding his left ankle. "Damn, I think it's broken!" he howled.

A cursory examination by myself and several interested pedestrians indicated otherwise. A bad sprain, but no breakage. Coltrin hobbled back to the bar, where he downed two tumblers of Scotch and claimed to feel better.

The race completed, Ferrari and his crowd carried on a celebration at the bar. In the middle of the melee I spotted Diana, leaning on the arm of a rotund, balding man I did not recognize. The party went on, with me a silent bystander, until Ferrari and a small group of men broke away and headed for the grand staircase leading to the mezzanine.

Diana suddenly appeared and grabbed my hand. "This will be fun," she said, hauling me toward the stairs.

"More racing?" I laughed.

"Better yet," she said. "There's a guy in town named Alessandro deTomaso. Argentinian. Wild man. Escaped to Italy when he and some other revolutionary nuts apparently tried to bomb Peron's palace with a stolen airliner. Now he's here with his girlfriend, Elizabeth Haskell. Ford family. Big money. Everyone thinks he's got her on the line to back him in the car business. He and Enzo don't get along, as you might expect."

"So what's going on?"

"More Italian messing about." The group, numbering perhaps ten, including Diana and myself bringing up the rear, climbed more stairs to the second floor, where Ferrari made a gesture for silence. Skulking down a darkened hall, he stopped in front of room 202 and silently signaled to a small man behind him. He was handed a wad of newspapers, which he carefully stuffed under the door.

"Oh my God, he's going to light them," whispered Diana in horror.

Ferrari scratched a large kitchen match and set the papers on fire. Stepping back from the little inferno, a wide smile on his angular face, Ferrari waited in silence with his co-conspirators until the inevitable screams began issuing from inside the room.

The sound of furious stomping and the shrill voice of a woman ended with the door bursting open. A naked man in his thirties, well-muscled, his face stiff with rage, kicked the smoldering papers toward Ferrari. Behind him, frantically draping herself in a bed sheet, was Miss Haskell. DeTomaso made a move toward Ferrari, his fists clenched and in prize-fighter's stance, until he realized he was completely naked in front of an audience now bent over with laughter.

"Bastard! Bastard!" DeTomaso yelled hysterically, followed by curse words in a jumble of Italian and Spanish drowned out in the hilarity of his tormentors. Realizing that the confrontation was hopeless, deTomaso slammed the door.

Easing toward the stairs, Diana said, "Now you can see that the great Commendatore isn't quite the regal 'pope of the north' that some people envision." She stopped and, before I could say a word, pecked me on the cheek and said, "Now it's past my bedtime. Early day tomorrow at the Autodrome. Sleep tight."

She swept away down the darkened hallway, taking with her any fantasies I might have harbored about being asked to follow.

My room was small and airless. I thought of my lodgings in Le Mans, along with the sound and fury of the crash and the hysterical cries of the wounded. But they were soon overwhelmed by more pleasant thoughts of the beautiful woman who had brought me here. Images of Diana Logan would not leave me as I tried futilely to sleep and put an end to the erotic dreams about what might have been.

The next morning, as I finished a customary Italian breakfast of hard bread rolls and coffee strong enough to power a locomotive over the Alps, Coltrin hobbled in, employing a small cane to support his swollen ankle.

"You look like you just spent two years on the Russian front," I joked.

"Make it that and the Gulag and you'd be right," he said, lighting a cigarette. "Where's Diana?"

"Haven't seen her. Maybe she left early."

"No score last night?"

"*Niente.*"

"She's a hard one to figure."

"What's Castellotti doing here? I thought he was driving for Lancia," I said, changing the subject, but still wondering if he had been with her last night.

"Weird things going on. He was Ascari's teammate at Lancia, but now there's word that the company is in deep shit financially and, with the death of Ascari, the owner, Gianni Lancia, is rumored to be quitting racing. Rumor has it he'll turn over the race cars and equipment to Enzo. That would be a godsend, because his current cars aren't worth a shit against the Germans."

"I thought all the Ferraris were world-beaters. That's what you hear in America."

"His Grand Prix cars are rejiggered versions of a four-year-old design. And Mercedes-Benz is cleaning the table. Enzo is in a panic. Worse yet, he's about to lose his long-term tire contract with Pirelli. I think Castellotti is coming back with the Lancia deal. That could save his ass."

There was a guttural rumble outside the window, and a *carbinari* began waving traffic to the side of the street as he tooted frantically on his whistle.

"Here it comes, the big parade," said Coltrin.

"An Italian holiday?" I asked.

"Hell, no. Ferrari is headed for some testing at the Autodrome. They're driving the car to the track."

"A race car on the street?"

"No problem here. They paint a *prova* number on the tail, meaning it's an experimental car, and drive the damn thing in the middle of traffic. Like right now."

Snarling like a leashed tiger was a squat, long-nosed, single-seat racing car, its wire wheels glistening in the morning sunlight.

"The new Tipo five-five-five Super Squalo Grand Prix car, out for another test run," said Coltrin as the outrageous shape rolled up in front of the hotel, its engine howling at high revs to keep its spark plugs from fouling.

"Who's that driving?" I asked, spotting a gray-haired man with a blue beret tucked over his ears.

"Bazzi. Luigi Bazzi. Ferrari's longtime shop chief. His best friend and confidant. The only really steady hand in the whole operation. He'll drive the car to the track, but somebody else—maybe Castellotti—will actually drive it at speed."

Directly behind the Ferrari race car idled a large Fiat four-door sedan. In the passenger's seat was the unmistakable profile of Enzo Ferrari.

"That's Ferrari. But who's driving?"

"His chauffeur, Pepino Verdelli. Been with him for thirty years. Knows all his secrets. Ferrari seldom drives himself. After all, why should a man of his stature go anyplace without a chauffeur?" Coltrin asked, his voice thick with irony.

Behind the race car and the sedan came a ragged fleet of honking automobiles. Among them I spotted what seemed to be Diana's Mexico.

"That mob scene behind them. They must all be going to the track," I said. "Is that Diana's coupe?"

"Yeah, all the press and the mechanics are headed out there, too. That's Diana all right. She wouldn't miss a show like this. We'll head out there in a while. They won't start any serious running for another hour."

The Mexico drew up parallel with the window. Seated beside Diana was Eugenio Castellotti. I stared in shock, trying to deny my senses.

"Little Gino got himself a ride," chuckled Coltrin. "And you were wondering what happened last night?"

My stomach churning, I tried to make light of the scene. "Well, I guess he had to get to the track somehow. Better than taking a bus."

"A lot better."

Suddenly my interest in going to the Modena Autodrome disintegrated. It was the last place on earth I wanted to be. "I've changed my mind. I don't think I'll go to the track. There's a ten o'clock train to

Milan. If I catch it I can get a late-night flight to London. I'm wasting too much time here," I said weakly.

Coltrin looked at me, his eyes squinted knowingly. With a crooked smile he said, "So, ol' Gino's got himself a beautiful babe's Ferrari and the best you can do is a coach seat on an Italian train. But you're probably lucky. The more beautiful they are, the more trouble they are. You can quote me on that."

As I checked out of the Albergo Real, I couldn't resist leaving my business card. "Would you mind delivering this to Miss Diana Logan's room?" I asked the concierge. And then Coltrin drove me to the station and I headed back to California and an attempted re-entry into the real world.

CHAPTER ELEVEN

THE RISE OF THE "LITTLE BASTARD"

BY THE TIME I TUMBLED OFF AN AMERICAN AIRLINES DC-8 at Burbank airport, my whole world had changed. Two days of semi-sleep on a series of flights that had zigzagged from Milan to London's Heathrow to New York's Idlewild to California had left me semi-comotose. The incessant din of the big radial engines that powered airlines in the pre-jet days had left me with a piercing headache, while days would pass before my digestive track purged itself of airline food.

After a day of sleep in my apartment, I rose to face a the gray assault of smog that blanketed the Los Angeles basin. Relief came only after a Santa Ana wind boiled off the high desert, shoving the acrid clouds into the Pacific and replacing them with sunny, 100-degree temperatures. I tried to write, but my thoughts were too fragmented by the nightmare at Le Mans, the wacky frivolity at Modena and, worst of all, the incredible Diana.

She had been right about James Dean. *East of Eden* had opened to rave reviews for the sulky kid who played Steinbeck's Cal Trask with an intensity that rivaled another new Method actor, Marlon Brando—who had already attained stardom with his debut the year before in another Kazan masterpiece, *On the Waterfront. East of Eden* opened at New York's Astor Theatre in all its Cinemascope grandeur on March 9, 1955. No less a superstar than Marilyn Monroe was stationed in the lobby to hand out programs to the black-tied VIPs who had been invited to the premiere. The reviews were mixed, mostly due to the complex plot, which offered Kazan little time to broaden the characters played by veterans Raymond Massey, Burl Ives, and Julie Harris. But Dean's performance as the wayward, outcast son elicited raves. Said the master French director and cinema immortal François Truffaut in his *Cahiers du Cinema* review, "James Dean has succeeded in giving commercial viability to a film that would otherwise have scarcely qualified, in breathing life into an abstraction, in interesting a vast audience in moral problems treated in an unusual way . . . this shortsighted star prevents him from smiling, and the smile drawn from him by dint of patient effort constitutes a victory."

One American movie critic exclaimed that Dean radiated the "innocent grace of a captive panther," while another labeled him the possessor of "bastard robustness."

A local horse trainer, movie wrangler, and occasional stunt man was amazed at Dean's performance. While shooting *Eden* in Steinbeck's home town of Salinas, Monty Roberts had been employed by Kazan to work with Dean in an effort to acquaint the small-town Indiana kid with the ways of the West. Dean was an adept student for the man who would rise to world fame of the creator of a revolutionary form of passive horse training called "the language of Equus" and who would be the basis for the Robert Redford character in the hit movie *The Horse Whisperer.* Dean was quick to learn complex rope tricks like the butterfly, but to Roberts, who had worked on numerous films, including the "Red Ryder" serials and "My Friend Flicka," Dean seemed to possess no talent as an actor. They became good friends, but Dean was so introverted, so blank an emotional canvas, that Roberts seriously doubted Kazan's judgment in enlisting the young man for the starring role. During the Salinas shooting, Dean bunked with Roberts and his new wife, Pat, in their small spread near the local airport. A strong bond developed between the trio, but Roberts remained skeptical about Dean's future in the movie business. One day, he was invited to watch the daily uncut film. He watched in stunned silence as the explosive personality of James Dean lit up the screen.

So introverted off the stage and screen that he seemed talentless to Roberts and others, Dean's performance in *East of Eden* was so vivid, so electrifying, so overwhelmingly commercial that Jack Warner and company immediately signed him to a long-term contract and announced that he would star in *Rebel Without a Cause,* while plans were laid to give him major roles in productions of *Giant, Somebody Up There Likes Me,* and *Left-Handed Gun.* (The latter two films would later be handed off to Paul Newman.)

With the Warner Brothers publicity machine in top gear, Dean was billed not as an existential outsider but as a bobby-soxer idol in the mold of Tab Hunter, Robert Wagner, Rock Hudson, and Paul Newman. Dean, deeply serious about his acting, hated the vapid typecasting and resisted Hollywood culture. He was living with his father, Winton Dean, a widowed dental technician, at 1667 South Bundy (a street to become infamous forty-five years later, thanks to O. J. Simpson) and was becoming increasingly interested in sports car racing as a way to escape the glitz. Following his mother's early death in 1940, when he was nine years old, Dean had been moved to the tiny Indiana town of Fairmount, where his aunt Ortense and her husband, Marcus Whitman, raised him through high school. Riding his Whizzer motorbike and driving a friend's "souped-up" 1934

Plymouth through a series of ess-bends they dubbed "Suicide Curve," Dean quickly displayed the balance and daring to become the fastest driver of the lot.

This scrawny high school basketball and track star from Fairmount, Indiana, exploded on the American scene as the newest anti-hero, radiating repressed, volatile anger and rejecting the increasingly plastic and vinyl "good life" permeating the national psyche. At the same time that a gaudy group of writers and poets were gathering in Greenwich Village and Haight-Ashbury coffeehouses and calling themselves Beatniks, young male actors like Brando, Dean, Newman, and Sal Mineo brilliantly expressed the latent restlessness, alienation, and anxiety that helped trigger the angry, drug-fed revolution of the hippies, which lay ahead in the next decade.

Dean had come to Hollywood in 1954, carrying his meager belongings in a paper bag, after starring in an adaption of Andre Gide's *The Immoralist* on Broadway and making a mark in a number of television dramas. In April he signed with Warner Brothers for the *East of Eden* part, receiving an advance of $700. He used some of his newfound wealth to purchase a used MG TD roadster and began dating Italian starlet Pier Angeli. The romance ended when the dazzling brunette married singer Vic Damone in late November of that year. By then, Dean had become the source of enormous buzz in the film colony and had no trouble finding dates—including the exquisite German actress Julie Harris, Eartha Kitt, Ursula Andress, and Liz "Dizzy" Sheridan, who would find stardom forty years later playing Jerry Seinfeld's mother on television.

His first motorcycle was a small single-cylinder purchased in Indiana, but he soon traded up to a series of faster, British-built Nortons. He then moved on to a larger English Triumph, like the one Marlon Brando had ridden in the Stanley Kramer hit of 1954, *The Wild One*. Brando's role as the outcast leader of a motorcycle gang that terrorized a small California town (based on the actual Hollister riot of July 4, 1947) had introduced the American public to disaffected youth, and surely influenced Dean's acting style, if not his entire public persona.

Using his Truimph motorcycle and later his MG, Dean honed his skills on the notorious Mulholland Drive, where he vented his frustrations with the movie business and what he believed to be its crass commercialism. In late May 1954, he wrote a girlfriend in New York named Barbara Glenn about his new possession. "Honey!! A new addition has been added to the Dean family. I got a red '53 MG (milled head, etc. hot engine) My sex pours itself into fast curves, broadslides and broodings; drags, etc. You have plenty of competition now. My motorcycle, my MG and my girl. I have been sleeping with my MG. We make it together. (signed) Honey."

Before *East of Eden* had been released, Dean began studying for the *Rebel* role, and on March 1, 1955, traded the MG for a new, 1,500 cc Porsche 356 Speedster-S roadster—a lightweight German sports car built by the son of Volkswagen creator Ferdinand Porsche. Dean became a fixture on Mulholland, sometimes running the nearly forty-mile round trip on the insanely convoluted roadway as often as twenty times a week.

One of his regular passengers was Lew Bracker, an insurance salesman who Dean had met in the Warner Brothers commissary restaurant. The same age as the young actor, Bracker was loyal and unthreatening. His connection to the movie business came through his cousin, Leonard Rosenman, who had composed the music for *East of Eden*. Bracker, who was driving a Buick convertible when he met Dean, was soon drawn into the world of high-speed driving and sports cars.

Bracker accompanied his friend to Palm Springs on March 26, where the California Sports Car Club was staging an amateur road race on a 2.3-mile circuit laid out on the runways of the local airport. Dean drove his new Porsche to the fashionable high-desert resort and entered a "novice" race for the first time. There being no formal training required for racing in those days, Dean simply dropped the Porsche's convertible top, snapped a seat belt in place, donned a helmet, and went racing.

The skills he had demonstrated on Mulholland were instantly apparent on the racetrack. Wearing glasses to correct his nearsightedness, Dean started sixth in the twenty-one car field. Before halfway in the six-lap race, he had powered his way into a solid lead. When the checkered flag fell, he had a full straightaway lead, with the second-place car barely in sight.

After an evening of celebration with Bracker, starlet Lilli Kardell, and new friend Lance Reventlow, the megarich son of Woolworth heiress Barabra Hutton and a fledgling race driver himself, Dean made ready for Sunday's twenty-seven lap "feature" race for sports cars under 1,500 cc. Again Dean was in his element, running an easy third behind a pair of lightweight MG specials driven by veterans Ken Miles and Cy Yedor. When the race was finished, it was announced by Cal Club officials that Englishman Miles's "Flying Shingle" machine had violated some obscure technical rule and had been disqualified. Dean was thus elevated to second place in the final standings. He and his retinue returned to Los Angeles that evening with first- and second-place trophies for his weekend's labors and a rising confidence that he had legitimate talent as a race driver.

Working closely with Bill Hickman, the expert stunt driver he had met on the *Rebel* set, Dean enthusiastically reran his Mulholland route to develop smoothness and rhythm. Two weeks later, he and Bracker drove the Porsche to Bakersfield's Minter Field airport, a defunct World War II B-24 bomber base. Saturday's six-lap qualifying race was run in a pouring rain that lashed the normally arid city. Driving with considerable alacrity on the slick pavement against larger and more powerful cars, Dean finished third overall and won his class for 1,500 cc sports cars. This qualified him for Sunday's main event. His chief rival in the thirty-lap was veteran Springer Jones, also driving a Porsche Speedster. Jones's experience paid off, and he was able to beat Dean to the finish line by half a car length.

Nevertheless, his performance won him grudging respect among the Cal Club crowd. Over the years, numerous movie types had tried racing and failed. But James Dean was different. He came to the races to compete, not to pose in the pits. He remained reclusive, seeking no attention or special treatment. This gained him admiration from the skeptics in the sport. He would later tell a friend, "The only time I really feel alive is when I'm racing." Based on his easy adaptation to the environment of speed, noise, heat, and danger, there was no reason to doubt him.

As shooting for *Rebel without a Cause* began in late March, it was almost invitable that a torrid affair would develop between Dean and co-star Natalie Wood. While studio publicists touted an off-screen romance, it was actually more of a brief, intense shipboard romance between the pair that culminated, according to Dean, in the Porsche on Mulholland Drive. The following morning he slouched into the Warner Brothers commissary for breakfast with Bracker and playwright Joe Hymans. Lounging in a chair and lighting a cigarette, Dean said softly, "Well, you guys, it can be done."

"What are you talking about?" asked Bracker.

"They said a Porsche is too cramped to get it on with a girl," said Dean. "That's bullshit. If you don't believe me, ask Natalie."

There was a faint smugness in his voice, since it was well known that both the director of *Rebel*, Nicholas Ray, and co-star Dennis Hopper were in pursuit of the comely Miss Wood.

Principal photography for *Rebel without a Cause* ended in Los Angeles on May 25, permitting Dean to rush north with the Porsche to Santa Barbara where a Memorial Day weekend of Cal Club races was scheduled for the 2.2-mile airport course on the edge of the city. Dean planned to run on Saturday in a six-lap qualifying race and in the one-hour final on Sunday for cars 1,500 cc and smaller. He was involved in a blind drawing for starting position and pulled the number 18 out of the hat, placing him deep in the field. By the second lap, he had gained fourth place. Then a car spun in front of him, forcing him off the course and into a pile of haybales lining the circuit. Driving with his usual fury, he had regained fourth place when the Porsche's engine gave way under the pounding. With one of its four pistons badly fried, the Porsche was sidelined for the weekend and ultimately towed back to Johnny Von Neumann's Competition Motors on Vine Street in Hollywood for repairs. The car would be placed in the hands of the shop's finest mechanic, a German transplant named Rolf Wutherich who had prepared race cars for the Porsche factory to be run in some of Europe's most challenging races.

Dean then packed up his gear and headed to the desolation of west Texas, where, in the tiny village of Marfa, director George Stevens and crew had constructed an elaborate set for *Giant*. Fearing the worst for the now cocky young race driver, Stevens had written into Dean's contract that he was forbidden to compete in any sort of motor sports event until shooting for the immense production ended in mid-September.

In the meantime, Bracker had been bitten with the racing bug. He had purchased his own Porsche Speedster and was embarking on a career that would bring him several Cal Club championships in the ensuing years. Monty Roberts joined Dean on the Marfa set, and many hours were consumed in conversation about the actor's desire to purchase a horse ranch in the Salinas area. Roberts and his wife, Pat, were assigned the task of locating property to fulfill Dean's increasing rapture with Western cowboy life. On the *Giant* set, he spent many hours in the steamy Texas sunshine demonstrating the rope tricks he had learned from Roberts.

The Los Angeles summer was cooler and cloudier than usual, which some weather experts blamed on the increasing smog that was blocking out sunlight. Below the dingy, foul-smelling cloud layer, the strange, outrageous world of rock and roll was driving conventional big bands out of business, while the movie studios clung to wide-screen Cinemascope as their only hope to repel the exploding interest in television. The two new threats were linked when a pouty, sideburned, hip-swiveling kid from Memphis appeared on Ed Sullivan's top-rated CBS variety show. Before the year was out, Elvis Presley's "Hound Dog," and "Don't Be Cruel" would elevate him to superstar status rivaling that of the aging Frank Sinatra.

"Elvis the Pelvis" soon displaced Bill Haley—whose "Rock around the Clock" was the first rock and roll hit—as the latest outrage to middle America. Already, millions of teenage boys were emulating the fashion of Marlon Brando in *The Wild One*, with leather jackets, Levi's, motorcycle boots, and T-shirts, and the dreaded, slicked-back "duck's-ass" haircut. While "decent" young men still favored brush cuts, button-down shirts, khakis, and white bucks, the trend was clear—a new and shocking cultural shift was under way in the nation.

The *Los Angeles Herald Examiner* had openly hated automobile racing ever since the 1930s, when its boss, William Randolph Hearst, had created shocking headlines whenever a driver died or was injured. The *Examiner* remained true to form when it trumpeted the death of Jerry Hoyt on July 10. The Indiana native, who had won the pole position at the 1955 Indianapolis 500, had embarked on a barnstorming tour of the Midwest with a friend and Indy winner Bob Sweikert in a matched pair of black Offy-powered sprint cars. Running in a ten-lap heat race on the half-mile Oklahoma State Fairgrounds dirt track, Hoyt's car hooked a light pole exiting a corner and flipped. The young driver, unprotected by a roll bar or cage, received massive head injuries that took his life the following day. More cries rose up from the Hearst editors—and a few legislators—that the sport ought to be banned.

Detroit ignored the cry. Ford's new Thunderbird, billed as a "personal car" with more luxuries than the Chevrolet Corvette, featured an optional 198 horsepower V-8. Chevrolet countered with a V-8-powered Corvette, rated at 195 horsepower, but the luxury and power accessories of the T-bird overwhelmed the noisy, hard-riding two-seater from General Motors. While both were reviled by the sports car crowd as overweight, poor-handling "Detroit iron," the Thunderbird was an instant hit with the public. When the sales figures for 1955 were finally tabulated, 16,155 Thunderbirds had been sold, while a mere 675 Corvettes rolled off Chevrolet dealers' lots.

As horsepower ratings rose toward 200 for even the most mundane sedans, the national media began to fret about the increasing rates of death and injury on the nation's highways. The year would end with 36,600 Americans dying in automobile crashes, over 3,000 more than in 1954. Part of this was due to 43.6 million more miles driven (561,963,000 vs. 605,646,000) thanks both to the rising prosperity of the nation and cheap, stable gasoline prices.

The death rate rose slightly, to 6.06 fatalities per 100 million miles driven—far below the record high of 45.33 per 100 million set in 1909, but way above the less than 1 per 100 million to be obtained in the early twenty-first century, thanks to advances in automotive technology, improved roads, and severe crackdowns on drunk driving.

In 1955, when seat belts were essentially unknown in passenger cars, airbags unthought of, tires, suspensions, and brakes essentially unchanged for twenty years, and Interstate highways in their infancy, the fact that the exploding performance of high-powered cars did not produce even more carnage is a testament to the innate good sense of the American driving public.

Concerns over the drumbeat of criticism from the national press about racing deaths and highway safety prompted AAA president Andrew J. Sordoni to announce on August 2 that the American Automobile Association would cease all involvement with motor sports by the end of the year. Its sanctioning of major American races had dated to 1902, and the news sent a ripple of panic through the Indianapolis establishment. There were, however, smiles of satisfaction at the Daytona Beach headquarters of Bill France's struggling NASCAR. A gap would have to be filled, and initially it was believed that France might step in to fill it. But Tony Hulman, the owner of the Indianapolis Motor Speedway, was not about to put his legendary event into the hands of a former Florida gas station operator and his gang of bootleggers. He hastily pulled together a meeting of Midwest business associates, wealthy race team owners, and promoters and formed the United States Auto Club, a nonprofit body that would assume sanctioning of the 500 and other races on the former AAA championship trail.

After having lunch at the Brown Derby in mid-August with friends in the movie business, I drove the MG back to Studio City, where I found a business card stuck in my door. It was my own. On the back, written in a decidedly feminine hand, was the message, "Tried to call. Back in town. Love to hear from you. Diana."

A Hispanic maid answered my phone call to Diana's Beverly Hills home, an elegant Georgian manse on North Beverly Drive in the so-called flats of the posh city. "Miss Logan not home. I take your number," she said, struggling with her new language.

Her call came an hour later.

"Sorry I missed you in Modena," she said brightly.

"It seemed like you were pretty tied up and I had to leave anyway."

She ignored the comment and said, "I just got back. Called twice but no answer. So I came by and left your card. You're a hard one to track down."

"That makes two of us."

She laughed easily and said, "I've got an idea. Remember when I told you about James Dean and you and Peter scoffed?"

"So you called up to gloat?"

"My dad was right. He's gonna be a monster. The studio is having a private screening of *Rebel Without a Cause* this evening. Want to go?"

"Let me check my schedule. There's a dinner with Zanuck at Chasen's about my new screenplay. A date with Marilyn Monroe. And a discussion about my secret inheritance from John Paul Getty. But to hell with 'em. I'll cancel. Where and when?"

"I'm flattered. I hope Marilyn won't be jealous. The Coach & Horses for a drink at six. On Sunset, three or four blocks west of LaBrea. Veddy English in a Hollywood kind of way. But fun."

I hunted up a freshly laundered button-down shirt and a decent pair of gray flannel slacks, and polished up my Bass Weejuns in an attempt to make a presentable appearance for the lovely Miss Logan and the movie crowd that was bound to show up for this screening.

The Coach & Horses was a mass of red leather, dark wooden beams, and wrought-iron fixtures, as Diana had inferred. Out front were parked a few sports cars—a Cadillac-Allard, a new Alfa Romeo Giuiletta coupe and a shimmering silver Mercedes-Benz gullwing. The valets had been instructed to park the trio curbside to amplify the restaurant's reputation as a hangout for the sports car crowd.

My MG was unceremoniously hustled to the back lot as I made my way to the bar. The chatter involved gossip about millionaire John Edgar dominating California sports car racing with his sub rosa team of professionals, headed by a transplanted Texas chicken farmer named Carroll Shelby. Diana arrived. I played it cool.

"Long time no see," I said.

"Busy, busy," she said, laughing.

"So what's the plan?" I asked, as I ordered her a tall vodka tonic.

"We'll drive over to Warner's in the valley and then there's a party at Nick Ray's."

"Nick Ray's? Sorry, but the name . . . "

"The *Rebel* director. Hot property in this town. At least this week."

"A short shelf life in this business," I said.

"Tell me about it."

"Still got the Ferrari?" I asked.

"Sure. It came in a week ago on Flying Tigers."

"You had it flown over from Italy?"

"Doesn't everybody?"

"No. I actually had my last Ferrari brought over on my private yacht. Airlines are too crassly commercial for me," I said.

"A little sarcasm there?" she asked.

"Naw, we Communists all think like that."

Her face darkened. "Are you on the blacklist?"

I laughed hard. "Me and Dalton Trumbo. Actually, not quite. Us upstate New Yorkers are all trained from childhood to be rock-ribbed Republicans."

The banter drifted on through two more drinks before I followed the blunt tail of her Ferrari over the Cahuenga Pass into the San Fernando Valley. A zigzag of streets into Burbank and through the Warner Brothers gates off Olive. Diana waved my MG through and we parked in the executive lot on the edge of a row of white stucco Bauhaus buildings. I had expected to rub elbows with a mass of Hollywood celebrities, but instead found myself easing into a leather chair in a small private theater filled with a collection of ordinary businesspeople—theater chain owners, middling Warner's executives, salespeople, and selected nobodies like myself. It would be one of dozens of private screenings of a rough cut of *Rebel*. The only celebrity of any kind was the director, Nicholas Ray, a forty-four year-old with curly hair and the edgy good looks of a movie tough guy. Ray spoke briefly, explaining that the final version of the picture was weeks away and that some scenes would either be cut or color-edited, while voice matching, sound effects, background music, and other details had to be attended to before the planned release in October.

Ray had gained good reviews the year before with the Sterling Hayden Western, *Johnny Guitar*. He had co-written *Rebel*, which ended up a personal favority of his, with playwright Irving Schulman, seeking to expand on the theme of angry young men that formed the core of Stanley Kramer's *The Wild One.*

I watched Dean's pouting presence overwhelm the picture. His race against a rival in the "chickie run" provided the centerpiece of the action, along with a final knife fight staged on the steps of the Los Angeles Planetarium. Those scenes provided the action sequences needed for the great mass of unwashed male moviegoers while Dean's romance with Natalie Wood was sure to please the female audience. The story line involved restless, disaffected teenagers rebelling against the conventions of middle-class life—"the bad boy from a good family," as the Warner's publicists promoted it. *Rebel* was avant-garde in the context of the mid-1950s. Surely other young actors might have handled the Dean role, but it was his incendiary, introverted rage that carried the picture. As the lights came up, a round of cheers and applause filled the room. "Didn't I tell you?" said Diana as she tugged my arm. "He's gonna break a million hearts," I said, little knowing how right I would turn out to be.

Nick Ray's elegant, sprawling, ranch-style house, complete with the obligatory swimming pool and tennis court, was on Abington, halfway up the mountain in the better section of Beverly Hills. He had made it in the business with such hits as the 1949 Humphrey Bogart drama *Knock on Any Door*, and was one of Warner's prized contract directors. As it turned out, *Rebel* would be his high-water mark in the industry, followed by a slow descent into B-picture limbo with his sexpot actress wife, Gloria Graham.

We took Laurel Canyon over the mountain, with the MG straining mightily in every gear to keep up with Diana's Mexico coupe. Valet parking awaited at Ray's curbside, and I handed off the keys to a Mexican attendant who acted as if he was climbing into a farm tractor. In the heady world of California cars, MG roadsters ranked somewhere between Studebaker sedans and Yellow Cabs. As we walked up the driveway, the guttural rumble of an unmuffled Porsche exhaust rose in the distance. A white Speedster, its top down, screeched to a halt. On its door, the black number 33 was neatly pasted in place, marking it as a car that had been raced.

"How about that," said Diana. "The star has arrived."

The tousled brown hair, the sharp chin, and the heavy brows were instantly recognizable. A cigarette dangling from his lips, James Dean slid out of the seat and slouched into the house. He was shorter than I had expected, no more than five feet six, and carried himself with a shuffling, head-down walk as if seeking anonymity.

"Can you believe it? There he is," said Diana, breathing hard.

"I thought you said he was in Texas shooting *Giant*."

"He was, but they fly back and forth. Must be a break in his shooting. I hear he's leased a house in Sherman Oaks. So now he's part of the Hollywood scene."

"He looks more like one of the parking attendants."

"Jealous?"

"If that's the new sex symbol, I'm Rudolph Valentino."

"You saw him on screen. Totally different. You'll see when we meet him," she said, grabbing my arm and heading for the door.

We plunged into a sea of beautiful people. Perfectly coiffed blond heads bobbed above tanned faces and flawless bodies. Black waiters in tuxedos drifted among the flotsam of perfect human forms with trays of drinks, while in a corner of the large, pastel-colored living room a balding man played show tunes on a grand piano roughly the size of Catalina Island. Diana identified him as Leonard Rosenman, the composer for *East of Eden*. Jim Backus, the character actor who would later gain fame as the screen voice for the myopic cartoon character Mr. Magoo, eased among the mob with a pudgy, soft-faced woman on his arm that had to be his wife. The rest remained anonymous—production people, wannabe actors and actresses, studio moguls and the inevitable pilot fish who floated in such waters around the world.

Diana chattered her way through the crowd until Dean's small frame came into view. He was speaking with a skinny young man with a large nose, curly black hair, and pouty lips that I recognized as Sal Mineo, another of the nouveau punksters starring with Dean in *Rebel*. They were in intense conversation, their heads nearly touching while both dragged on cigarettes hand-wrapped in brown paper. Marijuana, "Mary Jane," "dope," "weed," "pot," etc. had first been brought to the public's attention with the 1936 film *Reefer Madness* which had hysterically depicted how a single toke on a so-called joint could send a teenager on a suicidal death spiral. Twenty years later, most American kids were still swilling beer, with widespread use of drugs awaiting the counterculture revolution of the next decade. The film colony had long experimented with morphine, cocaine, amphetamines and marijuana; Robert Mitchum had been briefly jailed for his involvement with the dreaded "weed" in 1949.

Automobile racing seemed on the surface to be an activity that would not tolerate even the slightest loss of reflexes, yet drugs had intruded over the years. Achille Varzi, the great Italian Grand Prix driver, had become addicted to morphine in the mid-1930s, while Indianapolis driver Billy Winn was, at around the same time, known to use amphetamines or "speed." During the pioneering days of the sport, before World War I, Grand Prix drivers Jules Goux and Vittorio Lancia were believed to have refreshed themselves with champagne during pit stops, while in the mid-1960s a scandal hit the lesser leagues of European open-wheel racing when the death of Frenchman Bo Pitard revealed widespread use of speed among young, crazily competitive drivers.

I watched as Dean and Mineo dragged on their joints until the glowing tips nearly burnt their fingers. Then they tossed the butts into a nearby ashtray and separated with a strangely affectionate touch of the fingers that left me wondering if the rumored bisexuality of Dean was in fact true.

Diana seized the moment to rush up to him, and made a quick, cursory introduction. He eyed me, head down, eyes shifting.

"Diana tells me you're into cars," he said.

"Yeah. A little. I do some writing. I was at Le Mans."

Dean nodded and took a drag on a freshly lit Chesterfield. "Bad shit," he said.

"The papers say you're gonna start racing after *Giant* is finished," I said.

"Bet your ass. Stevens has me locked down until late September. Then I'm going. And fuck the studio."

"You gonna stay with Porsche?"

"Yeah. I tried to buy one of the new Lotuses. Cool. Lightweight. Quick. But they're fucking me over with getting one in time so Von Neumann's got my Spyder coming."

He was talking about Johnny Von Neumann, the transplanted Austrian who ran Competition Motors on Vine Street in Hollywood, where Dean had purchased his current Speedster.

"Another Porsche?"

"A 550 Spyder. He's got five of 'em coming from Germany. Runs like a raped ape. They're winning everything in the small-displacement classes in Europe. It'll be a winner. With any luck I'll have it by the end of September. There's a Cal Club race in Salinas on the thirtieth. Gonna try to make it. Twin cams. Alloy body. Runs 130 easy. Really quick for a little car."

Dean was relaxing, away from the artifice of the movie industry and speaking about a subject he truly cared about. He seemed to become a normal human being, released from his role-playing. Or was he merely assuming yet another role in his chameleon-like repertoire? That of hard-core car nut and race driver?

"I'd like to see the thing when it comes in. Maybe do a story on it," I said.

"Hell, come to the race if you want. Me and a bunch of guys are planning to go, if we can get our schedules set and the movie is over on time."

"Von Neumann do you a deal?" I asked, figuring that movie people got discounts on everything.

"Your ass," Dean scoffed. "Johnny doesn't cut a deal for anybody. Guys are lined up to get one of those Porsches. Seven grand on the barrel head. Cash money. Yeah, he'll cut me a little slack on the Speedster by offering me three grand on the trade-in. But still, seven grand is a lot of money."

He was scanning the room like most of the guests, who, while seeming to be in deep conversation, were constantly shifting their gaze to determine if an upgrade to more important, more prestigious, more potentially rewarding partners might be possible. A tall blonde woman eased up to him and spoke in a soft German accent. I recognized her as Ursula Andress, with whom Dean had been carrying on a much-publicized affair. "See you in Salinas," he said, turning away and into the grasp of the rangy beauty.

The *Hollywood Reporter* would soon quip that "Jimmy Dean is studying German so that he can fight with Ursula Andress in two languages."

A buzz swept through the room. Heads turned toward a couple. I recognized the blonde with the large bust and the wide mouth. It was Zsa Zsa Gabor, one of the famed Gabor sisters, who, along with their mother, had gained reputations as aristocratic courtesans in every city in the civilized world. The man beside her was less familiar— small, with a flat nose and a dark complexion.

"Oh my god," gasped Diana. "It's them."

"Them?"

"Zsa Zsa and Rubi. Don't you read the papers? Where have you been?"

"I don't get out much," I said. "But would that be Porfirio Rubirosa?"

"Nice guess," she laughed. "But you're right."

Porfirio Rubirosa was the former-son-in-law of longtime Dominican Republic dictator Rafael Trujillo. Rubirosa had risen to power in 1932 by marrying the ruthless dictator's daughter, Flor de Oro, "Gold Flower." When the marriage broke up in 1937, Rubirosa remained a favorite of Trujillo, who launched him on a career as an international playboy, polo star, sometime diplomat, and legendary lover of rich and beautiful women. In the late 1940s and early 1950s, he shattered world records as a Lothario by marrying tobacco heiress Doris Duke and Woolworth millionairess Barbara Hutton for brief but highly profitable interludes.

Rubirosa considered himself a racing driver and was a prized customer of Enzo Ferrari. He had competed both in Europe and in California amateur races, where posing in the pits and staying out of the way of the more serious competitors appeared to be his primary goals. "Rubi," as he was known, had caused a major tizzy in the film colony by luring the beautiful Zsa Zsa away from her actor husband, George Sanders. Their affair, tempestuous and punctuated by screaming matches and slugfests, would be the source of Hollywood gossip for years to come.

"They're trying to make a movie together," said Diana as the couple vamped their way into the crowd.

"I didn't know they could act."

"They can't. They call it *Western Affair* and Rubi plays a bar owner and elegant gambler. Kind of like Bogey in *Casablanca*. But they can't get studio financing and the immigration people are giving him trouble about working here as long as he's a foreign national. My father says the whole thing is a joke."

"The little bastard must have something going for him if he can hook all those babes."

"He's a legend."

"Meaning what?'

Diana brushed my crotch. It was a feint, an easy move that offered surprising encouragement. "Meaning that the next time you're in a good restaurant and the waiter hands you a large pepper mill, there may be people in the dinner party who'll call it a 'Rubirosa.'"

"You mean . . . "

"A legend."

"Hung like a bull moose. Is that what you're trying to say?"

"You could put it that way," she said, smiling.

I pondered Diana's revelation as Rubirosa and his spectacular girlfriend mingled. Like countless so-called gentlemen sportsmen, he considered motor racing to be an essential component of his social dossier. He was able to afford high-priced cars like Ferraris and Maseratis and to compete in racing at a relatively high level, depending simply on the superior power and handling of his machinery to outperform poorer competitors. While he had true skill at polo, which demanded some athletic ability, driving a racing car at modest speeds was easily achieved. But when maximum performance—called driving at $10/10^{th}$ in the trade—was demanded, only the best professionals could rise to the top. Poseurs and part-timers, the ones that the Indianapolis pros called "strokers and brokers"—like Rubirosa—could play at motor racing but never win.

The party gained in intensity as Rosenman labored at the grand piano, his tinkling finally giving way to the general din of conversation. Defeated, he left his bench and closed the keyboard. Unnoticed in a corner, four young men had installed a set of drums and were quietly tuning a bass and two guitars.

The apparent leader was a gawky kid wearing horn-rimmed glasses topped by a shiny pile of Brylcreemed hair. Like the other three, he was dressed in an Ivy League–style three-button blue blazer. On a signal, Nicholas Ray stood on the vacated piano bench and called for attention. After a few lusty shouts, the room noise dropped to a soft background murmur and Ray began: "Ladies and gentlemen, as you may know, a new kind of music is sweeping the nation. Bill Haley and the Comets started it with "Rock around the Clock," and in doing so, coined the phrase 'rock and roll.' There are others coming along, including Elvis Presley, whom some of you may have heard about. But tonight I'd like to introduce four boys from Lubbock, Texas, who have just signed a big contract with Decca Records. Many in the business think they're on their way to the big time. Please give a big Hollywood welcome to J. I. Allison on drums, Joe B. Maudlin on bass, Nicki Sullivan on rhythm guitar, and the leader of the group on lead guitar and vocal, Mr. Buddy Holly and the Crickets."

The quartert of skinny kids from nowhere in Texas powered up with what was to become their trademark song, "That'll Be the Day," which had a hammering beat that soon had the crowd shimmying and foot-pounding in frenzied participation. At nineteen years of age, Charles Hardin Holly was a prodigy, whose compositions, including his rock and roll classic, "Peggy Sue," would elevate him to immortality in the music world. Sadly, his pyrotechnic career would end in a frozen cornfield near Clear Lake, Iowa, a mere four years later.

Automobiles would play a role in only one early rock and roll tune—"Maybelline," released by the brilliant St. Louis guitarist Chuck Berry in May 1955:

> As I was motoring over the hill
> I saw Maybelline in a Coupe de Ville
> Power down the open road.
> But nothin' outrun my V-8 Ford

Buddy Holly and the Crickets played four hard-driving sets that lasted until well after midnight. Exhausted, their tidy blue blazers soaked with sweat, the foursome gave up in the face of deafening cheers and demands for more. It was over, and the crowd drifted back to drinking and talking.

"That was fabulous. Holly is an unbelievable talent. They're already talking about him doing a movie," said Diana, brushing back her hair, which had become frazzled with enthusiasm. She grabbed my arm. "Let's get out of here," she said.

"My place or yours?" I asked.

"Oh god, give it up," she laughed. "That line went out with Gable and Lombard. Just follow me."

We left the party, still at full din, and raced back south on Laurel Canyon and into a night that I will remember forever.

CHAPTER TWELVE

CROSSROADS
OF DESTINY

I GOT UP LATER THAN USUAL. JUANITA, THE MEXICAN maid, offered me a cup of coffee while Diana slept. She admitted to being an illegal, having crossed the border from Tijuana two years earlier and hoping to seek citizenship once her English improved. Aside from Diana, myself, and Juanita, the house was deserted. Diana's parents were on vacation in Italy, which had opened the door for my late-night arrival and a magical interlude with their daughter. She was beyond my wildest dreams.

Seated beside the pool, with only the distant murmur of traffic on busy Wilshire Boulevard to the south breaking the morning solitude, I reflected on my good fortune. A struggling writer hooks up with a Hollywood beauty for a night of insane passion. Then she eased onto the patio, wearing only a terry cloth bathrobe and a wide smile.

"You were up early," she mused.

"You had me up all night," I said.

"So I noticed. How could I forget? You were wonderful," she said, smiling.

"You weren't so bad yourself."

"Thanks. I guess you bring out the best in a girl."

"When you're a house guest, you have to do your best to please the hostess," I said.

"Hump the hostess. I've heard about that," she laughed.

The conversation was going nowhere. Diana took a long sip of coffee and looked away. "So what now?" she asked.

"Back to work, I guess. Up to my garret and writing. What about you?"

"I'm leaving today for New York. Gwen Verdon is opening in the musical *Damn Yankees*. Lots of parties. It'll be the big hit of the Broadway season."

"So maybe I'll see you when you get back."

"Sure. That'll be fun."

And so it ended. At least for the moment. Diana Logan was on the move. Her life was an endless roundelay of parties, premieres, intercontinental travel, and elbow-rubbing with the rich and famous. Later in the day, following a long and amusing lunch at Musso and Franks, she dropped me back at Nick Ray's house, where I retrieved my MG. From there it was a descent, socially, psychologically, and financially, from Beverly Hills into the mundane world of Studio City, where reality greeted me like a stray dog.

As September arrived, humid and hot, the Yankees and the Brooklyn Dodgers were headed for the World Series. The Dodgers, who would soon shock the baseball world by defecting to Los Angeles, had already rattled the establishment to its very foundations in 1947 by hiring the first black player, the brilliant Jackie Robinson. A supremely talented athlete, Robinson was destined to lead the Dodgers to their first World Series victory later that October, beating the hated crosstown Yankees four games to three and thereby shaking what was believed by many to be a curse against the beloved "Bums."

Sadly, the savagery in racing would not let up. A major sports car race was run in early September on the Irish Dundrod circuit, a 7.4-mile patchwork of narrow public roads closed off for competition. Many of the same machines that had raced at Le Mans were entered; the lethal Mercedes-Benz SLRs for Moss and Fangio, Hawthorn's winning D-type Jaguar, Castellotti in his Ferrari, and other top-ranked European professionals. Also in the field was the usual collection of gentlemen amateurs, semi-professionals, and struggling nobodies in manifestly slower cars.

News of the race was carried in two paragraphs in the *Los Angeles Herald Examiner* under the headline, "Three Die in Irish Car Race."

A cluster of slower cars often ridiculed as "back-markers" were heading down a straightaway toward a narrow cleft slicing through peat banks and a blind drop-off called "Deer's Leap." Two of the machines, driven by veterans Ken Wharton and Jim Mayer, had tried to squeeze past a Mercedes-Benz gullwing coupe being driven lazily by a French aristocrat and rank amateur, the Vicomte de Barry. As they poured over the brow and into the trough, Mayer's Cooper was squeezed by de Barry's Mercedes up an earthen bank. In a wink, Mayer slammed into a concrete post on the roadside and his car disintegrated in a ball of fire. Two more cars, driven by the experienced Peter Jopp and a rising British star, Bill Smith, sailed into the melee. Somehow Jopp skated through the inferno, but poor Smith slammed into the Mayer wreckage and was killed instantly. Later in the race, which was dominated by Mercedes-Benz with Moss and John Fitch teaming for the victory, another British amateur, Richard Mainwaring, died in a single-car rollover.

The Dundrod circuit, such as it was, would never again stage a motor race and would serve as a classic example of how a network of public roads could no longer accommodate a field of modern, high-speed racing cars. Automobiles running 170 miles an hour on country lanes lined with every conceivable roadside hazard simply could not be tolerated in the modern world. By the end of the decade, most major automobile racing would be run exclusively on dedicated circuits designed specifically for the sport.

But amid the increasing death and carnage on the world's race-tracks, carmakers in Detroit and in the European industry continued to build faster road cars. Not only were Ferrari, Mercedes-Benz, Jaguar, Corvette, and Porsche creating two-seaters that would exceed 150 mph on the open road, but even fusty old Pontiac, the long-maligned "maiden aunt's" car from General Motors, was experiencing a shot of engineering hormones. The last of the major domestic brands to resist the shift to high-powered V-8 engines, Pontiac finally relented with the introduction of the 200 hp "Strato-Streak V-8."

The Division's revival and its sale of 553,000 vehicles helped the industry reach record-shattering sales of 9,188,571 vehicles for the year. Total revenues exceeded $11 billion, with nine-hundred thousand workers across the nation receiving paychecks from the automakers.

By that time, one in six American businesses was connected to the auto industry. The powerful V-8s, with their advanced automatic transmission, were added to flashy models offering a plethora of power options. Svelte four-door hardtops with their wraparound windshields, outrageous frostings of chrome, and lurid three-tone paint work, triggered what economists described as an "explosion" of business.

But universally ignored by the moguls in Detroit was a strange, egg-shaped, wheezy-powered economy car from Germany. Designed prior to World War II as a "people's car" for Adolf Hitler's Third Reich, the Volkswagen Beetle sold 25,000 units in the United States in 1955—a paltry number when compared to the domestic industry's output. But the Beetle was the triggering mechanism for an invasion of imported automobiles that would, in twenty years, completely alter American automobile commerce. In 1955, a total of 57,115 imported cars were sold in the United States. Four years later, that number would escalate to 668,070 units and the floodgates would open in the heretofore provincial and isolated Detroit automobile industry.

For the short term, however, flashy, over-the-top, mega-powered, multi-colored "insolent chariots" would dominate the highways of wildly optimistic America. Pontiac's headquarters staff, in its namesake Michigan city, was abuzz with the expected elevation of forty-two year-old Semon "Bunky" Knudsen to the general managership of the division. The son of General Motors powerhouse William "Big Bill" Knudsen, "Bunky" was a certified car enthusiast who would soon introduce the Pontiac Bonneville "Wide Tracks" with 300-plus Tri-Power engines.

Meanwhile, Bill France's NASCAR circuit was becoming a major battleground for the Detroit manufacturers. Pontiac joined the wars with factory-sponsored teams competing against similar operations from Ford, Chrysler, Oldsmobile, and Buick. The slogan "Win on Sunday, sell on Monday" was becoming gospel in the sales offices of the car companies. Hudson, which had dominated NASCAR in the first years of the decade, was now aligned with Nash and headed for bankruptcy in 1957. Its demise fortified the contention that racing victories in fact could *not* substitute for saleable vehicles. No matter. Enthusiasm for high-performance cars of all sizes, shapes, and prices was the basic sales philosophy in the middle 1950's despite the endless news of catastrophic racing crashes here and abroad.

Diana Logan and the world of automobile racing drifted out of my consciousness until late September, when she returned from New York and we met for dinner and drinks at the Coach & Horses. She reported that Warner Brothers was preparing a James Dean promotional tour for the opening of *Rebel without a Cause* in October and that shooting of *Giant* had wrapped in Texas. Because her parents were now back home, a repeat of the beautiful night following the *Rebel* preview was not possible, although we agreed to meet the following morning at Von

Neumann's Competition Motors. Dean and Rolf Wutherich would be preparing the Porsche 550 Spyder that "Jimmy," as she called him, planned to enter at the Cal Club races scheduled for the Salinas road course on the last weekend of the month.

We arrived late in the morning. Because of the buzz surrounding both Dean and his new car, a security guard kept the small crowd of enthusiasts at the curb. Thanks to Diana's friendship with Dean, we were admitted into the shadowy confines of the race shop, where the sharp odors of lubricants, solvents, and high-octane fuel permeated the stark space. In the middle of the room sat a stubby silver two-seat roadster bereft of top, windshield-wipers, roll-up windows, bumpers, or other normal automotive amenities.

The Porsche Spyder serial number 550-0055 was one of a limited run of sports racing cars that had been introduced by the Zuffenhausen, Germany–based company at the Paris Automobile Show in 1953. Now 550s dominated small-displacement class competition at the international level, and had gained mystique among sports car lovers after Max Hoffman, the American distributor for Porsche cars, dubbed the little machines "Spyders." Weighing only 1,500 pounds thanks to their feathery aluminum bodywork and carrying a highly sophisticated rear-mounted, double-overhead-camshaft, air-cooled, 1.5-liter four-cylinder engine, the Spyders were reliable as anvils in long-distance endurance races and capable of dazzling top speeds over 140 mph.

Jimmy was already there when we arrived, wearing his horn-rimmed glasses and puffing on an unfiltered cigarette. The well-known Los Angeles custom-car builder and painter George Barris had already painted large "130s" on both doors and inscribed "Little Bastard" on its stubby tail—a trenchant reference to Dean's own self-image as a scrawny outsider.

Wutherich had pounded out a small dent in the right front fender, the result of a minor collision with a woman driver on nearby Sunset

Boulevard during an initial test drive. While theoretically a pure racing car, the Spyder carried California license plate 2Z77767, which, coupled with its rudimentary driving lights, permitted it to be driven on the public highways long before rigid safety and emissions laws limited such use.

The car was ready for its first outing at Salinas, although Dean had not formally entered the race and some doubted that he would be allowed to compete, based on his limited experience. Cal Club rules stated that three novice races had to be completed before a driver was allowed to race a car as potent as the 550 Spyder. Because Dean had failed to finish his third race at Santa Barbara, some among his retinue warned him that the trip to Salinas might be futile. Others, including Von Neumann, felt otherwise, considering Dean's excellent performances and his obvious skill behind the wheel. That, coupled with his newfound celebrity, would surely allow him entry into the starting field.

Diana was awestruck at the sight of the Spyder. Its shiny, unpainted body was accented only by a pair of red stripes running across the rear fenders. Wutherich started the engine, which awoke with a guttural rumble. He watched the oil pressure gauge as he blipped the throttle, the powerful little engine responding with ominous growls. Satisfied that the power plant was perfectly tuned, he switched it off as a small cheer arose from the crowd at the curb. To them, the thumping exhaust note, coupled with the screech and whine of gears, pistons, valve springs and bearings, all singing a chorus of mad cacophony, was a mechanical symphony.

On September 17, James Dean had recorded a television commercial for the National Safety Council with fellow actor Gig Young. It was aimed at young drivers, imploring them to drive sensibly. Dean concluded the spot by advising, "And remember, drive safely because the life you save may be . . . mine." A day later, he, Elizabeth Taylor, and Rock Hudson finished the famous "Last Supper" scene for *Giant* at the studio, thereby releasing him from his non-racing contract. Firm plans were then made to make the Salinas race on the last weekend of September. Dean and Wutherich would drive the Porsche to the race, thereby breaking in the fresh engine on the way. Studio photographer Sanford Roth and Dean's friend, stuntman Bill Hickman, would follow with a white 1953 Ford station wagon and a car trailer to be used to haul the Spyder back to Los Angeles following the race.

Roth had met Dean on the *Giant* set in Texas and was assigned by *Collier's* magazine to record the young star's weekend of racing with his new Porsche.

I accepted Diana's offer to drive with her to Salinas, figuring that a story on Dean's debut in his new Porsche might be saleable. Based on his performances in his first three races, it was possible he might become a major star in the sport even before the year was out. There being little doubt about his passion for fast driving and his latent talent, his future as both a race driver and a superstar on the silver screen seemed assured.

James Dean's last day began early. At eight o'clock on the morning of Friday, September 30, 1955, he was with Wutherich at Competition Motors, having driven over the mountain from his newly rented home at 14611 Sutton Drive in Sherman Oaks. He had been up late the night before attending a private party in Malibu, but, being young and fit, appeared ready for the 325-mile run north to Salinas. Before picking up the Porsche, he had stopped at the Competition Motors race shop on Ventura Boulevard, where future world champion Phil Hill was working on a Ferrari Monza he was planning to run at Salinas. Hill later recalled the brief meeting. "It was the only time I ever talked with him other than a few grunts at the racetrack. Generally he'd show up with a great retinue of hangers-on, and I had no interest in that sort of thing. I needed to be a great racing driver and that was my sole preoccupation. I'd seen dozens of these so-called godlike creatures from Hollywood, and I'd been inclined to treat him as sort of a mutation. But on that day we talked about racing without all the usual distractions."

After meeting Wutherich later that morning, Dean had lunch at the Farmer's Market with his father, Winton, and his uncle, Charlie Nolan Dean. He talked about the day before, when he had visited his friend Jeanette Mills and presented her with his Siamese cat, Marcus, which had been given to him on the set of *Giant* by co-star Elizabeth Taylor. Following this leisurely interlude with his father and uncle, he returned to Competition Motors, where he met Roth, Hickman, and Wutherich. After Roth shot a photo of Dean and Wutherich in the Porsche raising their joined arms in a victory salute, the little group headed north, planning a late-day arrival before practice for the races began the following morning.

Diana picked me up in the Ferrari Mexico early that same afternoon, hoping to miss the rush hour traffic heading out of the valley. We ran north on Sepulveda Boulevard, following the route taken earlier by Dean. Route 99 took us over the Tejon Pass and the notorious Grapevine into the broad San Joaquin Valley. From there it was west on Route 166, a two-lane toward Taft and Maricopa, then north on Highway 33 to Blackwell's Corners and a stop for a tank of Richfield high-test and a Coke.

We got there an hour after Dean and his retinue had left. An excited kid with a scruffy crew cut told us that Dean and two guys in a Ford wagon had met up with Lance Reventlow and fledgling movie director and racer Bruce Kessler. He reported that Dean had laughed about a speeding ticket he had received on the Grapevine from California Highway patrolman O. T. Hunter, who had written him up for doing 65 mph in a 55 mph zone. Hunter also wrote up Hickman, who was driving the Ford wagon. Hunter registered curiosity about the tiny Porsche, but gave no indication he recognized its driver.

After polishing off a Coke and an apple at Blackwell's Corners, Dean put on the red windbreaker he had worn in *Rebel Without a*

Cause. It was donned simply as protection against the late-afternoon chill, but would later be ascribed to his belief that the garment brought him good luck—yet more of the lore and legend attributed to every aspect of his short, tragic life. With a quick wave to Reventlow and Kessler and a promise to meet them for dinner in Salinas, Dean skittered out of the sun-baked parking lot and accelerated onto Route 466 toward Cholame and the fateful intersection with Route 41.

Somewhere up ahead, a twenty-three year-old student at California Polytehnic had left the San Luis Obispo campus and pointed his two-tone black-and-white 1950 Ford Tudor coupe toward home and his pregnant wife at 1001 Academy Street in Tulare, south of Fresno. Little did young army veteran Donald Turnipseed imagine that he was headed for involvement in perhaps the most famous car crash in history.

Dean drove the Porsche over the barren Diablo Range, where the San Andreas Fault rises out of the earth like half-buried dragon jaws, with his customary verve. He was not running flat-out, following the orders of Wutherich to break in the fresh engine at sensible speeds.

As Dean rolled off the twisty section called Polonio Pass, Highway 466 yawned wide toward the Highway 41 intersection. On a crested hill to the west lay the tiny hamlet of Cholame, little more than a greasy lunch counter next to a hulking wooden automobile-repair garage. Dean overtook a slow-running Pontiac sedan being driven by Los Angeles CPA John Robert White. In a daring move, Dean made the pass, barely avoiding an oncoming Packard driven by Clifford Hord. White and his wife grumbled about the audacity of the red-jacketed driver behind the wheel of the strange, bullet-shaped roadster.

Turnipseed, who never spoke publicly about the accident before his death in 1995, later confided to Monty Roberts that he had spotted the Porsche approaching on his right, but had failed to judge its speed. At first he attempted to scoot across the intersection, then slammed on the Ford's brakes. Reassessing the situation, he floored the throttle and tried to make another crossing, but panicked as the Porsche bore down on him.

Dean, driving hard, spotted the Ford jiggering at the intersection and said his last words to Wutherich. "That guy up there has gotta see us. He's gotta stop."

Turnipseed *was* stopping, his brakes locked in a skid that later measured twenty-two feet. The Ford veered right, but was still in Dean's path. Understanding that a brake lockup would spin the Porsche out of control, Dean tried to veer right around the yawing Ford, but at the last second rammed its left front fender almost *broadslide.* The impact sent the Porsche spiraling into the air, spilling Wutherich onto the pavement while Dean's crushed body remained on board. The rumpled machine slammed to earth near a lone telephone pole while the Ford, its left front fender shattered, pinwheeled to a stop in the middle of the intersection.

The Whites had watched in horror as the accident unfolded. They stopped to find Turnipseed wandering aimlessly, his nose bloodied, but otherwise unhurt. Wutherich dazedly lay on his belly like a beached whale, his left leg crushed and his jaw broken. Only the shredded red jacket of James Dean was visible inside the mangled cockpit of the Porsche.

The world's most famous car crash had occurred at 5:59 P.M. at the deserted intersection of two anonymous highways in the middle of the California high desert. Only four eyewitnesses were present—Turnipseed, Wutherich, and the Whites. They would produce contradicting stories that would help generate endless bizarre rumors about the incident.

Our first clue came when Diana sighted the flashing lights of police cruisers and smoking red flares as she descended Polonia Pass. "There's been an accident," she said, without emotion. As she braked the Ferrari to a stop in a line of four other vehicles, including the

Whites' vermilion Pontiac, the only visible indication of the crash was Turnipseed's wounded black-and-white Ford. Beyond it was parked a Cadillac ambulance, its rear door yawning open to accept a patient.

Three men in white jackets were wheeling a gurney toward the Cadillac. A young man in a black shirt I later learned to be Turnipseed stood by, holding his nose. The form on the gurney was covered with a blanket. Then Diana spotted the wreckage of the Porsche.

"Oh my god," she screamed. "It's Jimmy!"

Before I could stop her, she leapt out of the Ferrari and rushed toward the ambulance. A California Highway Patrol Officer intercepted her, grabbing her arms and holding her away from the scene. He did not release her until the ambulance departed, its siren wailing as it ascended the hill toward Cholame and the thirty-three miles to the War Memorial Hospital at Paso Robles.

Diana rushed back to the car and climbed in, her face dripping with tears. Jamming the Ferrari into gear and tearing past the barriers, she blubbered, "Jimmy's hurt. They're taking him to Paso Robles Hospital. I've got to be there!"

We caught up to the ambulance before it reached the city limits and followed it into the hospital parking lot. Still sobbing, Diana left the Ferrari and sprinted into the emergency room waiting area. By then others had gathered, proving yet again that bad news travels fast. A small man from the local paper with an ill-fitting sport coat and a Speed Graphic camera had already appeared.

Diana became reclusive, sitting alone in a corner. I waited outside in the gathering darkness, smoking. An hour passed before there was a flurry of movement inside. A doctor appeared, looking frazzled. He introduced himself as Dr. Bossert, the physician on duty, and said, without apparent emotion, "We admitted a patient, Mr. James Dean of Sherman Oaks, California, following an automobile accident near Cholame. I regret to inform you that Mr. Dean was dead on arrival."

A gasp arose from the tiny crowd. Diana screamed and rushed outside. I attempted to follow but was blocked by the mad cluster of bodies rushing toward the lone coin-operated telephone booth outside the emergency room. The first call was made by a reporter for KPRL, the local radio station, who alerted the world to the tragedy. By the time I made it into the parking lot, the Ferrari, and Diana Logan, had fled into the night.

CHAPTER THIRTEEN

THE AGONY CONTINUES

IT TOOK ME SEVERAL HOURS TO ACCEPT THAT DIANA was well and truly gone. She had left me stranded in Paso Robles, a tiny farming center over two hundred miles from Los Angeles. After waiting a day in a seedy tourist home, I managed to board a Greyhound bus that meandered through endless stops on busy Highway 101 before reaching the big city. Flustered and filthy, the memories of the gruesome crash scene and the hysterical Diana fried into my brain, I thought about trying to revive my flagging career. The James Dean story was out of the question now that every major media outlet in the nation was featuring spreads on his death.

The tabloids screeched headlines about Dean's reckless driving style, his suicidal tendencies, his fascination with doom—the latter mostly based on marginal notes found in his edition of Hemingway's bull fighting epic, *Death in the Afternoon*. He had scribbled four words, "death, disability, disfigurement, and degradation" in colored ink, with the word "death" underlined in red in other sections of the book. This served as rich fodder for the sensationalists who maintained that Dean was fascinated with his own demise. Adding to the frenzy, old girlfriends were dredged up to affirm that he took insane risks behind the wheel, suggesting that he was seeking the ultimate crash. In the end it all descended to the level of tabloid journalism at its worst.

Monty Roberts, who had expected to spend the weekend with Dean at the races, had received a call from the hospital reporting his death. Somehow, Roberts' address and phone number had been found in Wutherich's shirt pocket, and, because his broken jaw made speech difficult, a member of the hospital staff used the slip of paper to inform the cowboy of the tragedy.

Reports spread across the nation about how Dean had been driving over 100 miles an hour when the crash occurred. Pop psychologists insisted that the entire incident was an act of existential protest—a symbolic expression of youthful frustration and anger. Millions of schoolgirls reflexively mourned his passing, although his amazing rise to the pinnacle of popular culture would not occur until three weeks later, when *Rebel without a Cause* was released. James Dean had ironically created the ultimate publicity stunt by killing himself before two of his three motion pictures were released.

Endless replays and diagnoses would be made about the incident, which was not a cosmic act of strange metaphysics, but a simple car crash that would be repeated by more mundane players thousands of times across the nation. Two drivers misjudged each other's intentions and collided. It was that simple.

In the early 1990s the television series *What Happened?* attempted to analyze the exact cause of the crash. The producers retained Failure Analysis Associates of Menlo Park, California, to make detailed computer simulations of the incident using EDSMAC, an acronym for Engineering Dynamics Simulation Model for Automobile Collisions. Senior managing engineer Gary Kost and associate Erich Phillips recorded detailed measurements at the scene and made accurate calculations regarding the weight, structural integrity, impact positions, and damage of the two vehicles. An anomaly in the analysis was the fact that the Porsche had landed only fifty feet from the crash site, meaning that its speed at impact would have been only fifty-seven miles an hour, not the triple-digit velocities heretofore accepted to be the case. Had Dean been traveling at seventy-seven miles an hour at the time of contract, for example, the computer model placed the Porsche's landing a full 100 feet farther away from the scene.

But the debate over how fast Dean had been traveling at the last moment of his life started during an interview with Wutherich at the Paso Robles Hospital. Recorded by a group of law enforcement officers, Wutherich spoke with difficulty, constrained by his broken jaw and missing teeth. He told the officials that Dean was traveling "sixty to sixty-five"—numbers that implied a modest speed. But further analysis by Porsche expert Lee Raskin, who spent years studying the crash, indicated that Wutherich was speaking about engine rpms, not the car's speed. The 550 Spyder had a large tachometer centered on the driver's instrument panel. A smaller speedometer was mounted to the left. Raskin and others believe that Wutherich, seated to the right of Dean, would have had difficulty seeing the speedometer, and would have been watching the tachometer. The plan on the trip had been to "run in" the fresh engine at high rpms to ready it for the race. In an interview given in 1960, after he'd returned to Germany, Wutherich reconfirmed this contention. If this "sixty to sixty-five" statement meant 6,000-6,500 rpm, as opposed to "sixty to sixty-five" mph, the Porsche running in fifth gear would have been approaching Turnipseed at between ninety and ninety-eight mph.

Wutherich could not remember if Dean had downshifted into a

lower gear seconds before the crash; and eyewitness John White maintained that he and his wife saw no brake lights from the Porsche prior to impact.

How fast was James Dean going? The EDSMAC computer simulation had the Porsche ground-looping on the pavement rather than pinwheeling through the air before stopping. This radically altered the accident dynamics and speed calculations. At the end, based on the eyewitness reports of the Whites and Clifford Hord, and on Wutherich's testimony, it is believed that Dean came off Polonio Pass at somewhere near ninety miles per hour. Perhaps at the last minute he slowed somewhat as Turnipseed appeared. If the impact speed was in the seventy to eighty miles per hour range, the midair tumbling would explain why the car stopped so close to the impact location.

No matter, James Dean was dead. The coroner reported the cause as a broken neck, coupled with multiple fractures of the jaw and both arms, plus major lacerations. He somehow clung to life for a time and probably expired in the ambulance. The bleeding was so extensive that blood-alcohol tests were not possible, although there was no reason to believe that Dean had been drinking at any time since the Malibu party the night before.

Two weeks following the James Dean accident, automobile racing made anther oblique entry onto the front pages. On the sunny Monday morning of October 17, an outrageous playboy named Joel Wolfe Thorne took off his new Beechcaft Bonanza from the Burbank airport. Thorne had raced four times in the Indianapolis 500 in the 1930s and, thanks to a fortune stemming from New York's Manufacturer's Hanover Bank, had funded a series of ultra-fast Thorne Engineering Specials at the Speedway. Veteran George Robson had driven one of them to victory in the race's postwar revival in 1946. The survivor of multiple marriages, endless nightclub punch-ups and other social-page peccadilloes, Thorne somehow lost control of his plane moments after becoming airborne and nosedived into a North Hollywood apartment building. Thorne and three residents were killed in the crash, and several others were critically injured. While the accident had occurred far from any racetrack, Thorne's death reinforced the public perception that the sport was infested with lunatic risk-takers.

But it was James Dean's death that stunned the nation. Major coverage by periodicals like *Life* and endless stories in the Sunday supplements elevated young females of the population into a state of mass hysteria. Popular movie magazines like *Photoplay* and *Silver Screen* unleashed a barrage of stories on the late actor that would continue for years to come. His fan mail deluged Warner Brothers in volumes that remained at record levels long after his three movies had ceased distribution.

As expected, Dean's funeral, in his hometown of Fairmount, Indiana, became a spectacle. His body was flown to Indianapolis on the Tuesday following his death and placed in the hands of Wilbur Hunt, the owner of Fairmount's only funeral home. The service was set for the next Saturday afternoon at the Friends Church, with pastor Ken Harvey and Cincinnati television evangelist Dr. James A. DeWeerd presiding. With only six hundred seats available in the Church, loudspeakers were installed to permit the overflow crowd outside to hear the service. Funeral director Hunt summarily denied requests from various Hollywood celebrities for reserved seats, claiming that Dean's local friends deserved the same consideration and that his first-come-first-served policy would remain in effect. Burial would be in the Fairmount Cemetery.

Back in Paso Robles, Rolf Wutherich slowly recovered after surgeons decided that his shattered leg did not require amputation. His final few months of rehabilitation took place in Los Angeles after Johnny Von Neumann arranged for his return. But the emotional damage was more severe than anyone had suspected. Wutherich became moody and unruly. The Porsche management returned him to Germany to work in the race car testing department at Zuffenhausen. Journalists and other visitors to the facility were fore-warned not to discuss the Dean accident with him, lest they receive a violent reaction. On July 28, 1981, while driving at a high speed near the village of Kupferzell, Wutherich lost control of his Porsche and was killed.

As the years passed, the rumors about James Dean intensified, including the inevitable contention that he, like-Elvis, had actually survived, and was living as a disfigured recluse in a mental ward. Some claimed that his ghostly Porsche could still be spotted dashing down darkened roads near Paso Robles. Sal Mineo added to the lunacy when he told the tabloids that he was carrying on a conversa-tion with Dean from the great beyond. "Knowing Dean changed my life completely," he claimed. "At moments of doubt or insecurity he's a source of tremendous strength to me. After he died I became obsessed with him, trying to make contact with him, because he called me 'Plato,' the same name in the film." Sadly, Mineo met his own violent death in 1976, when he was fatally stabbed outside his Hollywood apartment.

Several tabloids maintained that Dean was alive, and offered a $50,000 reward for his location. This ploy produced grabber head-lines for the editors—with an absolute guarantee that the money would never have to be paid.

Even the big weekly magazines continued to troll for readers. A year after his death, the October 16, 1956 cover of *Look* magazine fea-tured his sulky face in a portrait for posed while shooting *Giant.* The blurb beside it proclaimed: "James Dean: the strangest legend since Valentino."

In the parking lot of Aggie's restaurant in tiny Cholame, a Tokyo businessman named Seita Ohnishi, who dealt in Dean souvenirs, erected a stainless steel monument twenty-two years following the accident. It carries a simple engraving: "James Dean 1931 Feb 8—

1955 Sep 30 PM 5:59." Surrounding the monument on a low stone wall are various quotations favored by Dean, including one from *The Little Prince*: "What is essential is invisible to the eye." Another is attributed to Dean himself and embodies the mystique that locks him in the public imagination: "Death is the one inevitable, undeniable truth. In it lies the only ultimate nobility for man. Beyond it, through immortality, the only hope."

As James Dean soared into the pantheon of endlessly fascinating, mystery-shrouded superstars, soon to joined by John F. Kennedy, Marilyn Monroe, Elvis Presley, and Princess Diana, the car that cost him his life became a part of the lore surrounding his death. After being briefly stored in the repair garage at Cholame, it was sold to a Beverly Hills surgeon after the Dean family had collected the insurance, and amateur sports car driver Dr. Troy McHenry, who also owned a Porsche 550 Spyder. After removing the engine and transaxle, McHenry later sold some suspension and steering bits to a friend, Dr. William Estrich of Burbank, who installed them on a special sports racing car. Estrich was later killed at Pomona, California, when he hit the only tree standing anywhere near the track. It was believed that a Pitman arm in the steering routinely failed, giving rise to the ludicrous rumor that the Dean car was "jinxed."

One legitimate mystery did arise from the tragedy. George Barris bought the engineless hulk and, after failing to repair it, turned it over to the Greater Los Angeles Safety Council for use as a display device to scare young drivers. The "James Dean Death Car" embarked on a nationwide tour, where it meandered from city to city for four years—a source of ghoulish curiosity but of doubtful value in the cause of teenage driving safety. In 1960, the car was loaded into a box car (or a truck—the story varies) in Florida to be returned to Los Angeles. It never arrived. The car was stolen in a Midwestern freight yard and disappeared. Forever. Some believe it was chopped into bits to be sold as souvenirs—which never reached the market. Others think it remains in the hands of a private collector. Historian Lee Raskin, who has delved deeply into the mystery, speculates that either the Dean family, tiring of the gruesome notoriety, retrieved the relic and had it destroyed, or more seriously that Barris, still active in Southern California's custom-car circles, collected the insurance and had it crushed. Barris refuses to comment. Whatever the case, the whereabout's of the world's most famous and notorious Porsche remains the single unsolved link in one of the most famous automobile crashes in history. Dean's first Porsche Speedster is also missing, although historian Raskin knows its serial number and remains on a trail that became blurred after Lew Bracker sold the car in the early 1960s.

Ironically, at the very moment that James Dean's vulnerable little Porsche was being folded into a lump of bent aluminum and steel, Ford Motor Company was embarking on a daring campaign to sell automobiles through safety. This was a revolutionary concept in Detroit in 1955, since many executive's believed that reminding customers of the potential of a crash was counterproductive, and that the liberating quality of automobile travel far transcended any concerns over safety. Talk of seat belts had been rejected, based on the conventional wisdom of the day that drivers and passengers did not want to be trapped in a wreck.

Ford and Chrysler had made feeble attempts to improve automobile safety, each donating $100,000 a year to the Cornell Aeronautical Laboratory in Buffalo, New York, where research chief Bill Milliken, himself a sports car driver, led a small team of auto-safety engineers. Sadly, the cash-strapped Milliken and his group could not make serious inroads on the issue. At one point, funds became so scarce that engineers had to drop cadaver heads down a stairwell to determine the benefits of various helmets and other head-protection devices.

Ford's new advertising campaign, launched in September 1955 along with their lineup of 1956 models, trumpeted "Lifeguard Design." This involved such product additions as dished "Lifeguard" steering wheels, optional "Lifeguard" seat belts (available in harmonious upholstery colors), "Lifeguard" door latches that helped keep the doors closed in the event of a crash and "Lifeguard" instrument and sun visor padding. Ford had already begun employing laminated windshield glass in 1927 (a move opposed by General Motors, who feared the effect of reminding the buying public about safety.)

As luck would have it, an indifferent public and intense pressure from crosstown rival General Motors caused the "Lifeguard Design" campaign to be quietly abandoned. In 1956, Chevrolet's new high-performance V-8 sedans swamped Ford, displacing it as the sales leader in the American market. Wags in Motor City sneered, "Ford sold safety, Chevrolet sold cars."

Death refused to leave the headlines as 1955 drifted away. In addition to the carnage on the highways and racetracks, the ugly specters of racism and of lethal drugs were arriving on the scene. The great jazz saxophonist Charlie Parker went down from an overdose of heroin. Black Americans celebrated the entry of the brilliant soprano Marian Anderson on the all-white stages of the Metropolitan Opera, and in December Alabama housewife Rosa Parks refused to give up her seat in the front of a Birmingham city bus. But they reeled in horror when Mississippi Klansmen lynched fourteen-year-old Emmett Till for a presumed affront to a white candy-store clerk. These incidents, good and bad, produced back-page news stories in the nation's press, but were harbingers of the epic civil rights struggles to come—as well as the nation's descent into a drug-fogged rebelliousness that would shatter tranquility during the wild and woolly sixties.

Unnoticed outside the tight little world of Southern California sports car racing was an accident at the Sacramento State Fairgrounds one month after the Dean fatality. David E. Davis Jr., a transplanted Detroiter who had come west to race sports cars while earning a living as an hourly worker at North American Aviation in El Segundo, flipped his new MG TF 1500 and suffered horrible facial injuries. Following his eighteen-month recovery he was hired by *Road & Track* as the magazine's West Coast advertising manager. That was followed by a brief but successful copywriting career back in Detroit at Chevrolet's Campbell-Ewald ad agency. In 1962 he assumed the editiorship of *Car and Driver* magazine, a struggling rival to *Road & Track*. Davis was a brilliant columnist and editor who elevated *Car and Driver* to the largest-selling automobile monthly in the world before leaving to start *Automobile* magazine for the Rupert Murdoch empire in 1986. Davis would be one of the few examples of serious injury on the racetrack diverting an individual from competition and into a field where he made a singular impact.

But it was not over. The grim reaper made one more selection before the deadly year ended. The 100-mile race at Phoenix, Arizona, was on the American Automobile Association's championship schedule as its final involvement with the sport. Set for the one-mile dirt oval at the State Fairgrounds, twenty-four of the best Indianapolis drivers were entered, including defending national champion Jimmy Bryan and the new title-holder, Bob Sweikert, whose victories at Indianapolis and Syracuse, plus other high finishes, had earned him the right to carry the coveted No. 1 on his car the following season. (It would be a brief reign: the brilliant but cocky Sweikert, who often claimed that he would never live to retire, tumbled to his death in a sprint car at the Salem, Indiana, high-banked speedway on June 6, 1956.)

In the Phoenix field was the steady, always competitive Jack McGrath driving Wichita, Kansas, sportsman Jack Hinkle's white No. 3 Kurtis-Kraft. Before leaving his Los Angeles shop with the car, McGrath had considered mounting a new front axle, but having received news that Hinkle was selling the machine after the Phoenix race, he decided to run one more time with the old unit in place. After qualifying third at over 100 miles an hour on the notoriously rutted and wooden-fence-lined horse track, McGrath seized the lead in the middle stages until he was passed by Jimmy Bryan and Johnny Thomson. Running a solid third on the eighty-sixth lap and only fourteen circuits prior to the finish, McGrath barreled into the third turn at the end of the backstretch, his car pitched sideways in its customary dirt-track broadslide. At that moment, the aged axle ruptured and the right wheel collapsed. The Hinkle began a series of vicious tumbles, in the process tearing loose McGrath's new jet-fighter-style crash helmet. Before emergency crews arrived at the scene, one of the most likable and respected race drivers of the era was dead.

Finally, the madness of the 1955 motor sports season was over, but the repercussions were just beginning.

CHAPTER FOURTEEN

THE LOST WARRIORS

WHO WERE THESE PEOPLE? WHAT SORT OF HOMO sapiens in civilized nations would engage in a sport that essentially guaranteed the death of half its participants—a mortality rate equaled only by Roman gladiatorial contests, dueling, and medieval jousting? A backward look of fifty years produces images of danger in a sport that would be intolerable today. The fatal crash of stock car icon Dale Earnhardt in the 2001 Daytona 500 produced angry charges that motor racing was too dangerous, despite the fact that only four drivers had been killed in major league stock car racing in almost two decades—even as speeds had increased more than 30 percent over the same span of time.

The reduction of risk in all phases of life has altered human behavior. We live longer, healthier lives, yet are haunted by fears of the latest virus, terror attack, nuclear threat—or even the slightest jiggling of our fragile emotional compasses. Aside from the vicarious thrills transmitted courtesy of risk-takers like astronauts or so-called extreme sportsmen, life for the average American citizen has devolved to such tepid adventures as carbohydrate counting, battling computer viruses, and remaining within the confines of political correctness.

Long gone are the days when audacity, physical courage, and the ability to tolerate physical pain and discomfort were components of daily life. The idea of early explorers probing into the unknown northern oceans aboard tiny sailing ships garbed in only the flimsiest of clothes and facing scurvy-inducing diets is unthinkable today to even the most adventurous sailor. The concept of a Charles Lindbergh launching his monoplane from Long Island on the first successful transatlantic flight with only a magnetic compass and pack of sandwiches borders on the insane. So too for Ernest Shackleton's escape from Antarctica aboard an eighteen-foot lifeboat, facing the wildest oceans on the planet. He and his iron-hearted crew are but one of a thousand examples of human daring and endurance that may have been erased from the psyche by the same technological advances that comfort and protect contemporary human beings.

In 1935 Alexis Carrell, the noted French scientist and 1912 Nobel Prize winner in medicine, published his international best-seller, *Man the Unknown.* His philosophical speculations about the future of mankind advised an intellectual aristocracy (a kind of twentieth century update of Plato's philosopher-king, proposed in his *Republic* several millennia earlier) that prompted widespread controversy and, perhaps, later Nazi experiments with eugenics. But beyond such ruminations, Carrell wrote at length about the rising frailties of the human mind and body; our loss of audacity in the face of adversity; our inability to withstand pain; and our increasing susceptibility to mental tensions.

The men who raced cars in the mid-1950s (there were no women competing at the top level of the sport at the time) rode 150-mph bucking broncos with no more protection than a rodeo rider. Dressed in street clothes and wearing leather helmets (that research in 1960s by the Snell Foundation revealed were actually more dangerous than no headwear at all), the human form was essentially naked in the face of high-speed impacts and fire. Seat belts were used by some and eschewed by others who believed that being tossed clear of a crashing automobile afforded a better chance for survival.

The mid-1950s race cars were archaic monsters. No power steering or brakes, no automatic transmissions, no protection from flying dirt or stones; nothing but a seat, a steering wheel, and rudimentary instruments. Behind the drivers were mounted fifty- to seventy-gallon fuel tanks loaded with either fiercely volatile gasoline or methanol-alcohol, which that burned with an invisible yet lethal flame. Many cars carried extra oil reservoirs mounted near the cockpit that could rupture and burn in a crash, meaning that drivers were literally ensconced in tubs of explosives.

Worse yet, the suspensions of the automobiles had changed little since the mid-1930s. Handling, such as it was, could not be easily pre-dicted. The tires were skinny and lacked cohesion. The slightest error could send a machine into an ugly, high-speed spin. Springing, either by conventional leaves or torsion bars, was minimal, meaning the driver would be pounded and pummeled even on smooth macadam, not to mention a rutted dirt track or the brick paving of the Indianapolis Motor Speedway. Add to that the unremitting heat of the engine, and the deafening drumbeat of the exhaust, and the phys-ical effort of steering, and a race driver of 1955 rode in a nightmar-ish, deadly environment that simply would not be tolerated today.

Protective headgear, first developed by British motorcycle riders in the 1920s, had not been required at Indianapolis until 1935. Cloth aviator's caps, useful only to prevent mussing of the hair, were employed in European Grand Prix motor racing until helmets came into universal use in 1952. Fireproof clothing was essentially unknown until the late 1960s when DuPont's Nomex synthetic material was developed. Full-face helmets would not be perfected until the same period. Six-point reinforced shoulder, lap, and crotch belts came into widespread use, as did self-sealing fuel bladders and onboard fire extinguishers, all of which radically reduced the fatality rate as speeds escalated to well over 200 mph in most forms of the sport. (In 1955 the lap record, set by Jack McGrath, was 142 mph. By the turn of the new century, lap speeds at Indianapolis commonly exceeded 225 mph.) In the mid-1990s before engine limits were imposed, several drivers had exceeded 235-mph averages, meaning that the cars were negotiating the four sweeping Indianapolis corners *over 80 miles* an hour faster than McGrath's overall average speed. Even at those enormous velocities, drivers are often able to survive crashes, thanks to ultra-strong carbon-fiber cockpit enclosures and the above-mentioned safety components.

The thirty-three men who started the 1955 Indianapolis 500 fit the profile of mid-1950s professional racecar drivers. They were essentially white Anglo-Saxons, with only Vukovich, his friend Ed Elisian, and fellow Fresno veteran Fred Agabashian tracing their roots to Eastern Europe. Seventeen were either native or transplanted Californians, where the automobile culture had its deepest roots. Jerry Hoyt, an Indiana native, and brash Oklahoman Jimmy Reece were both twenty-six years old. Agabashian and Duane Carter were, at forty-two, the senior citizens in the field. Most came from working-class families, although Ray Crawford, a former World War II P-38 fighter pilot and ace, was a wealthy West Coast supermarket-chain owner. (In contrast, many *sports* car drivers of the day came from affluent backgrounds.)

Most were World War II combat veterans who had returned home with a taste for adventure in an increasingly placid and peaceful nation. Most were married, although they remained on the road for most of the year. While they exhibited a warrior's camaraderie at the racetracks, few close friendships were formed. Said one driver of the day, "You don't want to get too close to these guys. You never know how long they'll be around."

It was an all-male, lily-white sport. Women were not allowed in the pits or the garage areas until the late 1970s. African Americans were almost unseen. In the 1930s, "Rajo Jack" deSoto had competed at the dangerous Legion Ascot track in suburban Los Angeles. In 1955, thirty-four-year-old Wendell Scott was laboring on backwater Virginia stock car tracks before his rise to fame in NASCAR Grand National competition and his ultimate recognition in the 1977 bio-pic *Greased Lightning* starring Richard Pryor. Fifty years later, little has changed in terms of racial, ethnic, or sexual diversity, although a great influx of South Americans, mainly from Brazil and Argentina, has had an enormous impact on motor racing worldwide.

Race drivers of the 1950s fit Hungarian psychoanalyst Michael Balint's description of "Philantasim," meaning the enjoyment of thrills in daily life. Balint recognized that high speed was a crucial component in the entire psychology of mobility. In his 1959 book, *Thrills and Regressions*, Balint divided civilization into the thrill-seeking Philobats and the nonaggressive Ocnophiles, who were repelled by high-intensity movement like automobile racing. The Philobat, by contrast, sought to develop skills that would permit high-speed movement in such sports as car racing, motorcycle riding, skiing, surfing, flying, etc. With this went an inability to relate to others and a selfish, introverted satisfaction gained from the activities. Balint maintained that the Philobat immersed him- or herself so completely in the task of driving that "skill should no longer require any effort," and even risky racetrack competition became "a kind of fairyland where things happen as desired." In so doing, the Philobat "exposed himself unnecessarily to real danger in search of thrills and confidence that he can cope with any situation."

Balint's observation about risk-taking behind the wheel of an automobile was but one of many examples of intellectual probing into the world of motor racing, most of which descended into psychobabble relating to exhibitionism, Freudian sexual innuendos, egocentrism gone wild, and overt death wishes. Poet Mario Leone skidded into the hyperbolic fence in 1914 with his "Fornication of Automobiles," in which he likened the collision of two motor vehicles to a kind of technological sexual encounter:

> Involuntary collision
> furious fornication
> of two automobiles—energy
> embrace of two warriors
> bold of movement
> syncopation of two heart motors,
> spilling of blood-gas.

Years later, the nonsense intensified when Ralph Nader artfully, if hysterically, assaulted the admittedly oafish and isolated leadership of General Motors and the entire automobile industry with his 1966 polemic *Unsafe at Any Speed: The Designed-in Dangers of the American Automobiles.* The book was a modest seller until it was revealed that GM had hired private investigators to trail Nader and had tapped his telephone. General Motors president James M. Roche was forced to make a public apology and a large financial settlement that funded several auto-safety efforts.

Energized by the Nader flap, Congress passed the National Traffic and Motor Vehicle Safety Act, which required automakers to offer seventeen major safety features, including seat belts, collapsible steering columns, paddled instrument panels, etc. This legislation opened the floodgates for government involvement an industry that should have had the foresight, in view of rapidly changing public attitudes in the 1960s, to have engineered its own safety components.

Literary contributions, absurd as most were, reached a nadir (no pun intended) with the 1973 publication of British novelist J. G. Ballard's *Crash*—a scatalogically bloody, schoolboyishly pornographic tale of a blitz through London motorways and occasional racetracks in a drug-fogged, blood-stained, metal-crunching, sex-soaked bash that one reviewer described as "the first pornographic novel based on technology." Ballard, writing in the first person, dealt with a "hoodlum scientist named Vaughan" (who, the reader learns in the first sentence of the book, is already dead) whose apparent mission is to engage in a fatal, psycho-sexual car crash with Elizabeth Taylor.

A half-century since the automobile revolutionized personal transportation on a worldwide scale, the carnage of 1955 finally triggered a response in the scientific community. Car crashes on the highways, racing cars tumbling into crowds, and champion drivers dying all contributed to a rising awareness of automobile safety—an issue that had been essentially ignored since Gottlieb Daimler and Karl Benz's pioneering machines had first rolled out in the years 1885–87.

In May 1955, Air Force colonel John Paul Stapp organized the first automobile-safety conference at Holloman Air Force Base in New Mexico. The year before, Stapp had subjected himself to stupefying feats of physical endurance on an Air Force rocket sled that had accelerated to 632 miles an hour before stopping dead in 1.4 seconds. This deceleration imposed an unbelievable 40 g (40 times the pull of gravity) on Stapp's body. This experiment, and others like it, proved that pilots could eject from jet fighters at up to 1,800 miles an hour and at altitudes of up to 35,000 feet.

Such courageous experiments prompted *Time* to feature Colonel Stapp on its September 12, 1955 cover with the description: "The fastest man on earth and No. 1 hero of the Air Force."

Stapp invited members of the automobile industry and the armed services, research laboratories, medical experts, and representatives from national safety councils to participate in the conference. It was clear to Stapp that crash injuries in automobiles involved massive decelerations. If automobile interiors and structures could be improved to absorb impacts while passengers were better contained, injuries and fatalities might be reduced. The meetings continued through 1957 and resulted in recommendations to relocate padded instrument panels away from front seat passengers; doors with rigid latches that would remain in place in crashes; anchoring seats more firmly to the chassis; and improving seat belt design to hold passengers in place.

After Colonel Stapp was transferred to advanced studies in the aerospace field, his auto-safety conference was taken over by University of Minnesota engineering professor James J. Ryan, who carried on as a leader in automobile-safety studies and research.

It was in March 1955 that Colonel Stapp and others at Holloman staged a breakthrough experiment using a World War II surplus Dodge weapons carrier vehicle and a pair of crude dummies strapped in the front seats. The tests used the instrumented dummies to measure impact and damage to the human form. Anesthetized pigs were later employed in violent crash tests to improve interior safety components.

Scientists learned that the average human body, if properly restrained by a seat belt, could survive a crash involving up to 30 g's with minor discomfort. A 40 g's impact would cause serious injuries to lungs, hearts, and abdominal organs, while anything over 50 g's would probably be fatal.

Meanwhile, engineers at Daimler-Benz AG in Germany had been conducting research that revealed new truths about automobile structures. Up until then, car bodies and frames had been unyielding masses of steel that refused to bend or deform in crashes. This transferred enormous deceleration forces to the most vulnerable component in the vehicle, i.e., the human bodies. Daimler-Benz began to build its Mercedes-Benz cars with "crush zones" that would deform and absorb energy in a crash—the exact opposite of orthodox engineering theory that a car body ought be made as rigid as possible.

It was these pioneering efforts in 1955 by Colonel Stapp and other engineers in and out of the automobile industry that slowly—and sometimes frustratingly—led to such current safety components as air bags, crushable, energy-absorbing body structures, three-point seat belts, better headlights, and safer interiors, plus radically improved anti-lock disc brakes, radial tires, traction and stability control, etc. These engineering advances, now common on all automobiles regardless of size or price, have been a major contributor to reducing the automobile death rate from 6.06 per 100 million miles driven in 1955 to under 1 per 100 million miles today—in a nation where motor vehicles have more than doubled, to over 220 million, and highway miles traveled per year have nearly tripled.

The shocking crash at Le Mans in June 1955, generated radical changes in track design. The Automobile Club d'Ouest, which operated the Le Mans 24-Hour race, widened the front straightaway where the Levegh tragedy had occurred and built larger and more effective barriers for spectators. Within a few years, the entire circuit would be lined with fences to further protect the crowds.

It was also obvious to millionaire Tony Hulman, the Terre Haute sportsman who owned the Indianapolis Motor Speedway, that his track offered the same potential for a major crowd disaster as Le Mans. Throughout 1956, plans were laid down for a major revision. The 1957 race was run with the pit area separated from the racetrack by a ten-foot grass apron and a low retaining wall. The new Tower Terrace grandstands, had also been moved well back from the Speedway and rigid cable fencing installed along the front straightaway grandstands. But the ancient track itself remained in a chute between the grandstands and many more crashes and fatalities awaited competing drivers in the years to come.

While spectator safety was improved, drivers remained as vulnerable as ever. The Unites States Auto Club, which in 1956 replaced the American Automobile Association as the sanctioning body for Indianapolis and other championship races, did not require rollover bars in race cars until 1959. Self-sealing bladders to contain fuel in crashes would not be adopted until they were perfected by the military for use on Vietnam combat helicopters that were susceptible to small-arms fire.

Back east, the small-town committee that organized the now-growing Watkins Glen Grand Prix realized that it was also operating on an obsolete network of narrow public roads. Plans were made to construct a dedicated 2.3-mile road course on vacant land overlooking Lake Seneca. In a mad dash of construction, the new track was completed in time for the October 1956 event. Crowd safety was a primary consideration, and the Glen circuit would rise to international stature when it hosted its first Formula One United States Grand Prix in 1961.

Yet it would be years before crowds would be totally protected from race cars. In the spring of 1957, international racontuer, celebrity, and racecar driver Count Alfonso de Portago, an heir to the Spanish throne, lost control of his Ferrari on a high-speed straightaway of public road during the running of the Mille Miglia road race around Italy. A blown tire at 165 mph sent his car scything through the roadside spectators, killing himself, his friend and navigator Eddie Nelson, and ten men, women, and children. The incident would end Italy's largest sporting event after authorities decided that crowd protection on open roads was impossible. In 1960 another Count—Wolfgang Von Trips—again driving for the Scuderia Ferrari, tumbled into the crowd at the Monza Autodrome on the second lap of the Italian Grand Prix, killing himself and fourteen spectators.

While innocent bystanders were slowly moved out of harm's way with new track designs in the late 1950s and 1960s, questions lingered: What kind of men were prepared to risk their lives in such a dangerous sport? Were they obsessed with a death wish, as some suggested? Were they mindless show-offs? Ignorant rubes? Simpleton playboys? Pure antisocial psychopaths?

As the establishment press, the Vatican, safety experts, and some politicians railed against the sport as a brutal, Neaderthal expression of technological savagery that encouraged irresponsible behavior on public roads, serious academics undertook studies to determine exactly who these people who raced automobiles actually were.

In the early 1960s Dr. Keith W. Johnsgard and Dr. Bruce C. Ogilvie, clinical psychologists at San Jose State College in San Jose, California, embarked on an extensive scientific examination of race drivers and their motivations. Johnsgard and Ogilvie chose to study 350 men and 7 women from the San Francisco Region of the Sports Car Club of America who were participating in amateur road-racing events. Also tested was a group of 30 professional drivers. The study would ultimately be expanded to include over 700 drivers, consuming more than 4,000 hours of tests and interviews.

The results amazed and baffled both supporters and critics of the sport. The tested drivers were found to be highly intelligent, ranging from the ninetieth to the ninety-fourth percentile. They possessed a need for achievement unmatched by other athletes. All were exhibitionistic and had intense, vivid desires for attention from the opposite sex. Contrary to public perception, the drivers indicated a strong sense of self-control. As a group, they indicated below-average needs for interpersonal relationships. This, coupled with fierce independence and with what Johnsgard and Ogilvie described as a "remarkable freedom of guilt," suggested that mildly psychopathic personalities were not uncommon.

Similar studies involving five top-ranked professional British

Grand Prix drivers by English psychologist Bernice Kirkler in 1965 produced similar results: above-average intelligence, reflexes, and hand-eye coordination. They also possessed superb self-control and all improved performance under stress. Kirkler also discovered that her five GP drivers had extremely strong urges to compete, were perfectionists, had intense needs to be in control, and possessed extremely high tolerance to all forms of physical discomfort.

Kirkler further speculated that the driver's ardent competitiveness extended to a subtle form of gambling with death. Winning affirmed, in her words, their "fantasy of omnipotence." This urge to duel with disaster and win was a far greater motivation for race drivers than any sort of "death wish." At the end of Johnsgard and Ogilvie's six-year study, none of the over six hundred amateurs studied had been killed in racing accidents. By contrast, among the thirty professionals examined during the same time frame, seven had died while competing and six others had been so severely injured, as to force retirement from the sport. The causes of death were roughly split between driver error and mechanical failure.

Among the professionals, both studies revealed significantly below-average scores for personal empathy toward others. Emotionally intimate and sensitive relationships were universally low priorities. They were self-reliant and realistic, with little need for dependence on others and feeling no abiding sensitivity to their needs.

All the professionals revealed an amazingly high capacity for performance under duress. This was further confirmed in the 1970s when a team of psychologists from the University of North Carolina worked with a small group of top NASCAR stock car drivers during the running of several Daytona 500-mile races. After wiring the subject drivers with sensitive telemetry, they discovered that during the race their body temperatures rose to over 110 degrees, while their blood pressures remained normal, even during wild 160-mph crashes. Years later, Rick Mears, a three-time winner of the Indianapolis 500, commented on what went through his mind at the moment of a major crash. "I think, what do I do next?" This was repeated by Tom Wolfe when writing about Air Force test pilots in his best-selling *The Right Stuff.*

Johnsgard, perhaps the most experienced academic in the study of race driver psychology, summed up the subject best when he wrote, "The dimension that separates them [professional race drivers] most clearly from the men on the streets is intelligence. In contrast to the general male population, the race driver has unusually high abstract intelligence, high achievement needs, strong heterosexual needs, high exhibitionistic needs, above-average needs for change and a high degree of self-sufficiency. He is very non-differential, dislikes nurturing others, and has a low need for order and planning ahead. He is quite expedient and free from guilt. He is reserved and very tough-mined as against being sentimental and dependent. Taken together, the profile is a rather classical 'masculine package.'"

After the James Dean madness, my life changed. I sold the MG and bought a Chevrolet business coupe. My writing switched to network television sitcoms. Their feathery plotlines and inane dialogue helped erase memories of the death and carnage I had witnessed at Indianapolis, Le Mans, and on the road to Cholame.

I never saw Diana again, although I heard through friends that she had moved to Europe and continued her groupie life with the Grand Prix crowd until March 14, 1957. It was on that day at the Modena Autodrome that, while testing a Ferrari protoype, Gino Castellotti crashed to his death. His goal had been simply to regain the lap record at the obscure circuit after Frenchman Jean Behra captured it for crosstown rival Maserati a day earlier. His demise, like most others in the sport, was the result of pure hubris and an affirmation that Alexis Carrell's "audacity" had not disappeared entirely from the human psyche.

Following Castellotti's death, Diana apparently abandoned motor racing entirely. Word drifted back to Los Angeles that she ultimately married a German banking mogul and settled into a reclusive life in Gstaad, Switzerland, skiing in the winter and hosting lavish parties in the summer. In the late 1980s, when Ferrari prices went off the Richter scale with mad speculation in the collector market, I recognized her Ferrari Mexico being auctioned in Monaco. It was sold to a Japanese businessman for $6,500,000.

It was in 1957 as well that the automobile industry rebelled against the steadily escalating horsepower race. Ford, Chevrolet, and Chrysler were engaged in a vicious battle for supremacy in the steadily growing NASCAR Grand National stock car series. Chevrolet and Ford were selling "special service" packages that included all manner of heavy-duty performance parts for racing cars. Chevrolet produced a limited run of lightweight, two-door 150 sedans, all in black-and-white paintwork, known as "Black Widows." Under their hoods were fuel-injected, 283 horsepower, race-tuned Corvette V-8s. Ford answered by equipping its similar two-doors with Paxton superchargers that boosted horsepower to over 300.

The Automobile Manufacturers Association, pressured by car companies that did not participate in NASCAR, voted to limit advertising involving bogus claims of power and speed. Bill France, the crafty boss of NASCAR, responded by banning special engines with fuel-injection and superchargers. General Motors, Ford, and Chrysler then suspended their racing operations, at least in public, to appease their stockholders, the media, and the noisy safety lobby. Sub rosa support would continue until 1963, when Ford denounced the hypocrisy and resumed official motor racing participation. The other manufacturers soon followed.

By the end of the decade, thousands of miles of Interstate highways had been constructed. Seat belts were slowly being installed in a few models, but another thirty years would pass before automobiles would include truly effective safety devices such as air bags, anti-lock disc brakes, better tires, and crush zones in the bodywork. Racing cars would also become safer, but a counterbalance of radically increasing speeds kept the grim reaper in the game.

As daily life became safer through advances in medicine, environmental clean-ups, and quantum leaps in technology of all kinds, the dangerous days of 1955 faded into the fog bank of history. The risks taken by men in the primitive machines of the day, be they racing cars, jet fighters, or motorcycles, or in the new sport of scuba diving, seem irrational today. Perhaps they were induced by chemical imbalances—if some current experts are to be believed. They claim that crossed circuitry in the brain's neurotransmitters causes such problems as Attention Deficit Disorder (ADD) and Attention Deficit Hyperactivity Disorder (ADHD), which in turn triggers risk-taking.

An extension of that logic implies that hiding under one's bed except to eat healthy foods is a shining example of sanity. If everyone behaved "normally," there would be no explorers, no astronauts, no test pilots, no Lindberghs, Francis Drakes, Colonel Stapps, Neil Armstrongs, ad infinitum. Truth be known, living is dangerous to one's health. This was best stated by the German philosopher Goethe, who said, "The dangers of life are infinite, and among them is safety." Tacitus noted, "The desire for safety stands against every great and noble enterprise."

The savage year of 1955 perhaps produced nothing of great benefit to the human race (aside, possibly, from fluoride-laced Crest toothpaste, Disneyland, Dacron, microwave ovens, instant oatmeal, and the first McDonald's fast food). But as men challenged the physical penalties of power and speed without fear, they perhaps in some small way affirmed the elemental value of audacity as a vital component of the human spirit.

The great racing driver Parnelli Jones, who was only beginning his dazzling career in 1955, once observed, "If you're under control, you're not trying hard enough."

That perhaps applies to everyone on earth.

BIBLIOGRAPHY

Automobile and Culture. Gerald Silk & Associates, Harry N. Abrams, 1981.

Cutter, Robert, and Bob Fendell. *Encyclopedia of Auto Racing Greats.* Prentice-Hall Publishing, 1973.

Brottman, Mikita, ed. *Car Crash Culture.* Palgrave Press, 2001.

Clarke, R.M., and Anders Ditlev Clansager. *Le Mans, the Jaguar Years, 1949-1957.* Brooklands Books, Ltd., 1998.

Dalton, David, and Rob Cayen. *James Dean, American Icon.* St. Martins Press, 1984.

Defechereux, Phillipe, and Jean Grafton. *James Dean, The Untold Story of a Passion for Speed.* Mediavision Publications, 1995.

Desmond, Kevin. *The Man with Two Shadows, The Story of Alberto Ascari.* Proteus Publishing Group, 1991.

Flower, Raymond, and Michael Wynn Jones. *100 Years on the Road, A Social History of the Car.* McGraw Hill, 1981.

Fox, Jack C. *Illustrated History of the Indianapolis 500, 1911-1994.* Carl Hungness Publishing, 1997

Grinnell, James. *John Fitch, Racing through Life.* Book Marque Publishing, 1993.

Halberstram, David. *The Fifties.* Fawcett-Columbine, 1992.

Mantle, Jonathan. *Car Wars.* Little, Brown & Co., 1995.

Jewell, Derek, ed. *Man and Motor, the Twentieth-Century Love Affair.* Walker and Company, 1966.

Ludvigsen, Karl. *The Mercedes-Benz Racing Cars.* Bond Parkhurst Books, 1971.

Lynch, Michael T., William Edgar, and Ron Parravano. *American Sports Car Racing in the 1950s.* MBI Publishing Co., 1998.

Marsh, Peter, and Peter Collet. *Driving Passion.* Faber and Faber, 1959.

Nixon, Chris. *Mon Ami Mate: The Bright, Brief Lives of Mike Hawthorn and Peter Collins.* Transport-Bookman Publishing, 1998

O'Malley, J.J., and Bill Green. *Watkins Glen:* Private publication, 1990.

Peters, George, and Henry Greuter. *Novi: The Legendary Indianapolis Race Car, Volume One.* Bar-Jean Enterprises, 1991.

Popely, Rick, and L. Spencer Riggs. *Indianapolis 500 Chronicle.* Publications International, Ltd., 1998.

Trager, James. *The People's Chronicle.* Henry Holt, 1999.

White, Gordon Eliott. *The Kurtis Kraft Story.* MBI Publishing, 1999.

White, Gordon Eliot. *Offenahuaser, the Legendary Racing Engine and the Men Who Built It.* MBI Publishing, 1966.

Wise, David Burgess, William Boddy, and Brian Laban. *The Automobile, The First Century.* Greenwich House, 1983

Wallen, Dick. *Fabulous Fifties, American Championship Racing.* Dick Wallen Publishing, 1993.

Wollen, Peter, and Joe Kerr, eds. *Autopia, Cars and Culture.* Reaktion Press, 2002.

Wollen, Peter, and Joe Kerr, eds. *Autopia, Cars and Culture.* Reaktion Press, 2002

Numerous back issues of *Car and Driver, Road & Track, Speed Age, Autocar, National Speed Sport News,* and other motoring periodicals.

INDEX

NORTH COUNTRY LIBRARY SYSTEM
Watertown, New York

CENTRAL LIBRARY
WATERTOWN

FEB   2005